Postcollectivity

Studies in Critical Social Sciences Book Series

Haymarket Books is proud to be working with Brill Academic Publishers (www.brill.nl) to republish the *Studies in Critical Social Sciences* book series in paperback editions. This peer-reviewed book series offers insights into our current reality by exploring the content and consequences of power relationships under capitalism, and by considering the spaces of opposition and resistance to these changes that have been defining our new age. Our full catalog of *SCSS* volumes can be viewed at https://www.haymarketbooks.org/series_collections/4-studies-in-critical-social-sciences.

Series Editor
David Fasenfest (York University, Canada)

Editorial Board
Eduardo Bonilla-Silva (Duke University)
Chris Chase-Dunn (University of California–Riverside)
William Carroll (University of Victoria)
Raewyn Connell (University of Sydney)
Kimberlé W. Crenshaw (University of California–LA and Columbia University)
Heidi Gottfried (Wayne State University)
Alfredo Saad-Filho (Queen's University, Belfast)
Chizuko Ueno (University of Tokyo)
Sylvia Walby (Lancaster University)
Raju Das (York University)

Postcollectivity

Situated Knowledge and Practice

Edited by
Agnieszka Jelewska
Michał Krawczak
Julian Reid

Haymarket Books
Chicago, IL

First published in 2024 by Brill Academic Publishers, The Netherlands
© 2024 Koninklijke Brill NV, Leiden, The Netherlands

Published in paperback in 2025 by
Haymarket Books
P.O. Box 180165
Chicago, IL 60618
773-583-7884
www.haymarketbooks.org

ISBN: 979-8-88890-361-2

Distributed to the trade in the US through Consortium Book Sales and Distribution (www.cbsd.com) and internationally through Ingram Publisher Services International (www.ingramcontent.com).

This book was published with the generous support of Lannan Foundation, Wallace Action Fund, and the Marguerite Casey Foundation.

Special discounts are available for bulk purchases by organizations and institutions. Please call 773-583-7884 or email info@haymarketbooks.org for more information.

Cover design by Jamie Kerry and Ragina Johnson.

Printed in the United States.

Library of Congress Cataloging-in-Publication data is available.

Contents

Acknowledgements   VII
List of Figures   VIII
Notes on Contributors   IX

Postcollectivity
New Ways of Gathering and Practicing in Times of Crises   1
    Agnieszka Jelewska, Michał Krawczak and Julian Reid

PART 1
Resistivity

1   Resistance   15
    Julian Reid

2   Carnivalesque Postcollectivity
    Reenactment as Decolonial Subversion   27
    Adela Goldbard

3   Collecting Crumbs of Lost Knowledge
    Learning from Postindustrial and Postsocialist Disruptions   45
    Andrzej W. Nowak

4   Borderforms   68
    Grant Leuning and Pepe Rojo

5   The Networked Public Sphere and the Sectarian Public   86
    Stephen Dersley

PART 2
Co-existence

6   Collective Co-existence, Climate Apocalypse, and a Nature-Relational Way Forward   111
    Peter H. Kahn, Jr., Sarena Sabine and Carly E. Gray

7   As I Sit Down to Write a Monsoon Story without Cloud Bands   128
    Harshavardhan Bhat

8   A Meteorology of Media   137
    Brett Zehner

9   Not-Only-Human-Habitat, or Pedagogies of Vulnerable Collectives in the Age of Extractivist Fantasies   148
    Anna Nacher

10 Media Warfare
    The Coercive Coexistence of Radiation and Memory   165
    Agnieszka Jelewska

PART 3
Transversality

11 The Right to Breathe Is the Right to Speak
    The Transversality of Environmental Pollution and Postdigital Infrastructures   187
    Michał Krawczak

12 Transversal Physiognomies and the Postcollective Self   206
    Jan Stasieńko

13 The Silicon Gender
    Technological Species and the Transgression of Model Sexes   224
    Ania Malinowska

14 Towards a Postmonetary Collectivity   236
    Jens Schröter

    Index   249

Acknowledgements

Postcollectivity: Situated Knowledge and Practice is the result of research carried out under the NPRH grant of the Polish Ministry of Education and Science, entitled *Mediated Environments. New Practices in Humanities and Transdisciplinary Research* (no: 0014/NPRH4/H2b/83/2016).

Figures

2.1   Still shot from RINXUI [*into the night*] by Adela Goldbard, 2019–20   28
2.2   Still shot from RINXUI [*into the night*] by Adela Goldbard, 2019–20   30
2.3   Still shot from RINXUI [*into the night*] by Adela Goldbard, 2019–20   31
2.4   Still shot from RINXUI [*into the night*] by Adela Goldbard, 2019–20   36
2.5   Still shot from RINXUI [*into the night*] by Adela Goldbard, 2019–20   38
2.6   Still shot from RINXUI [*into the night*] by Adela Goldbard, 2019–20   39
2.7   Still shot from RINXUI [*into the night*] by Adela Goldbard, 2019–20   41
2.8   Still shot from RINXUI [*into the night*] by Adela Goldbard, 2019–20   43
4.1   *Experimental Subjectivation*, NS channel still, by Grant Leuning   69
4.2   *Raw Assemblage*, detail, part of the *Occupy Thirdspace II/Ocupa Tercer Espacio II* 2022 exhibition at the San Diego City Library, curated by Sara Solaimani, photo by Viviana González Gómez   71
4.3   *Untitled*, found during a flag-making event, 2016, photo by Grant Leuning   73
4.4   *Untitled*, part of *We All Sleep Today/Hoy todos dormimos,* 2016, photo by Omar Pimienta   75
4.5   *Untitled*, part of *La procesión / Procession* 2016, photo by Grant Leuning   78
4.6   *String smear*, found during a flag-making event, 2018, photo by Grant Leuning   79
4.7   *Untitled*, part of *Celebración de la derrota/Celebration of Defeat*, 2017, photo by Grant Leuning   83
7.1   Image of the cloud, by Harshavardhan Bhat   134

Notes on Contributors

Harshavardhan Bhat
is a researcher and writer interested in the social study of monsoonal futures. He is currently a Postdoctoral Fellow at the Translational Data Analytics Institute at The Ohio State University.

Stephen Dersley
is a researcher at the Faculty of Anthropology and Cultural Studies, and at Humanities /Art /Technology Research Center, Adam Mickiewicz University in Poznan. His doctoral thesis was an interdisciplinary work that applied Ludwik Fleck's theory of thought collectives and thought styles to the study of cultural change. His areas of interest include the philosophy of culture; discourse analysis; technology, media and cultural practices; and what makes us think what we think. Recent publications include: *Mutating Scepticism – the Strains and Determinants of UK Euroscepticism, Lockdown Scepticism and Vaccine Scepticism* (Kontekst, 2022) and "A Discourse Analysis of News Media Articles on the Polish 'Rule of Law Crisis'", *Comparative Legilinguistics, International Journal for Legal Communication*.

Adela Goldbard
is an interdisciplinary artist-scholar from Mexico, Associate Professor at the Rhode Island School of Design and fellow of the National System of Art Creators of Mexico. With her research/practice, Goldbard investigates how radical community performances can subvert the imposition of hegemonic narratives, and how performances of violence and destruction can become aesthetic tools of resistance against power. She is especially interested in how collectively building, staging, and destroying has the potential to generate critical thinking and social transformation, and is currently working on an emergent *poetics of violence*. Recent art commissions include a pyrotechnic play with/for the Mexican community of La Villita, Chicago (University of Illinois, 2019–20), and a socially engaged art project with/for the P'urhépecha community of Arantepacua (FEMSA Biennial, 2020–21). Recent publications include: *PARSE Journal* 2022, *Law and the Senses*: *Explorations in Sensori-Legal Studies* website (Centre for Sensory Studies at Concordia University), *Repair: Sustainable Design Futures* (Routledge, 2022) and *Inoculaciones* (Universidad Iberoamericana, 2021). She lives and works in the US and Mexico. www.adelagoldbard.com

Carly E. Gray

is a doctoral candidate in the Department of Psychology at the University of Washington in Dr. Peter H. Kahn, Jr.'s Human Interaction with Nature and Technological Systems (HINTS) Laboratory. Her research has investigated the importance of interacting with nature (a) for children during the COVID-19 pandemic, and (b) for adolescents in a group home context to enhance coping and resilience. She has also been part of a research group conceptualizing and developing a new scale to measure the construct Presence. Currently she aims to understand how natural and technological environments shape, facilitate, and hinder emotion regulation.

Agnieszka Jelewska

is Professor at the Adam Mickiewicz University in Poznań, Poland, Deputy Dean of the Department of Anthology and Cultural Studies, and director of Humanities/Art/Technology Research Center AMU. She has served as a visiting fellow at Kent University, Canterbury, UK. She held lectures and workshops at Mahindra Humanities Center at Harvard University, Emerson College Boston, Folkwang Universität der Kunst, Essen. Jelewska has authored the books: *Sensorium. Essays on Art and Technology* (AMU Press, 2012), *Ecotopias. The Expansion of Technoculture* (AMU Press, 2013), *Art and Technology in Poland. From Cybercommunism to the Culture of Makers* (AMU Press, 2014, as editor), *Nuclear Gaia. Media Archives of Planetary Harm* (INTELLECT BOOKS, forthcoming, as co-author with M. Krawczak) and *Aesthetics of Radical Truth. Collaborative Media Practices Against Violence* (forthcoming, as co-author with M. Krawczak) and a number of articles. She examines the transdisciplinary relations between science, art, culture and technology in the 20th and 21st centuries, their social and political dimensions. She is also a curator and co-creator of art and science projects: *Transnature is Here* (2013); *Post-Apocalypsis* (2015) – awarded a golden medal from PQ 2016; *Anaesthesia* (2016); *Artropocene* (2017), *PostHuman Data* (2019).

Peter H. Kahn, Jr.

is Professor in the Department of Psychology and the School of Environmental and Forest Sciences, and Director of the Human Interaction with Nature and Technological Systems (HINTS) Laboratory at the University of Washington. He is also Editor-in-Chief of the journal *Ecopsychology*. His publications have appeared in such journals as *Science, Developmental Psychology, Human-Computer Interaction, Environmental Health Perspectives, Child Development*, and *Journal of Systems Software*. His five books (all with MIT Press) include *The Human Relationship with Nature, Children and Nature,* and *Technological Nature: Adaptation and the Future of Human Life.*

Michał Krawczak

is an assistant professor at Anthropology and Cultural Studies Department (Adam Mickiewicz University in Poznań, Poland), co-founder and program director of Humanities/Art/Technology Research Center. His main research fields are modern forms of mediatized violence, grassroots media practices and cultural consequences of climate change from the perspective of postdigital studies and media ecologies. Author of articles about media arts, sound design; editor of book *Post-technological Experiences. Art-Science-Culture* (AMU Press, 2019), co-author (with A. Jelewska) of books *Nuclear Gaia. Media Archives of Planetary Harm* (INTELLECT BOOKS, forthcoming) and *Aesthetics of Radical Truth. Collaborative Media Practices Against Violence* (forthcoming). He also works as designer, and curator of art and science projects, such as *Transnature is Here* (2013), *Post-Apocalypsis* (2015), *Anaesthesia* (2016), *Artropocene* (2017), *PostHuman Data* (2019), *Solastalgia* (2021).

Grant Leuning

is an artist and Ph.D. Candidate in Communication at UC San Diego. His research concerns the Gangjeong Village Peace movement in South Korea, and the role of media production in experimental democracies and anti-imperialist movements. His films have been screened in Hong Kong, South Korea, and the United States, and as a member of Comité Magonista, his artwork has been shown and performed in San Diego, London, Mexico City, and at the Judd Foundation in Marfa, TX.

Ania Malinowska

is a cultural theorist with an interest in the semiotics of feelings and author of *Love in Contemporary Technoculture* (CUP, 2022). She is a Professor of Media and Cultural Studies at the University of Silesia in Katowice (Institute of Culture Studies and Centre for Critical Technology Studies), and a former Senior Fulbright Fellow at The New School in New York. Malinowska's work is associated with critical posthumanism and cultural semiotics, gathering approaches from media and cultural studies, anthropology, philosophy of technology, and digital humanities. Her writing focuses on technologically shaped love practices and emotional traditions under digitalism. She also writes about robot cultures using her own approach termed "roboneutics".

Anna Nacher
is an Associate Professor at Jagiellonian University, a 2020 Fulbright alumna, and a member of the Board of Directors of the Electronic Literature Organization. Her research interests include: contemporary art, digital aesthetics, new media art, electronic literature, and sound art. She also ventures into ecological humanities and postcolonial theory. She has published in journals (*European Journal of Women's Studies, Hyperrhiz, Electronic Book Review, Acoustic Space, communication +1*) and contributed chapters to edited volumes. She is also a musician and sound artist. Since 2021 she has been collaborating with Victoria Vesna on various projects, such as Alien Star Dust Online Meditation, Noise Aquarium Meditation, and Breath Library. Since 2014 she is an active member of permaculture community in the Pieniny mountains. More information and a full list of publications: http://breathlibrary.org

Andrzej W. Nowak
is a professor at Adam Mickiewicz University. A scholar active on the intersection of social philosophy and philosophy of science and technology, he is interested in the social and political dimensions of materiality. An important part of his research is the study of scientific and social controversies and processes of producing fears, doubts and ignorance, as well as attempts to combine the ontological sensibility of posthumanism with the Promethean promise of modernity and the Enlightenment. Nowak is a populariser of Immanuel Wallerstein's modern system-world theory in Poland, with a particular interest in the study of semi-periphery. Author of the books (in Polish): *Wyobraźnia ontologiczna* (2016) and *Podmiot, system, nowoczesność* (2011), and co-author of books: *Czyje lęki? Czyja nauka? Struktury wiedzy wobec kontrowersji naukowo-społecznych* (2016) (together with Abriszewski and Wróblewski) and (in English) *Polish Science and Technology Studies in the New Millennium* (Peter Lang GmbH, 2022) (with Abriszewski and Derra), he is also the author of several dozen scientific articles, and is an active participant in scientific and public life, occasionally a publicist, and also present in the blogosphere.

Julian Reid
is a political theorist, philosopher, and professor of International Relations; he is renowned for his advance of the theory of biopolitics, contributions to cultural theory, postcolonial and post-structural thought, critique of liberalism, and seminal deconstruction of resilience. He has occupied the Chair in International Relations at Lapland University since 2010. In 2006 Reid published *Biopolitics of the War on Terror* (Manchester University Press), and in 2009 *The Liberal Way of War: Killing to Make Life Live* (coauthored with Michael

Dillon; Routledge). *Resilient Life: The Art of Living Dangerously* (coauthored with Brad Evans) was published in 2014 (Polity) to wide critical acclaim. In 2016 he published his latest monograph, *The Neoliberal Subject: Resilience, Adaptation and Vulnerability* (coauthored with David Chandler; Rowman & Littlefield). He has edited collections on *The Biopolitics of Development* (with Sandro Mezzadra and Ranabir Samaddar; Springer, 2013) and *Deleuze & Fascism* (with Brad Evans; Routledge, 2013). He is co-editor of the journal *Resilience: Policies, Practices and Discourses* (with David Chandler, Melinda Cooper and Bruce Braun).

Pepe Rojo

is a writer and artist currently lecturing at UC San Diego. He holds a Ph.D. in Communication and an MFA in Creative Writing, both from UCSD. His research and work centers around conceptual, material and performative borders, particularly in California. He has published seven books and 300+ texts: fiction, non-fiction, experimental and academic. His work has been shown and performed in different venues, including Ex-Teresa in Mexico City, the San Ysidro border crossing in California, and the Judd Foundation in Marfa, TX (as a member of the Comité Magonista).

Sarena Sabine

is a 4th year Psychology Ph.D. Student at the University of Washington in Dr. Peter Kahn's Human Interaction with Nature and Technological Systems (HINTS) Laboratory. Sarena's primary research focus has been developing a scale to measure Presence, a newly identified construct, with the HINTS lab. She earned a Psychometrics and Applied Analytics Graduate Certificate and a Quantitative Psychology Minor, informing this research. She now plans to study why some nature experiences can be psychologically so enriching, and suspects that Presence is a key component to answering this question.

Jens Schröter

is Chair for media studies at the University of Bonn since 2015. Director (together with Prof. Dr. Anna Echterhölter, Prof. Dr. Sudmann and Prof. Dr. Alexander Waibel) of the VW-Main Grant "How is Artificial Intelligence Changing Science?"; Senior-fellowship IFK Vienna, Austria. Winter 2018: Senior-fellowship IKKM Weimar. Winter 2021/22: Fellowship, Center of Advanced Internet Studies. Research topics: History and theory of digital media, History and theory of photography, media philosophy, mushroom studies. Recent publications: *Medien und Ökonomie* (Springer, 2019) and *Media Futures. Theory and Aesthetics* (coauthored with Christoph Ernst; Palgrave, 2021).

Jan Stasieńko

is a full professor and the Director of Research in the Department of Media and Communication, University of Lower Silesia. He also holds the position of the Head of the Centre for Games and Animation, ULS. In 2010/2011 and 2013/2014, he was a visiting fellow at SUNY Brockport Department of Communication (USA) and the Centre for Digital Media and Simon Fraser University, Vancouver (Canada). He is a member of Beyond Humanism Net as well as the Game Research Association of Poland. In his research, he focuses on posthumanism and media technologies, the narrative structure of video games, educational and therapeutical contexts of gaming, animation history and anthropology, video games, and CGI in the context of disabilities. He published several books and reports: *Media Technologies and Posthuman* Intimacy (Bloomsbury Academic, 2021), *Posthuman Studies Reader: Core Readings on Transhumanism, Posthumanism, and Metahumanism* (eds. with Sampanikou) (Schwabe, 2021), *Fragile Avatars? Representations of Disability in Video* Games (with A. Dytman-Stasienko, K. Madej, A. Flamma, M. Śledź; University of Lower Silesia Press, 2021), *Capturing Motor Competencies. People with Disabilities as Actors in Motion Capture Sessions* (ULS, 2015).

Brett Zehner

is a postdoctoral fellow at The Ohio State University. His research focuses on critiques of whiteness and white supremacy in relation to big data, abolitionist aesthetics, and critical theories of subjection. His work has been published in *Que Parle, Media-N,* and he has exhibited at Transmediale. He is currently working on his manuscript *Digital Abolitionism: Technological Resistance to Behavioral Data Mining and White Racial Capitalism.*

Postcollectivity
New Ways of Gathering and Practicing in Times of Crises

Agnieszka Jelewska, Michał Krawczak and Julian Reid

Postcollectivity is an attempt to capture and name the tendency leading to the formation of the temporary assemblages and groups that emerged in many spheres of social, political, economic and cultural life in the first two decades of the new millennium. Most of these phenomena have arisen as a result of various crises, disasters, threats and forms of violence, both long-term, such as progressive environmental pollution and the devastating practices of anthropogenic drive; and direct, such as wars, refugee crises and the destructive forces of political regimes. Others are a form of response to new political, social and cultural changes that we experience due to the rapid development of technology or progressive economic stratification.

This book, which addresses the need for critical studies of collectivity, proposes the perspective of postcollectivity as an interdisciplinary reflection and study of this tendency in relation to groups of human subjects, but also to human and non-human (including material-digital, human-technological, human-plant, human-animal, human-environmental) assemblages that are involved today in producing different types of relations, dependencies and interactions. In the book we show how these dependencies are mediated by technological devices, digital interfaces, while also being determined by infrastructures that are anthropogenic, anthropocenic and postcolonial. What these new formations have in common is not so much the production of material goods and commodities (which was the purpose of collectives in the twentieth century and maintained today by co-operatives) but rather new practices of knowledge production for times of crises, and thus of communicative and cultural models. As such, postcollectivity can be located within three sets of contemporary phenomena.

The first is related to attempts to regain political and social agency. This encompasses both the search for new strategies of resistance exemplified by groups of citizens that organise themselves in protests and demonstrations, in the streets and on the Internet, as well as artistic practices and performative actions of a political and social-creative character. Postcollectivity is realised here in conjunction with the mediatisation of these processes at different stages of their realisation, and in this aspect the question arises of the possibility of producing a new agency of the collective imagination as a form of resistance. The second tendency, which co-constructs new assemblages of the human and non-human, involves the production of speculative narratives that allow us to re-name and re-think, within this collective, anthropogenic environmental violence and its consequences for organisms cohabiting on the planet. In many cases, speculative narratives collide with knowledge co-produced by specific models of legitimating science, or postcolonial infrastructures that forcibly connect humans and the environment. The third area concerns the coexistence of the human and the technological (Simondon 2017), within the frameworks of new postcollectives that are emerging in situations involving human interaction with robotic and digital technologies, but also through the strong development of online platforms as a new environment for establishing algorithmically stimulated and maintained postcollective relationships.

For us, postcollectivity designates the transition phase between, on the one hand, disintegration and critical reflection on traditionally understood collectives as groups of people who act together and produce certain goods or resources, and, on the other, a move towards new, emerging contemporary communication models and forms of knowledge production as need to regain agency in difficult circumstances.

1   Collectivisation

The concept of the collective, and especially of collectivisation, is historically associated with processes involving force and coercion aimed at the accumulation of people (mainly rural populations and workers) in a given area for the purpose of producing material goods or commodities, as was the case in the Eastern Bloc countries until 1989 and in China during the Mao era and continues today in North Korea. At the same time, however, the concept of the collective is also used to describe voluntary groupings of people, who were united by common values and work ethics to form cooperative farms, as in the case of the Kibbutz in Israel. Another historical manifestation emerged in the 1960s, with artistic, anarchist and eco-utopian collectives that shared political and social beliefs and attempted to form groups that were self-sufficient in terms of food and commodity production, thereby fulfilling the basic needs of life. In each case, the idea was to produce material goods, to engage in economic and industrial activity, and for anarchist and eco-utopian collectives the point was also to negate the political and economic system by trying to 'live differently', on their own terms, outside the system.

The processes of top-down collectivisation that took place in the Eastern Bloc countries, especially in the USSR, where the first of such projects were implemented in the Stalinist era, from the 1930s onwards, are still employed today in authoritarian regimes which make no attempt to hide the strategies of slavery and violence or the resulting human exploitation (Livi-Bacci 1993) (exploitation and over-working for the state), economic destruction (mono-farming, mono-commodity production leading to biodiversity degradation), as well as environmental exploitation, which included exhausting the collectivised land and then abandoning it, without ensuring the necessary recultivation. In Israel, the concept of collectivism implemented within the framework of the Kibbutz achieved certain economic and social successes and provided an opportunity to learn how to self-organise in difficult environmental conditions. However, the movement fell into crisis in the 1980s, and in the following decade many aspects that had been developed earlier influenced the specificity of the civic relations formed within the state of Israel and neighbouring states (Levy 2017). Twentieth-century collectives were first and foremost defined by the production of material goods and attempts to develop models of self-sufficiency, yet they also involved dangerous exploitation of the environment at the local level, and in extreme totalitarian and regime cases the exploitation of people. Artistic, anarchist and eco-utopian collectives are still a permanent feature of grassroots social and political practices in many parts of the world, gathering people around beliefs and values. Grassroots collectives have also become sites for experimenting with new forms of community building based on shared labour, production and values, and have had a strong utopian aspect, which, as researchers point out, has transformed over time into a dystopian vision (Zilbersheid 2007).

From this brief overview of examples, it is evident that in the 20th century there were roughly two types of formation and emergence of collectives: top-down, i.e. managed by state policy, and bottom-up, based on self-organisation and experimentation, attempting to search for new social forms outside the main system.

2 Collectives vs. Communities

Collectives should be distinguished from communities. Communities tend to be united by a long-term process, often historically conditioned, whereas collectives are formed temporarily, to produce goods, for cooperation and collaboration. Individuals forming communities do not need to cooperate and produce goods, the most important thing is the connectivity – based on common residence, shared values and beliefs, or traditions and customs. Recently, many publications have been written on the subject of communities and community.

Decolonial studies and especially indigenous studies have become an important field for this reflection. Especially in the latter there is a strong return to – and deep redefinition of – social agency and the political and epistemic value of communities. In the decolonial perspective, there is a shift towards knowledge and situated science, collective actions based on dynamic relationships, bringing together materiality and languages, local stories and histories, rejecting paradigms of colonial oppression, and creating new concepts of possible existence. However, this important turn towards communities would benefit from supplementary studies on new forms of collectives.

3 Postcollective Knowledge and Practice

The postcollectives we write about are grouped around the production of knowledge and new cultural, political, and economic practices. Therefore, we propose the perspective of postcollectivity – as a critical interdisciplinary sphere for the formation of knowledge about new processes involved in the emergence, duration and disappearance of the collectives that form between human and more-than-human subjects. As a research modus, postcollectivity grows out of, firstly, posthuman knowledge, where subject relations are recognised as open, transversal (Braidotti 2019) and more-than-human (Latour 2004; Puig de la Bellacasa 2017), and where the importance of situated practices is emphasized (Haraway 1988; Ward 2018; Tsing 2015); secondly, a postdigital perspective (Cramer 2015; Jandrić et al. 2018), which considers the transgression and blurring of the boundary between the digital and the material, and investigates these practices in relation to new networked collectives (Couldry 2015); and, the social consequences of, among other things, data capitalism (West 2019; Crain 2018), and surveillance capitalism (Zuboff 2019).

The postcollectives discussed in the book are therefore not the result of top-down planning; they most often arise from a specific situated need, often a crisis or a threat, and sometimes a desire to mark cultural, historical or political distinctiveness (Jelewska and Krawczak 2014). In terms of human and non-human relations, they relate to struggles with the climate crisis and new understandings of collectivity and planetary injustice. This dimension also reveals an affective psycho-physical condition based on an increasingly experienced need for contact with the habitat and the environment. With regard to the lost indigenous practices of being with the environment, which have frequently been obliterated due to the dominance of colonial settlers' knowledge, we are increasingly looking for new possibilities to activate a postcollective agency for tackling the pressing problems of the climate crisis (Chandler and Reid 2019).

From the perspective of postdigital studies, the postcollective condition is manifested in the entanglement of the material and the digital. Many of the processes that determine human and non-human subjects also result from their functioning at the interface of these two spheres. Hence, the phenomenon of postdigital ecosystems emerges, enmeshing and transversalising human and nonhuman subjects (Jandrić and Ford 2022), which are determined by the structures of the ontological hierarchies of data capitalism or algorithmic colonialism. Postdigital ecosystems have become part of contemporary habitats; their forms of organization are one of the factors shaping the condition of inter-and infra-subjective relations. For this reason, a critical analysis of these systems is extremely important. The postcollective perspective enables a multifaceted analysis of this phenomenon, on the one hand due to its theoretical openness to transversality and interrelationality, and on the other hand by virtue of its situated practices (of adaptation, resistance, political agency). Such an analysis stems from the practice of negotiation and debating, involving the search for non-hierarchical methods directed against the "universal machine" (Cramer 2015).

The research perspective proposed in *Postcollectivity* draws on the approaches of all the authors, who combine academic and theoretical discourse with social engagement, and artistic practice with critical thought, as they also focus attention on political and cultural exploitation, as well as areas of manipulation. The researchers also have experience of practices of being on the ground (in the broad sense) and of different ways of engaging with issues of societal formation. The examples of practices analyzed in each chapter are carefully selected. They have a very important local aspect which opens up the possibility of building discourses based on knowledge practices. The book presents critical studies of various forms of new collectivities. There are three types of complementary narratives in the book – analytical (diagnostic and pertaining to data and facts), performative (being at the same time a testimony to community art projects), and critical-speculative (revealing the possibility of getting out of the impasse and opening new, unpredictable perspectives). This is a coherent but multidimensional narrative, and its aim is to present both lost and new elements of community created as a result of dynamic socio-political processes.

The search for methods of describing the phenomena of postcollectivity is also noticeable in the structures of individual texts, which often depart from the traditional academic style in favor of more prototypical forms. The book includes scientific and artistic texts, as well as those that, through an experimental approach, try to find a new language and narrative for the collective shaping of knowledge. What is important, however, is that all the boundaries between the various approaches, perspectives and methodologies proposed here in this book are transversal, which means that all authors, regardless of their professional practice, jointly shape the critical and theoretical image of postcollectivity.

4 Resistivity, Co-existence and Transversality

The book is divided into three parts: *Resistivity*, *Co-existence* and *Transversality* which are focused on notions that could serve as microtheories for understanding and analyzing postcollectivity.

Part 1 describes the theories and practices of *Resistivity*. We chose this notion to refer to resistivity as a process, but also to the property of resisting the action of external factors. The term is also clearly related to electrical resistivity, where it is defined as the property of a body that causes it to resist the flow of an electric current. While in physics resistivity is a characteristic property of each material and is thus useful for comparing various materials on the basis of their ability to conduct electric currents, in the case of postcollectivity we study the resistance of newly formed collectives to various factors that affect, haunt, co-constitute them. This part includes texts by practicing artists and researchers depicting forms of intervention, resistance, and decolonization.

The opening chapter by Julian Reid is focused on the image of resistance as trouble one for western knowledge. He argues that "in the modern era at least, ideologies have tended to emerge from and as a response and resistance to the oppressions of myth" (Reid) which we have to re-think and re-practice in the contexts of new postcollective knowledge. What we need, Reid proposes, is a new practice of resistance based on decolonial approach to the western imagination.

Adela Goldbard in her text, based on her own ethnographical and performative research and practises, is focused on new forms of collectivity in terms of violence against migrants, colonial trauma. She shows how the power of "carnivalesque postcollectivity" can be a strategy for new forms of resistance based on "an active construction" and "postcollective communal organization." Goldbard also experiments with the form of the text, proposing a narrative spread between critical theoretical discourse, fragments of interviews and original visual documents.

This part also contains an analysis done by Andrzej W. Nowak of what is lost from the knowledge that was co-constituted by working collectives after the deindustrialization process in Polish cities in the 1980s and 1990s. As a case study he shows his own hometown Konin, where through the process of deindustrialization disappeared " not only the knowledge" of the people "but also the confidence in technology, factories, and knowledge as transformative agents that could change our lives and shape the future."

Another chapter analyses the examples of using practice as a critical metatheory of postcollectivity, in which doing and thinking become entangled. In such a designed frame, as Grant Leuning and Pepe Rojo convince us, various forms of resistance are created through postcollective doing-thinking, through "artwork-in-common." The metadiscourse proposed by the authors is intertwined with the analysis of historical facts, autoethnographic and performative narratives and visual documents.

The closing text by Stephen Dersley in this part discusses the different historical and contemporary conceptions of "the public" to shed light on new practices, forms of agency and postcollective organizations such as grassroots groups using OSINT (open-source investigation) that produce new ways of sharing knowledge about violence.

Part 2, *Co-existence,* discusses speculative theories of "multispecies postcollectives" tie up in between human and no-human beings. This part gathers articles on many different understanding of nonhuman beings, from monsoon and tornado, through permaculture and green environment in the urban planning to radiation and memory as coercive postcollective co-existence.

In the first chapter, Peter H. Kahn, Jr., Sarena Sabine, and Carly E. Gray analyze the importance of people interacting with nature for their physical and psychological well-being. The authors stress the immediate need for seeking a new postcollective ethical approach as the remedy to the "environmental generational amnesia." They also offer five transformational ideas to position us for hard years of climate change to come.

The following chapter proposes thinking through the monsoon's flood and the states of depression as a speculative postcollectivity created by this troubling coexistence. As Harshavardhan Bhat writes from his long-lasting research, the monsoon "read through political figuration is more-than-cloud, more-than-water and is definitely more-than-a-fluid-measure" become not just a methodology for understanding particular aspects of climate crisis but also reveals the deep history of postcollective tensions between human and nonhuman.

Another analysis of the co-existence of the chaotic and distractive entanglements between nature and humans is brought by Brett Zehner as he focuses on tornado chasers. For him, they can be looked into as producers of new nomadic science. In the crisis moments, they are a part of the process of producing postcollective knowledge about handling the situation.

The next contribution in this part discusses permaculture practices perceived as creating an environment for the coexistence of various entities as a "vulnerable collective." Anna Nacher is particularly interested "in tracing how the possibility of counter-extractivist practices located at the very core of permacultural design can be transplanted into digital pedagogy" in her own courses at the university.

In the closing chapter of this part Agnieszka Jelewska analyses the case of the coercive coexistence of radiation and memory in the context of the recent act of nuclear terrorism in Chernobyl and Zaporizhia Nuclear Power Plant. As Jelewska emphasizes "new postcollective approaches and methodologies" projected in the frames of postnuclear media studies "are needed to overcome the epistemic impasse that has arisen as a result of the 'cementing' of many discussions on nuclear energy in the face of political and military pressures."

In Part 3, *Transversality*, the collected texts refer to the notion that spaces and species can intersect while being simultaneously enmeshed in technological and economic interdependencies. The authors in this section critically describe the concepts of technologically mediated collectives.

Michał Krawczak analyses the transversality of environmental pollution and postdigital infrastructures in case of climate crises in western Siberia in the historical context of Soviet collectivization and contemporary political oppression done by RuNet (Rusian Internet) closing access to information from outside of the country. In the text, Krawczak also refers to the ways new postcollective practices are against these historical and contemporary forms of violence.

Jan Stasieńko, in his chapter, follows the transversality research on technology, and analyses transversal physiognomies both in the digital imaginary and the medical prosthetics of the face, opening up questions of identity in the technologically reconciled collective self. The examples of postcollective activities such as designing or art interventions he refers to aim "at indicating the interpretative capacity and diversity of the area of research on this part of the body in technological and cultural context."

The emergence of new postcollectives between humans and robots based on the problematic idea of silicon and fluent gender in comparison to anthropocentric biological and fixed gender became Ania Malinowska concern in her contribution to the book. According to her research, we should more look into the robotics fluent gender to be more conscious about new postcollectives (human-robotic) to come.

Transversality in this part of the book also means new speculative concepts of postcollective economies as transverse to the data capitalism, and algorithmic government. In this field, Jens Schröter proposes a theory of post-monetary collectivity. Refering to the concept of the commons he offers "the form of a speculative narrative that tries to bring different theoretical fields into discussion through addresses questions associated with the bottom-up self-organization of collectives and their medializations."

The arrangement of parts and chapters we propose is just one of the possible problematized paths that readers can follow when reading the book. It is also possible to read the book in a non-linear way – moving between texts and sections, thereby opening up different methods and forms of narration between, through and across the proposed layout. On the one hand, the collected texts strongly indicate possible forms of resistance to the top-down systems of managing communities – political, economic, and technocratic and towards situations of crises and violence. Thus, various forms of postcollective knowledge production and local social and cultural practices are described in the texts: the potential and threats of the coexistence of humans and nonhumans in multiple cultural, geographic, and technological contexts; forms of bottom-up shaping of multi-species habitats; and speculative models of the community economy, new political agency as regaining the knowledge of violence as decolonial practices. As we can understand it from each of the texts gathered here, contemporary postcollectivity is also marked by the coupling between matter and technology, which results in the production of new infra-actions (Barad 2007) in postdigital reality. The disclosure of communal practices on many levels will show that the bottom-up organization of postcollectives and their practices are of particular importance for resistance to top-down policies. Our proposal is not a description of the model of a new society, it shows how minorities, margins and even everyone and everything that is not usually perceived as society and citizens are organizing themselves today in critical and violent situations. It also reveals a closer relationship with the environment – that which is the immediate habitat, but also that which is seen in a broader, planetary perspective. Therefore, the set of the above texts should be understood in terms of the theory of postcollectivity practices, based mainly on the experiences of authors derived from participation in community projects, field research, and activities in such postcollectives.

5 Between Top-Down and Bottom-Up

Postcollectivity: Situated Knowledge and Practice proposes a multiversal perspective, but one that is always precisely located in a geographical, cultural, and problem context. The image of the postcollectivity which emerges from the book is not a homogeneous and stable one, as it depends on cultural, social, economic, geographic, historical, and political contexts. Therefore, the book indicates the need to operate with theories and practices that are always situated, and which should be understood in this way. The book is not addressed only to academics, but also to all those interested in changes concerning community and collectivity. Everyone for whom the production of knowledge and cultural practices has a communal and environmental significance, related to their local and situated contexts. Postcollectivity is also a self-analytical project. On the one hand, it is characterised by creative speculation on the future of societal relations, opening up possibilities for metanarrative and interdisciplinary studies. On the other hand, postcollectivity embraces the need for critical reflection on their very essence and causality, as well as the inevitable entanglement of collectives in the operational systems of late capitalism, neoliberalism, neocolonialism, data management, and dominant modes of communication.

Indeed, addressing that entanglement and seeking to disentangle themselves from these power relations to regimes of late capitalism and neoliberal colonialism, among others, is arguably the most pressing task faced by postcollectives today. In the twentieth century the conflict between top-down and bottom-up forms of collective was stark and obvious with battlelines that were relatively easy to trace. In the present, by contrast, it is not always obvious where postcollectives begin and where the forms of power they seek to resist ends. Often, the narratives on which postcollectives draw for their sustenance leach into those of the powers they oppose. Understanding how regimes of neoliberal capital and settler colonial function today requires considering how postcollectivity serves their strategies. Which is why the problematisation of forms of resistance, transversality, co-existence and power has to also be key to the task of critical reflection in an era of postcollectivity as a new form of gathering, being-with, and creating knowledge for critical and violent situations, as this book also seeks to draw out.

References

Barad, Karen Michelle (2007) *Meeting the Universe Halfway: Quantum Physics and the Entanglement of Matter and Meaning.* Durham: Duke University Press.

Braidotti, Rosi (2019) *Posthuman Knowledge.* Medford, MA: Polity.

Chandler, David and Reid, Julian (2019) *Becoming Indigenous: Governing Imaginaries in the Anthropocene.* London; New York: Rowman & Littlefield International.

Couldry, Nick (2015) The Myth of 'Us': Digital Networks, Political Change and the Production of Collectivity. *Information, Communication & Society* 18, no. 6 (June 3, 2015): 608–26. https://doi.org/10.1080/1369118X.2014.979216.

Crain, Matthew (2018) The Limits of Transparency: Data Brokers and Commodification. *New Media & Society* 20, no. 1 (January 2018): 88–104. https://doi.org/10.1177/1461444816657096.

Cramer, Florian (2015) What Is 'Post-Digital'? In: Berry D.M. and Dieter M. (eds) *Postdigital Aesthetics*, 12–26. London: Palgrave Macmillan. https://doi.org/10.1057/9781137437204_2.

Haraway, Donna (1988) Situated Knowledges: The Science Question in Feminism and the Privilege of Partial Perspective. *Feminist Studies* 14, no. 3 (1988): 575. https://doi.org/10.2307/3178066.

Jandrić, Petar and Ford, Derek R. (2022) Postdigital Ecopedagogies: Genealogies, Contradictions, and Possible Futures. *Postdigital Science and Education* 4, no. 3 (October 2022): 692–710. https://doi.org/10.1007/s42438-020-00207-3.

Jandrić, Petar, Knox, Jeremy, Besley, Tina, Ryberg, Thomas, Suoranta, Juha and Hayes, Sarah (2018) Postdigital Science and Education. *Educational Philosophy and Theory* 50, no. 10 (August 24, 2018): 893–99. https://doi.org/10.1080/00131857.2018.1454000.

Jelewska, Agnieszka and Krawczak, Michał (2014) The Difficult Relations Between Art, Science and Technology in Poland. In: Jelewska A. (ed.) *Art and Technology in Poland: From Cybercommunism to the Culture of Makers*, Poznań: Adam Mickiewicz University Press.

Latour, Bruno and Porter, Catherine (2004) *Politics of Nature: How to Bring the Sciences into Democracy*. Cambridge, Mass: Harvard University Press.

Levy, Mordechai (2017) Political implications of new social thinking: byproduct of the privatization of the kibbutzim. *Przegląd Politologiczny*, no. 4 (December 15, 2017): 87. https://doi.org/10.14746/pp.2017.22.4.7.

Livi-Bacci, Massimo (1993) On the Human Costs of Collectivization in the Soviet Union. *Population and Development Review* 19, no. 4 (December 1993): 743. https://doi.org/10.2307/2938412.

Puig de la Bellacasa, María (2017) *Matters of Care: Speculative Ethics in More than Human Worlds*. Posthumanities 41. Minneapolis: University of Minnesota Press.

Simondon, Gilbert (2017) *On the Mode of Existence of Technical Objects*. Translated by Cécile Malaspina and John Rogove, Minneapolis: University of Minnesota Press.

Tsing, Anna Lowenhaupt (2015) *The Mushroom at the End of the World: On the Possibility of Life in Capitalist Ruins*. Princeton: Princeton University Press.

Ward, Shelby E. (2018) Re-Locating Haraway: Situated Knowledges in the Questions of Democracy and Development. *Community Change* 2, no. 1 (September 24, 2018): 2. https://doi.org/10.21061/cc.v2i1.a.9.

West, Sarah Myers (2019) Data Capitalism: Redefining the Logics of Surveillance and Privacy. *Business & Society* 58, no. 1 (January 2019): 20–41. https://doi.org/10.1177/0007650317718185.

Zilbersheid, Uri (2007) The Israeli Kibbutz: From Utopia to Dystopia. *Critique* 35, no. 3 (December 2007): 413–34. https://doi.org/10.1080/03017600701676845.

Zuboff, Shoshana (2019) *The Age of Surveillance Capitalism: The Fight for a Human Future at the New Frontier of Power*. London: Profile books.

PART 1

Resistivity

CHAPTER 1

Resistance

Julian Reid

Resistance, today, has an image problem. What is it, where is it, who does it, to whom and what and how? How do we know what is resistance and what is not? Each of these questions is a question of the image of resistance. Research in the social sciences on resistance commonly points to the limits of our imaginaries when it comes to the question of resistance, and the ways in which those limits lead us to the issue of form.

A recent article by the geographer Sarah Hughes provides a classic example. She complains of the "predetermination of form that particular actions or actors must assume" to be considered as resistance (Hughes 2020, 1). She points out what it is we risk missing or ignoring in having succumbed to such "predeterminations of form", and then proceeds to revisit fundamental assumptions at work in concepts and practices of resistance, before making an argument for an engagement with a wider understanding of resistance, one that does away with traditional images of resistance, as linear, intentional, oppositional forms of agency, to focus instead on new, different and better ones, such as incoherence, multiplicity, becoming and emergence. The basic idea is that the emergence of alternative forms of life are held back by resistance once resistance is shut off from these alternatives on account of the limits of the imaginaries framing it (Povinelli 2011, 14). "Traditional framings" of resistance are seen as problematic in these literatures, as new "intersectional" framings are championed (Taylor 2017, 20–21). The struggle over the image, form, and frame of resistance is all about making it more "accessible" to its own potentials (Taylor 2017, 14), as theorists of resistance call for a mobilisation of the imagination to release images of resistance from the confines of the myths which condition it.

This kind of problematisation of form is not confined to resistance. Much has been made in recent years of how 'the West' in its entirety has been shaped by a certain understanding of the origins of forms. The anthropologist, Philippe Descola, has argued that what defines the West, and what distinguishes it from other civilizations, is its belief in what he calls "the heroic model of creation"; the idea, that is, of "production as the imposition of form upon inert matter" (Descola 2014, 323). Descola demonstrates the peculiarity and cultural specificity of this idea, discussing how foreign it is to, for example, Chinese culture, but more especially to that of the Indians of Amazonia, for who there is no heroic imposition of forms onto anything, but simply reciprocal processes of co-creation (Descola 2014, 321–325). Another anthropologist, Tim Ingold, has made a similar kind of critique of such 'hylomorphism', the theory according to which form is that which is simply imposed onto matter by practitioners (Ingold 2010, 20–21). Indeed, Ingold's work is a classic example of an attempt to make us think differently about the processes through which forms themselves are engendered. Practices of deformation, themselves emergent through the agency of the matter acted upon, are today seen as intrinsic to the processes by which form evolves. Arguing for exactly this, Ingold drew significantly on the work of Deleuze and Guattari, for whom the resistance of matter was key to the processes by which form develops (Ingold 2010, 25; Deleuze and Guattari 1999).

In terms of the political theory of resistance, the question of the connections between form and image is doubtless an essential one. The theorist and historian of Black radicalism, Cedric Robinson, makes this point very well. In his now classic text, *Black Marxism*, he describes how the Europeans who bore historical witness to the resistances of African peoples to enslavement were perfectly able to understand why those peoples would rebel, and yet, how they could not comprehend the forms which African resistance took (Robinson 2021, 309). The limits of European imaginaries when it came to resistance meant those forms were dismissed, not as resistance, but as the expressions of madness, of insanity, of savagery, and satanism (Robinson 2021, 309). Yet, as Robinson well maintains, the invention of those forms were themselves the expression of the combination of a power of imagination with an ability to conserve what was most fundamental to a culture, that of black African culture (Robinson 2021, 309). Within western scholarship on slavery a mythic and false image of the docility of slaves has been perpetrated at the cost of a real understanding of the multiplicity of forms which resistance took (Owens 1976, 70–105).

The argument as to the importance of form and the peculiar limits of European abilities to comprehend and enable its plasticities can be applied to every possible kind of resistance. There would seem to be something intrinsic to the limits of the European imagination when it comes to resistance which has made it difficult to see resistance for what it is, whenever a given act of resistance has not complied with those limits. Imagination and form are, in this sense, highly interrelated when it comes to the question of resistance. Resistance requires imagination to be inventive, yet it easily runs up against the limits of dominant imaginaries in the forms it takes. And those limits have racial determinations. White thought is inflexible while Black thought is eminently elastic. Robinson's argument continues to reverberate in contemporary literatures on resistance.

The argument goes that we have been taught to imagine resistance in highly particular ways, and that these ways are no longer adequate for our present. In short, we are told that we need to make new images of resistance, as well as learn to deploy the imagination in ways that can change practices of resistances, killing off those mythic, tired and clichéd images of resistance as merely linear, intentional opposition to power, devised by autonomous agents, with preconceived plans as to 'what is to be done', which lead to the same tired and mythic forms of politics. We also, it is said, need to contribute to the creation of new intersectional subjects of resistance endowed with the abilities to free us from those now outdated practices. This is a line of argument about the relations between imagination, resistance, form and myth that is fairly ubiquitous today. Numerous works express these kinds of sentiments – the need to recover the imagination, as a source for resistance, and in the process, reimagine what resistance is and how it takes place, in order to free it from the limitations of imaginaries which would otherwise stifle it.

This task is often foregrounded in relation to issues of the fight against neoliberalism. Mark Fisher, for one, argued it very well. The problem for Fisher was that resistance today, and for some time, has been reduced to the limits imposed by an imaginary of 'anti-capitalism'. Shaped so, it has no alternative vision to offer, or 'positive political project'. All of which means it possesses no better image of how society might be organized to that of its opponent. Which is why, as he argued at least, it has become such a subdued hostage to neoliberalism and its peculiar yet deeply naturalized image of the human as a competitive, self-preserving and endlessly enterprising entity (Fisher 2018). Franco 'Bifo' Berardi makes a similar kind of argument. For Berardi, Europe has become a dogmatic project of reassuming and reinforcing neoliberal ideology, of a neoliberal regulation that leads to the impoverishment of European societies: to the slashing of salaries, to the postponement of retirement, but most crucially, to the project of colonizing the imagination itself (Berardi 2012, 38–9). The future where Europe is concerned has become unimaginable as anything other than the further extension of this project. This is all testimony to the power and success of neoliberal strategies that depend not simply on the application of a set of economic rules and functions but "the internalization of a certain set of limitations, of psychic automatism, of rules for compliance" (Berardi 2012, 58).

Traditionally we have been taught also to see resistance as a peculiarly human capacity. However, images of humans achieving forms of sovereignty and security dependent on their distinction from, and exploitation of, other life forms are no longer particularly in vogue today within critical theories of resistance, as research into resistance chases after other more posthuman commodities; vulnerability, perseverance, adaptation and resilience, for example. Discourses of resistance which involve recourse to ideas and concepts of independence are dismissed as ableist, romanticized and anthropocentric, as much as dependence becomes a capacity to be valorized (Taylor 2017, 205–218). Much of this has, of course, to do with the racial underpinnings of humanist discourses on resistance. The human which has claimed sovereignty over nature is the same white human which has dominated and exploited other races of humanity on the basis of the understanding that whites are more human than others; others whose lesser humanity renders them closer to a nature which it is the right and responsibility of a white race to lord over. As we have become more aware of the ways in which racism has shaped discourses on the political left as much as on the right, so the humanism of leftism has been brought further into question, as the construction of a posthuman subject has become an ever more urgent task for leftist critique on racial grounds. As Rosi Braidotti puts it:

> not all humans are equal and the human is not at all a neutral category. It is rather a normative category that indexes access to privileges and entitlements. Appeals to the "human" are always discriminatory: they create structural distinctions and inequalities among different categories of humans. Humanity is a quality that is distributed according to a hierarchical scale centred on a humanistic idea of Man as the measure of all things. This dominant idea is based on a simple assumption of superiority by a subject that is: masculine, white, Eurocentric, practicing compulsory heterosexuality and reproduction, able-bodied, urbanized, speaking a standard language. This subject is the Man of reason that feminists, anti-racists, black, indigenous postcolonial and ecological activists have been criticizing for decades.
>
> BRAIDOTTI 2020

The task of the political imagination when it comes to imaginaries of resistance is quite clear then. Resistance must be deformed and re-imagined. The limits of its dominant imaginary must be exploded; the image, that is, of its subject, the white urban hetero able-bodied European man, and his servile politics, his anti-capitalism, his economistic diagnosis of the limits of neoliberalism. In its place a new kind of subject must emerge, one that can reconcile the differences between the trans feminists, the anti-racists, the blacks and the indigenous, and the ecologically minded, and fight for the creation of a new politics, one formed upon a different kind of image, capable of birthing a world beyond and outside of capitalism, neoliberalism, but also colonialism, racism, sexism, anthropocentrism, and so on.

The indigenous tend to play particularly specious roles in these kinds of prescriptions. Indigenous peoples have been crucial to the narratives, mythologies and ideologies of western states and their societies since the discovery of the New World. We know much by now about the ways in which the indigenous have been deployed to create the myth of a contrast between the old and the new, the primitive and the developed, past and future. However, it is a fact, as one of the great chroniclers of that mythology described, that the ideological needs of western regimes have undergone significant changes since that discovery, and that the functions of the indigenous in practices of western mythmaking have changed much too. Their function in the 20th century was not that which it was in the 19th, nor the latter that which it was in the 18th century, and so on (Slotkin 1998, XVI–XVII). To understand how colonialism continues to operate today we need to attend and be wise to the narrative adaptation strategies of these regimes and changes in their operative languages, in ways that Slotkin's research was historically, and which we can see affecting the new science and theory of resistance.

In the modern era at least, ideologies have tended to emerge from and as a response and resistance to the oppressions of myth. As Slotkin put it, ideology is the product of a discontent with a world dominated by myth, and the expression of a desire to free that world from myth (Slotkin 1998, 25). Problems persist however with the ways in which ideologies tend to end up generating their own myths based on their own narrative formulas (Slotkin 1989, 25–31). Going beyond the kind of deconstruction of classic and nationalist structures of myths which Slotkin's research achieved, has to mean, however, examining how ideologies mask themselves in a narrative of the deconstruction of myth itself, and the deployment of new and old myths in discourses of resistance.

A classic example of this kind of paradox can be found in the work of Braidotti, whose work *Posthuman Knowledge* entails significant references to what she calls the "creative imagination" (Braidotti 2019, 132) as well as the struggles of indigenous peoples, those "people who live closest to the earth" (Braidotti 2019, 164), the alternatives which indigenous peoples supposedly offer to critical imaginaries today, and the need of resistance movements to learn from them about their ways of thinking and living (Braidotti 2019, 7). The indigenous are, Braidotti argues, peoples that are or have been missing; "subjects whose knowledge never made it into any of the official cartographies or genealogies" (Braidotti 2019, 162) and she situates their struggles "for visibility and emergence" as the driver of what she calls a "radical politics of immanence, aimed at actualizing minority-driven knowledges through transversal alliances" (Braidotti 2019, 162). Similar demands to make indigenous peoples and their indigeneity more visible, learn from them, and build alliances with them, have been made by a host of other thinkers concerned with resistance, including Judith Butler (Butler and Athanasiou 2013), Elizabeth Povinelli (2011), Bruno Latour (2017), Donna Haraway (2016), Timothy Morton (2017), and Anna Tsing (2015).

Are the indigenous of these discourses on resistance the people who were missing and are now being given presence by such authors, or do they remain, simply, a figment of western myth-making? A point well made by Slotkin was that myths are never simply tools of conservative ideologies, but also of radically critical ideologies too. Indeed, the same myths tend to reinforce both kinds of ideology simultaneously. In the 1960s, to give an example which Slotkin dwells on, "counter-cultural radicalism" deployed the myth of the frontier, and that of the "Noble Savage" to critique a form of society which had "gone wrong" (Slotkin 1998, 17).

The iconography of beads and headbands, the adoption of "tribal" life-styles as a form of communalism untainted by political association with communism, the rationalization of drug use as a form of mystic religiosity, the linkage of political and ecological concerns, the withdrawal to wilderness refuges and the adoption of an "outlaw" or "renegade" stance towards the larger society – all of these phenomena so special to the sixties were acted out as if they were not innovative at all, but merely repetitions of an older pattern (Slotkin 1998, 17).

It is a fiction to assert, as Braidotti does, that the knowledge of the indigenous never entered into official cartographies of power. By contrast it had a very crucial function in the construction of western myth making, as a weak and negative counterpart to positive and superior western forms. The problem is that the counter-cultures of today are simply trying to reverse the structures of western mythologies in much the same ways that those movements of the 1960s did which Slotkin well describes.

Much of this latest turn to indigeneity is motivated by the underlying desire of thinkers including Braidotti to advance what they call "posthumanism". Indigenous peoples are said to possess a radically different cosmology to peoples in the West, one that does not support the human/non-human distinction supposedly so central to Western political imaginaries since at least the Enlightenment, and which is held to blame for a great deal of historical damage (Braidotti 2019, 7; Descola 2014). Indigenous peoples never bought human exceptionalism, it is argued; they understand intrinsically the depths of human vulnerability, the need to build caring relationships with each other as well as other species, and act as custodians for the environments on which they depend for survival.

All of this is myth. There is plenty of more balanced and empirically grounded research, both anthropological and otherwise, to demonstrate that indigenous cultures are as complex in their constructions of the purpose of the animal as their western counterparts (Reid 2020). One particularly dangerous myth of indigeneity coshared by Left and Right today, is that of the resilience of indigeneous peoples. Resilience has in fact already been widely exposed across the social sciences as a key component of the ideology of neoliberalism (Cretney 2014). And much of the discussion around the topic has headed in the direction of the question of how precisely to resist resilience (Slater 2022). Meanwhile however, fashionable works continue to treat resilience as if it is some kind of partisan property of those working on the outside of power. Marquis Bey's recent book, *Black Trans Feminism*, which is another attempt to articulate a politics of the multitude is a case in point. As Bey puts it, "(T)he multitude carries with it a resilience via its plasticity, its ability to be more than and excessive of the unitary. In black trans resilience, an embodied 'antagonism of subjectivity' ... there is flexibility" (Bey 2022, 214).

Resistance is not the source of resistance. It is that which is to be resisted. Resisting resilience, however, requires the indigenous turning on these oppressive sources of critique in which the resilience agenda is now advancing. And a complication of doing that is that these sources of critique also come garbed in a discourse of resistance, and a discourse of resistance itself cloaked as a critique of existing and predetermined forms. As we are told, today we have to be wary of pertaining to forms of resistance that do more damage than good. Resistance is something but it's not enough, to paraphrase Braidotti. "Politics", as she puts it, "requires not just resistance, but the effort to activate the generative force of virtual possibilities" (Braidotti 2019, 177). As such a politics of resistance which does not simultaneously function to activate "the generative force of virtual possibilities", we have to assume, is a politics which is lacking: a politics which is not enough, and indeed if it is a politics which connects with and draws support from "the sovereign power of the master signifier which means what it says and says what it means" (Braidotti 2019, 174–175) then it is a politics which resistance itself has to be tasked with dismantling; the object of opposition for the kinds of resistance Braidotti is calling for.

Thou shalt not speak in the language of the master signifier, is one of the fundamental 'do not's' of this present discourse on resistance, which seeks to adapt us to the harsh realities of the Anthropocene, bend us to accommodate the new forces emerging, which exceed anthropocentric perspectives, and rid us of the white western humanisms which led to the Anthropocene in the first place. The source of resistance, from now on, once the subject has swallowed this message, and adapted itself to the new world and its conditions, will be as Braidotti also informs us, not just the indigenous, but "the resilience of *zoe*" (Braidotti 2019, 177).

That is an interesting turn of phrase; "the resilience of *zoe*". Derrideans might choose to dwell a while on that phrase and wonder at it. Does Braidotti mean that *zoe*, in its infinite resilience, is the source of resistance? Or is it that resilience is the subject here? That resilience, being always derivate of, and an expression of, *zoe*, is the source of resistance? Is resistance another word, in a way, for resilience, and vice versa? And what of the relationships of indigenous peoples to *zoe*? Are they mere *zoe*? Or have they just digested their Agamben better?

Braidotti's philosophico-political alignment with the powers of *Zoe* goes back some way in her work. In her relatively early book, *Transpositions*, for example, she elaborated on *Zoe* as that which "marks the outside" of a "particular vision of the subject"; that is, the outside of "male, white, heterosexual, Christian, property-owning, standard-language-speaking citizens" kinds of of subjects (Braidotti 2006 37). *Zoe* is to *bios* "the poor half" in a couple, she argues, wherein *bios* claims the mantle of intelligence and sociability while *Zoe* is left at home to do the laundry (Braidotti 2006, 37). The struggle to free *Zoe* from its subjection within its coupling to *bios* is akin to that which Deleuze and Guattari theorized in terms of the nomad to the state (Deleuze and Guattari 1999). Resistance, in this vein of thought, is a practice which connects those who find themselves, contemporarily, on this outside, being neither male, white, heterosexual, christian, property-owning, standard language speaking, with all those historical nomads of yore on which Deleuze and Guattari constructed their own theory of grand historical struggle. And indeed, this connection to the nomadic is not incidental to Braidotti's thought either, going back some way, and being essential to her contribution.

For Braidotti, the nomad has long been precisely the answer to the problem of "the poverty of the social imaginary", when it comes to resistance (Braidotti 2002, 5). The nomad is also a way to bring the outside in, at least in terms of her inhabitation of philosophy itself (Braidotti 2002, 7), and a way of avoiding the customary separation of reason from imagination which has so held back philosophy when it has come to the task of the apprehension of forms which break with established ideologies of resistance. An admittedly "iconoclastic, mythic figure", the nomadic subject is nevertheless *the* subject capable of rescuing us from the conventions of established imaginaries of resistance (Braidotti 2002, 7).

What if this mythic and iconoclastic figure is not the liberator it is claimed to be, and itself a force for the colonization of imaginaries? Let us recall that Deleuze wrote not only of the people who are missing, in the present, but of the people which are to come, in the future, so to say (Deleuze,1989). The task of the people to come, Deleuze argued, was precisely to destroy dominant imaginaries. It is a community of iconoclasts which seeks to destroy icons in order to create a space for the consistution of a new regime of images. It imposes its own images with as ruthless a power as it destroys those of its enemies. Any serious theorist of resistance and power today has to engage with Deleuze (and Guattari), and yet soon runs up against the issue that Deleuze's work has become so iconic that it demands being destroyed itself, being so overwrought in its influence. One is not at the margins if reading and citing Deleuze, one is at the centre, and there to be attacked. Still, there are better and worse readings of Deleuze; those which are nuanced and allow for complex interpretation, and those which reduce him to one side in a binary struggle, between the nomad and the state, for example, or the imagination and reason.

When it comes to theorizing resistance today the imperative which governs thought is that of the necessity to be suspicious of forms, to work for deformation, to see and empower the materials within the forms, the emergent properties of which are only ever contained by form itself. Form has become in itself a conceit, an imposition of sovereigns, an expression of power, and a problem for resistance. Yet it bears remembering that we have known since at least, Foucault, that power itself incites resistance, and that it needs resistance, in order to be, and moreover that *it knows this* (Foucault 1990).

Foucault's thesis, so radical for its time, and so abstract in its formulation, is confirmed in the work of Ingold, which works through the problem of form via practices. Ingold describes, for example, how in learning to make a basket, the novice runs up against the resistance of the willow, only to discover that it is that very resistance which makes willow such a conducive material for basket making (Ingold 2010, 22). In the drive to make a theory of resistance which would exceed the limits of hylomorphic models the work is already complete, and there is little more to be done. As with the making of baskets, it is left up to the artisan to decide when to finish. It would be possible to go on forever, yet at some point, if only for the maker to go home and sleep, it is necessary to stop (Ingold 2010, 23).

There is a paradoxical problem with regards to the roles of imagination in resistance here. It is wrong, we learn, to attempt to impose an image onto resistance. This is what we Europeans have done historically, following the hylomorphic model, and it is this error of image-imposition which accounts for the many failures to recognize and comprehend practices of resistance which confounded the images we had made for it. Instead, imagination is supposed to follow the morphogenetic model which Ingold and others have developed. Adhering to this latter model means the image of resistance has to ally with whatever the practices of resistance produce. Images are, at most, participants in a field of forces combined with other tools and practices, working towards the production of emergent forms. They must not be allowed to become dominant or legislative in this process, as this would be to miscomprehend the ways through which resistance works (Ingold 2010, 126–127). However, on the other hand, imagination is needed, we are told, if resistance is to be truly creative (Robinson 2021; Braidotti 2019), and critics of the failures of resistance to neoliberalism berate the weakness of the imaginaries shaping it, and call for more imagination, and better, more potent images (Fisher 2018; Berardi 2012).

Which is it to be then? Does the image problem which besets resistance demand more imagination or less? The imaginaries which govern resistance produce a limitation of forms of resistance. Dominant and prescriptive images of resistance are held accountable for forms which fail us strategically, as well as for failures of apprehension when it comes to the encounter with truly imaginative forms of resistance. It is obvious, therefore, that one answer to the problematic has to be an expansion of the imagination in order to produce better images strategically, and as a means to increase the powers of apprehension by which we recognize resistance in all its multiplicities. Is there, then, a *nomadic imagining*, akin to what Maggie Nelson describes, after Braidotti, as "nomadic remembering" (Nelson 2021, 214), which would perform this work of reconciliation between strategy and ethics in the field of resistance? And yet, it is as obvious that this problematization of resistance, dominated by forms which function to limit and exclude, is itself today a legislative one, formative of an industry of critique, which functions to police images of resistance. Perhaps, therefore, it is time to revisit the supposedly Deleuzian critique of the hylomorphism on which so much of this problem seems to hang. Of all the authors, makers, figures who so inspired Deleuze to think about resistance, as well as about images, we might consider what he had to say about T.E. Lawrence, who defined himself "solely in relation to the force through which he projects images into the real", images he drew from himself and his friends (Deleuze 1998, 118). Yes, resistance requires images and imagination, if it is to escape being dragged into this quagmire of impotence where it now finds itself, deformed beyond all recognition, wedded to political power. But we also need to recognise the depths of the problem, when it comes to the functions of images and imagination in the strategies of the forms of political power which resistance is tasked with undoing. Too often what comes declared as resistance, and too often arguments and analyses claiming to be aimed at freeing up resistance from what it is not, reveal themselves too easily as dependent on myths and forms deriving from regimes of representation that are themselves already dominant and subjugating.

References

Berardi, Franco B. (2012) *The Uprising: On Poetry and Finance*. New York: Semiotext.
Bey, Marquis (2022) *Black Trans Feminism*. Durham: Duke University Press.
Braidotti, Rosi (2020) 'We' are in this Together, But We are not One and the Same. *Journal of Bioethical Inquiry* 17: 465–469.
Braidotti, Rosi (2019) *Posthuman Knowledge*. Cambridge: Polity Press.
Braidotti, Rosi (2006) *Transpositionsi*. Cambridge: Polity Press.
Braidotti, Rosi (2002) *Metamorphoses: Towards a Materialist Theory of Becoming*. Cambridge: Polity Press.
Butler, Judith and Athanasiou Athena (2013) *Dispossession: The Performance in the Political*. Cambridge: Polity Press.
Cretney, Raven (2014) Resilience for Whom? Emerging Critical Geographies of Socio-ecological Resilience. *Geography Compass* 8(9): 627–640.
Deleuze, Gilles and Guattari, Félix (1999) *A Thousand Plateaus: Capitalism & Schizophrenia*. Volume 2. London: Athlone Press.
Deleuze, Gilles (1998) *Essays Critical and Clinical*. London: Verso.
Deleuze, Gilles (1989) *Cinema 2: The Time-Image*. London: Athlone Press.
Descola, Philippe (2014) *Beyond Nature & Culture*. Chicago and London: The University of Chicago Press.
Fisher, Mark (2018) Foreword. In: Davies W (ed.) *Economic Science Fictions*. London: Goldsmiths Press.
Foucault, Michel (1990) *The History of Sexuality: An Introduction*. London: Penguin.
Haraway, Donna (2016) *Staying with the Trouble: Making Kin in the Chthulucene*. Durham: Duke University Press.
Hughes, Sara M. (2020) On Resistance in Human Geography. *Progress in Human Geography* 44(6): 1–20.
Ingold, Tim (2010) *Making: Anthropology, Archaeology, Art and Architecture*. London and New York: Routledge.
Latour, Bruno (2017) *Down to Earth: Politics in the New Climate Regime*. Cambridge: Polity.
Morton, Timothy (2017) *Humankind: Solidarity with Nonhuman People*. London and New York: Verso.
Nelson, Maggie (2021) *On Freedom: Four Songs of Care and Constraint*. London: Jonathan Cape.
Owens, Leslie H. (1976) *This Species of Property: Slave Life and Culture in the Old South*. Oxford: Oxford University Press.
Povinelli, Elisabeth (2011) *Economies of Abandonment: Social Belonging and Endurance in Late Liberalism*. Durham: Duke University Press.

Reid, Julian (2020) Constructing Human versus Non-human Climate Migration in the Anthropocene: The Case of Migrating Polar Bears in Nunavut. *Anthropocenes – Human, Inhuman, Posthuman* 1(1): 2.

Robinson, Cedric J. (2021) *Black Marxism: The Making of the Black Radical Tradition*. London: Penguin.

Slater, Graham B. (2022) Terms of Endurance: Resilience, Grit, and the Cultural Politics of Neoliberal Education. *Critical Education* 13(1): 1–16.

Slotkin, Richard (1998) *The Fatal Environment: The Myth of the Frontier in the Age of Industrialization 1800–1890*. Norman: University of Oklahoma Press.

Taylor, Sunaura (2017) *Beasts of Burden: Animal and Disability Liberation*. New York and London: The New Press.

Tsing, Anna L. (2015) *The Mushroom at the End of the World: On the Possibility of Life in Capitalist Ruins*. Princeton: Princeton University Press.

CHAPTER 2

Carnivalesque Postcollectivity
Reenactment as Decolonial Subversion

Adela Goldbard

Inside an unfinished motel room, a group of eight or ten people are closely sitting together. The green hue of the video–reminiscent of surveillance imagery–implies that it was shot in complete darkness and suggests the inconspicuous character of the actions that are taking place, discreetly, in the middle of the night. It is cold, as can be appreciated by the people's outfits. The white glow in the characters' pupils–an effect of infrared lights–gives them a ghostly and scary aura, adding to the frightened facial expressions revealed by the close-up shots. The aesthetics of the night-vision technology makes the subjects 'blurry', but they can certainly be identified as people of color, mostly men. The atmosphere is tense and the person who appears to be their guide talks on the phone and curses in Spanish with some interspersed words in Hñähñu. He then rushes the group to leave the room and to quickly hop on the back of two pickup trucks, urging them to be silent and hide. The infrared lights allow us to see, in the darkness, the terrified faces of the subjects who, trying not to move, lay awkwardly in the box of the pickup trucks (Figure 2.1). The old vehicles traverse a rough and remote semidesert landscape, brushing against tree branches, nopales and magueys, and lifting dense clouds of dust, stunningly visible by the effect of the headlights and the night vision cameras. The identity of the camerapersons is concealed, but the unsettling intimacy of the shots and their point of view places them in a privileged position: from above, imperceptible to others due to darkness, but able to see because of the cameras' night vision technology–similar to that used by the military and hunters.

After the pickup trucks come to a halt, the distressed subjects are brought inside an abandoned–and ostensibly looted–unfinished house, and are forced to sit down on the cold concrete floor, tightly packed together, once again. We can certainly sense that their journey is not pleasant and, through the guide's dialogue with the house custodian, we soon understand that they are trying to cross the U.S.-Mexico border without documents. The hand-held night-vision camera complicitly immerses the viewer in the *safe house,* providing, once again, a sensorial, baffling and problematic close-up view of the migrants, but

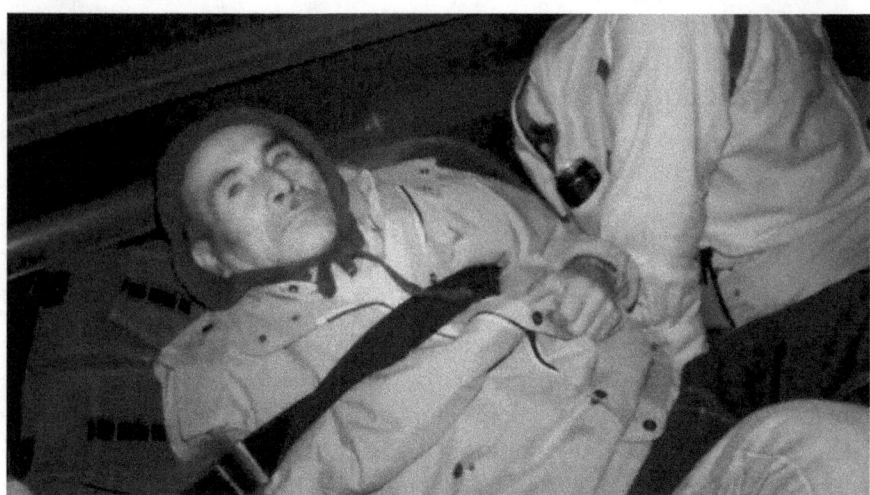

FIGURE 2.1 Still shot from *RINXUI [into the night]* by Adela Goldbard, 2019–20

not a hint about who is documenting the actions or about how is the camera allowed to follow the characters so closely. The safe house vigilante, before the puzzled eyes of the other *mojados* and with the endorsement of their guide–*coyote* or *pollero*–takes one of the three women that are part of the group to another room, presumably to rape her. We hear her screaming as the safe house–an American style architecture made of cinder blocks–is visible from outside.

> I was an immigrant who suffered a lot. When I left in '89, there was nothing. Nothing. All these houses you see here, there was nothing. This road, the pavement ... I left in '89; this road did not exist. The Gran Cañón Park did not exist. There was no drainage, there was no suspension bridge. I left when the town was at zero. There was no water to irrigate those milpas. When I left, I felt like crying. I went barefoot. My generation went barefoot. Without shoes. We wanted to leave to bring back dollars. It's the American Dream. All those houses that have an American style are the American Dream of people who are living in the U.S. All this was built with the money we brought. The roads too; the government didn't do anything. The community services we have were done with cooperation. I am sharing this story with you so you can rest. That's what I do when I bring a group, I tell them about my personal life to make it more real. And I tell them about the things you experience in the border, and it's really what I've been through. I lived 25 years in Las Vegas. Yes. I speak English.

When I left, I didn't speak Spanish or English. I first learnt English. My Spanish is not very good, but I try to improve it. When I was a *pollero* I was in jail for three years. My children in the U.S., abandoned, and me, in jail. Just think about that. This short talk is interesting, isn't it?
FEDERICO AGUSTÍN SANTIAGO, alias Commander[1]

A hand-held stabilized camera follows the subjects closely as they continue their journey through the semidesert, now hurriedly on foot, until they reach a barbed wire fence. This precarious device clearly differs from the grandiloquent imaginary of The Wall–a fortified and invincible border–inserting doubts about the film's spatial and temporal location. For the first time we observe two actions simultaneously, as one of the cameras now follows a border patrol car that is silently stalking the migrants from the other side of the fence. The *coyote* helps the migrants cross *la línea*, either by climbing a concrete column or by going under the barbed wire. But as soon as they set foot on 'U.S. soil', the border patrol siren goes off, and the migrants rapidly run to the hills to hide and erase their footprints with a branch. We then see the border patrol agents getting out of their cars, and searching, unsuccessfully, for the undocumented migrants with flashlights (Figure 2.2). "I want you guys come over here or go back to your country," is uttered, with a puzzling accent, by a border patrol agent using a megaphone. The precarious barb wire and the confusing identity of the border patrol agents become 'fissures' in the credibility of the actions, adding to the opacity and ambiguity of the documentation.

Here we explain to the people that they are already in the United States. This *is* the United States. They have already arrived, usually in Las Vegas. I tell them: "you are already in the United States, but you still have to be careful of border patrols." To be in the United States is to be afraid. Being anywhere illegally [sic], you see a light and you think it's Immigration. You see an ambulance, and you think it's coming for you. You see a city police car and you think it's Immigration. Being in the United States illegally [sic] is very scary. You are in your apartment and you see police outside and you think they are coming for you. Being in the U.S., once you've already crossed, it's not easy… without speaking English, even worse. You are in the store or in a restaurant and you don't even know what to ask for, and you have to give a 100-dollar bill because you don't know how much it

---

1 Fragment of personal communication between Adela Goldbard and Federico Agustín Santiago, 01.14.2019 (translation by Adela Goldbard; its syntax tries to convey the tone of the original conversation in Spanish).

FIGURE 2.2   Still shot from *RINXUI* [*into the night*] by Adela Goldbard, 2019–20

is, you don't know how to ask. Once you are in the United States, another challenge begins. Not only Immigration, not only the *cholos*.[2] Another way of life that you are not used to. You start to see the gringos saying: "look at that filthy guy, look at that *frijolero* [beaner]." If you are Mexican, they humiliate you. There is a lot of racism in the United States. It is not easy. A lot of people think it's just hard at the border. This talk takes an hour, it's to tell them about all the challenges in the United States. When you are in the United States you live in fear. You are not happy like when you were with your family. You are all the time with that fear of thinking: "At what time are they taking me?" Many challenges begin. Really, many challenges. The boss, he looks at you like you are too slow: "let's go outside, where's your social security [number]?" You want to drive a car. You don't have a license. You don't know English. You can't get your license because you're illegal [sic]. Just one mistake, you go to jail. Just one mistake, the American government doesn't forgive.

FEDERICO AGUSTÍN SANTIAGO, alias Commander

Violence and sadism escalate as the epic continues to unfold. *Cholos* threaten the *pollero* holding a knife to his throat, and point rifles at migrants after stealing their belongings (Figure 2.3). Hitmen from drug cartels and *rancheros*

---

2   *Cholo* is used in this context to name members of juvenile gangs on Mexico's northern border.

(minutemen vigilantes) violently pull and push the already shaken subjects, and fire their rifles to the air in order to scare them. In a cemetery, after harassing and robbing everyone in the group, *rancheros* retain two migrant women, sexually harass them, and are about to rape them when the moon, once again, appears from behind the clouds functioning as an ellipsis to the next action. In these scenes, 'unhidden' theatrical artifacts create more 'fissures' in the verisimilitude of the actions. For example, the fake gestures of the *pollero* when he has a knife held to his throat, the almost comically placed corpse on a pathway, and the visibly faked mourning tears of the widow (literally triggered with an onion), become theatrical incongruencies that question the artificiality of the documented scenes. The number, placement of the cameras and the crosscutting between images enable the disclosure of the staged nature of the film, complicating its documentary character. But even after these 'cracks' reveal the 'hoax' (the mise-en-scène), the narrative still feels inextricably and inexplicably real and harsh.

CHOLO:	Are you the fucking guide?
ADELA GOLDBARD:	No, we come alone.
CHOLO:	Tell me who the fucking guide is.
AG:	No, we came alone, the guide stayed back there.
CHOLO:	I don't believe you, bring me the fucking guide, because you won't leave here.
AG:	No, we have to go back, we... we are lost.

FIGURE 2.3 Still shot from *RINXUI* [*into the night*] by Adela Goldbard, 2019–20

CHOLO:	You are going back where?
AG:	That way, that way...
CHOLO:	What the fuck! You are going the other way! I don't believe you. All the fucking people say that.
AG:	They got us...
COMMANDER:	It was a small test, eh. How did you like it? Isn't it scary?
AG:	And what happens next?
COMMANDER:	They rape you.[3]
AG:	In there, in the tunnel?
COMMANDER:	Yeah. I can make a deal with him. If I have drugs or if I have money, I give him drugs and money. But if he asks me to give him two girls...
AG:	Do you negotiate with the girls?
COMMANDER:	No, not with the girls, with him. I don't tell the girls anything except: "two of you have to go with them, so that they let us all pass". Of course, everyone gets scared. Yes, they cry, everyone cries here. And we never tell the whole group that everything is a simulation. Normally in real life this does happen. But here we act it, some girls from our people come, and they pull them and they scream and cry. I didn't want to tell you, but I already told you. This is where a lot of fear starts, really. They [the *cholos*] bring guns and they bring knives... Most of them [the participants] are already crying here.

...

El Alberto is a self-governed Hñähñu community located in the great canyon of B'ot'ähi, the Mezquital Valley, in central México. El Alberto has resisted centuries of marginalization and oppression: in pre-Hispanic times, by the Toltecs and the Mexicas who demanded payment of tribute. Later on, by colonial governments who exploited their lands and labor, an operation that continued through the 19th century when the expansion of capitalism also meant the looting of land. There were also multiple attempts by post-revolutionary governments, especially since the 1950s, to assimilate and control the Hñähñu

---

3   Olivia Teresa Ruiz Marrujo estimates that 90% of the women that attempt to cross undocumented into the United States through Northern Mexico suffer sexual assault. (See De León 2015, 17).

communities of the region. But El Alberto established self-governance since the 1940s with a communal assembly as the ultimate horizontal decision-making body, and a straightforward set of rules for collaboration though communal labor that includes the creation of commissions and yearly communal charges without payment that each member has to hold every eight years. However, sovereignty is an ongoing struggle. The mentioned lineage of exploitation, racism and colonialism led the community to extreme poverty and isolation, which, in turn, resulted in a high level of migration to the United States. Since the 1980s, it became common practice for teenagers to follow the American Dream as soon as they graduated from middle school, and by the 1990s around 90% of the male adults of El Alberto had migrated to the U.S., transforming the community into a ghost town. Today, more than three quarters of the community live in the United States, mainly in Las Vegas, Utah and Arizona.

> To be a citizen in El Alberto you have to do social service. You have to be here personally to do a full year's social service; so, you come back to do the social service. One does not cross the border and forget. If you want to continue to be part of the community, you have to come back when you are appointed.
> ANTONINO[4]

In recent decades, El Alberto has strengthened its autonomy and communal labor through an array of commercial projects, all of them intimately connected to their territory and to the thoughtful use of its resources, "going from a passive resistance, to an active construction based on the principles of solidarity and reciprocity" (Gaete Balboa and Monroy Gaytán 2018, 11), a unique form of postcollective communal organization that looks into the past and into the present simultaneously. Some of the projects that the community has created in the last two decades include: the EcoAlberto hot springs, El Gran Cañón Eco-touristic Park (named after the Arizona Grand Canyon), a water purification plant also named EcoAlberto (in collaboration with Bonafont, a company from the transnational Danone), the women-led cooperative "Mujeres Reunidas" that sells their ixtle fiber products to Body Shop (another transnational company), and *La caminata nocturna* [the night walk], which, according to Netflix, is a *dark tourism* attraction–a form of tourism that involves visiting places that are historically associated with death

---

4 Personal communications, 12.23.2018 (translation by Adela Goldbard).

and tragedy. These communal projects have created jobs that have become the 'road back' to El Alberto for many migrants and have helped the community *delink* (Mignolo 2007) from Western modes of exploitation, extraction and patriarchal organization; they represent an *Indigenous modernity* that challenges the modern/colonial world-system (Quijano 2000), taking advantage of current capitalist trends (for example ecotourism, dark tourism, and 'socially responsible' companies) while preserving a holistic and respectful relationship to the land and the nonhuman. Breaking romanticized Western imaginaries of the Indigenous way-of-life, the Hñähñu of El Alberto–as may other Indigenous communities in the country–perform a unique and radical postcollectivity, their own modernity and sovereignty, interconnected (economically) but delinked (ideologically) from Mexico's and transnational neoliberal modernities, "decolonizing power by strengthening its autonomy of government and community work" (Gaete Balboa and Monroy Gaytán 2018, 101).

> "This is where the real truth begins. Here you are going to obey, if not, you go back. There are not going to be any more questions on the way, there are not going to be any more answers. Here you hold hands and team up; here we are going to start the real journey." After praying we have another conversation... We are going to talk about what you are going to do in the dangers. If I tell you that you have to run, you run. If you say: "I'm not going to walk anymore", I'll leave you there. I am not going to lose the whole group because you can no longer walk. I leave you in a small road if anything, so that the *migra* can pick you up. Right now, I'm telling you this softly, because when I'm an actor, it's different: a very deep voice, very heavy, very angry, no smile, no happiness. Like the guides, all the time at the border they are very drugged, so as not to be afraid. All the time they take out the cocaine and go to the nose. Marijuana and cocaine. All the time it is danger. There is no laughter, no play. All the time it's fear.
>
> FEDERICO AGUSTÍN SANTIAGO, alias Commander

Members of El Alberto have been reenacting their border-crossing experiences as a touristic attraction for more than 15 years, under the name of *La caminata nocturna* [the night walk] "to raise awareness among people... to make people aware of how difficult and hard it is to cross into the United States (Gerardo),"[5] but also as a collective, cathartic, and even sadistic carnivalization of trauma;

---

5 Personal communications, 12.23.2018 (translation by Adela Goldbard).

a regenerative and decolonial mode of memory making; and a source of economic wellbeing.

The reenactment takes place in El Alberto's canyon and valleys. Their semidesert ecosystem of mesquite trees, magueys and nopales, according to the ones who have crossed the border, very accurately resembles the Sonora/Arizona landscape. The Hñähñu people of El Alberto rely on their vast and embodied knowledge of their territory to trace the different routes for the reenactment. Without a map or a compass, they navigate the territory they have stewarded and defended for centuries: from the Toltecs, from the Mexicas, from the Spaniards, from the Mexican government, from exploitative companies, from neighboring communities (Figure 2.4). The Sonora Desert, with ICE's (Immigration and Customs Enforcement) nonhuman allies, is displaced to Hidalgo. The Tula River becomes Río Bravo, and El Alberto becomes Altar, the last town migrants usually stop at before advancing into the desert. In preparation for crossing, participants of *La caminata* pray at El Alberto's church; they buy water, crackers and canned tuna in the general store, and wait for the *pollero* in the only hotel in town; in the cemetery, they hide to rest. The unfinished Americanized local architecture becomes safe houses and drug trafficking facilities. Empty sewage tubes are traps where the *cholos* hide and corner migrants to rob and rape them.

Community members of El Alberto leverage human and nonhuman agency and employ the particularities of the local architecture to generate a subversive embodied *re-creation* of their border-crossing narratives–impossible to retell only verbally because of the incommunicability of extreme violence– more than two thousand kilometres away from their original location in the border. Time and space spiral in this reenactment.

Undocumented crossings of the border increased exponentially after the North America Free Trade Agreement (NAFTA) was signed in 1994, and the Mexican economy, once again, crashed. The U.S. government responded with the Prevention Through Deterrence (PTD) policy: fortifying the traditional urban crossing points through fencing and stationed border agents to redirect the routes of migrants into the Sonoran Desert and to 'discourage' migrants from crossing.

> The basic premise was, and continues to be, that if they can't stop the huddled mases, at least they can funnel them into remote areas where the punishment handed out by difficult terrain will save money (or so some foolishly thought) and get this unsightly mess out of public view, which it did.
> DE LEÓN 2015, 6

FIGURE 2.4   Still shot from *RINXUI* [*into the night*] by Adela Goldbard, 2019–20

This strategic and tragic policy enrolled nonhumans as perpetrators targeting migrants: the desert's extreme weather, lack of water, inedible vegetation and poisonous wildlife made the Border Patrol's job less strenuous, since they could "draw on the agency of animals and other nonhumans to do its dirty work while simultaneously absolving itself of any blame connected to migrant injuries or loss of life" (De León 2015, 43).

> Well, it was very difficult. We crossed during the cold weather... I imagine you have some idea of how cold it gets in a desert, right? At midnight, the coyotes howled, wild dogs, as we call them. We had to look for some nopales, roast them, eat them without tortillas, without salt, to endure those five days we were there.
> GERARDO

Costumes, props and mockups of border patrol cars add realism to an experience that for the reenactors tells their truth and *is* real. We witness how embodied memory *makes* history while narrating it, or as Natalie Alvarez points out:

> the overarching gesture of this reenactment is not recuperative so much as generative, instantiating conditions of possibility still to come. The reenactment operates in a transtemporal mode–a present-past that looks back on the reality of migration within the experience of the reenactment from a future perspective.
> 2018, 119

Every border-crossing experience condenses and expands in this performance in which individual experiences are collectivized and each body represents the community's body. "Historical memory is reactivated and at the same time reelaborated and resignified in subsequent crises and cycles of rebellion" (Cusicanqui 2020, 6). Truth, fiction and memory merge in a temporal spiral movement that *corrects* the past in the present and gazes into the future, producing a continuously regenerated, subversive, empowered, communal and thoughtful narrative of migration that integrates to the (contemporary) cosmogony and identity of the Hñähñu people of El Alberto. Events are reenacted from the interpreters' memories, but the perspective used is reversed: the victim becomes the oppressor, subverting power relations and empowering the oppressed. Reenactors *become* border patrol agents, *cholos*, drug dealers, and, as them, are violent and sadistic. When Hñähñu migrants play border patrol agents, speak in English, and use the words that the agents used to repress them, social roles are inverted, and reality is suspended and transformed. The victim/perpetrator dichotomy of border-crossing is subverted, and, in this *carnivalesque* world, we witness the defeat of power by performing power, by embodying the oppressor, by using violence to neutralize violence: reenactment as subversion.

> Here, pick-up trucks arrive. We 'load' people in them, but they are going to catch us. It's a show, it's an action where Immigration catches the migrant. Here a *corretiza* will take place. If you run, if you hide over there, as I told you, then you come back later, and we meet in the same place when Immigration leaves. I like this scene very much. If they catch you, they tell you that you will go to the detention center, to jail, that they will sentence you to three years, five years, for crossing the border, it is a federal crime. Here I like this show, because here Immigration acts half in Spanish and half in English. Here I like this show a lot. Well, I like everything.
> FEDERICO AGUSTÍN SANTIAGO, alias Commander

La caminata has been perceived by the government as an insurgent, rebellious and dangerous act of resistance–which it certainly is. This reenactment challenges the *politics of memory*–"who wants whom to remember what, and why" (Burke 1997, 56)–, questions imposed modes of memory-making, and gives community members access to the production of their own historical narratives. As many other forms of Indigenous communal storytelling (such as rituals, chants, and embroidery, to name a few), *La caminata* contests Western hierarchical and verbal-centered modes of memory-building. Non-written and

FIGURE 2.5 Still shot from *RINXUI [into the night]* by Adela Goldbard, 2019–20

non-verbal modes for the transmission of knowledge have been consistently ignored, discredited as non-valid, and systematically obscured by the Western cannon. This *epistemic violence* reveals how "part of the colonizing project throughout the Americas consisted [and still consists] in discrediting autochthonous ways of preserving and communicating historical understanding" (Taylor 2003 34). *La caminata* allows a shift from the verbal to the embodied, thus delinking from Western canonical modes of retelling and remembering. It is a structural refusal or *obstruction*: a form of *sensate sovereignty* "that is felt viscerally, proprioceptively, and affectively, to counteract the epistemic violence of normative writing" (Robinson 2020, 23–24) (Figure 2.5).

• • •

RINXUI [into the night] (Goldbard, 2019–20) is a collaborative exploration/re-elaboration of *La caminata* through the grammar of film: a translation of the embodied and live nature of the performance to an audiovisual, sensorial and immersive filmic language. Despite the lasting nature of film–which contrasts with the ephemerality of performance–*RINXUI*, due to its layered and ambiguous structure and to its sensorial aesthetic, delivers a shifting and immersive experience that somehow relates and complicates the experience of the live performance. *RINXUI* re-elaborates–for the video cameras and for a remote audience a communal *performance of oral history* constituted as a violent and radical mode of collective social remembering. By generating a meta-narrative where ambiguity plays a central role (the equivocal nature of the characters and actions is amplified and blurs the limits between fact and fiction), *RINXUI* immerses, critically disturbs, and challenges the viewer to 'read the politics between the lines' (Figure 2.6).

RINXUI was produced in collaboration with the board members of EcoAlberto Park, Federico Agustín Santiago, Francisco Ramón García and Eugenio Cruz García, and administrator Ivonne Castillo Hernández, and with the spontaneous help of Federico alias Commander (the guide or *pollero*), leading the actors, taking decisions about the camera positions and angles, and rushing the crew to keep up with the actions. To focus on the Hñähñu people's point of view and experience, in *RINXUI* the tourists have been purposely left out, reverting the reenactment to its original version when only community members participated.

In the last decade, *La caminata* has drawn attention from academia, the entertainment industry and the press. Academic articles have critically addressed *La caminata's* socio-political background and aesthetics from a decolonial standpoint (Gaete Balboa and Monroy Gaytán 2018) or pulling from performance studies (Alvarez 2018). Documentaries–such as Netflix *Dark Tourism* series–and news reportages usually rely on *experiential journalism,* framing the experience of the author as/with tourist(s), usually complementing it with pseudo-ethnographic materials (interviews and portrayals of characters in their every-day lives) to counterweight the sensationalizing of the reenactment. For *RINXUI*, the conversations with board members of EcoAlberto were

FIGURE 2.6   Still shot from *RINXUI* [*into the night*] by Adela Goldbard, 2019–20

initiated almost a year and a half before the shooting took place. I attended several meetings with them, with reenactors, and with El Alberto communal authorities to present my idea and start a dialogue about their expectations—both conceptual/creative and monetary—and to better understand the stakes of their performance and their holistic communal socio-economic project. During the community engagement and pre-production phases of the film, I carried out open interviews with several participants where they narrated some of their border-crossing experiences (some quotes in the previous sections of this essay are taken from those interviews). The impromptu conversation that I recorded while Federico alias Commander showed me, the cinematographer and the producer of the film the route of *La caminata* during the scouting, was a fascinating interdisciplinary practice of decolonial critique, oral history, and acting, in which time and place expanded and collapsed in a spiral, replicating the mechanisms that the reenactment implements. In a split second, Fede shifted back and forth between: interpreting/embodying Commander—a fictious character based on his real experiences as a *pollero*—explaining how he addressed tourists (and scared them) in the discursive parts of *La caminata*; making fun of my crew members for not being brave enough, for being tired or scared—similarly to how he mocks tourists, in a gesture of *decolonial revenge*—retelling his own experiences as a migrant; literally pointing out how El Alberto had changed over time due to remittances; and relating the success of their communal project, specifically of *La caminata*. When 'in character', Fede used a harsh and aggressive voice; when 'out of character', he switched back to his regular voice and employed a tone that was by turns condescending, sarcastic or serious. The layered complexities of this conversation-turned-monologue mirror the reenactment's multidimensional character: a communal and embodied oral history that functions both as a tourist attraction and as a decolonial/subversive device where spatial, temporal and ontological boundaries are blurred, while normative and hegemonic roles and rules are undermined.

An experiential documentation of *La caminata*—I argued in my meetings with board members—would strip the reenactment of these complexities. I instead proposed a cinematographic remake of the reenactment, with a structure and aesthetics that would add meta layers to the performance, complicating it, instead of simplifying it, for the audience. After several assemblies over months of negotiations, we agreed on the characters (only community members), method (real-time chronological filming with minimal repetitions), aesthetics/equipment (three night vision cameras plus additional infrared lights, stabilizers and tripod), logistics (one full night of shooting with two breaks), consensus (final edit of film would have to be approved by board members),

CARNIVALESQUE POSTCOLLECTIVITY 41

FIGURE 2.7 Still shot from *RINXUI* [*into the night*] by Adela Goldbard, 2019–20

and compensation for the community ($30,000 pesos fee for the location, the payment of accommodations for the crew in EcoAlberto's cabins, the payment of food for the crew and cast in their restaurant, a short-version of the film for the Park's social media to be delivered one month after the shooting, and the insertion of their logos in every version of the film). We signed a contract and sealed the deal sharing a couple of *caguamas* (1-liter beers).

On the day of the shooting, at dusk, when all ambient lights faded, the cameras' screens started glowing with an almost paranormal green shine (Figure 2.7). We spent the next hours in total darkness, only briefly interrupted by the headlights of the pickup trucks and the occasional use of small flashlights, until a crescent moon partially illuminated the canyon. Since infrared lights are invisible to the human eye, the spectral glow of the cameras' screens was our only means for visualizing the scene and its lighting. We carried three medium-size infrared LED panels–usually used for surveillance of ample locations–made portable with a DIY adaptation of heavy-duty hefty batteries. Our 'invisible lights' made some landscape features and architectural elements punctually appear in the cameras' screens, while keeping most of the landscape in the shadows. But for our bare eyes, the landscape was continuously concealed.

Although very different in nature, infrared light and x-rays have a shared *forensic aesthetic:* they both relate to the finding/revealing of corporeal visual evidence ultimately associated to violence and death–criminals, targets, accidents, diseases. The ostensibly translucent imagery of x-rays allows the doctor or technician to see fractures, tumors, etc. that are 'invisible' to the bare eye; while the capacity of infrared light to 'trespass' darkness allows the soldier, the police officer, or the hunter to see their prey. The 'revelatory' aspect of these technologies places the users of devices such as CT scanners and surveillance cameras in a position of power: *cyborg vision* allows them to observe what others cannot. Translucency, increased contrast, and glow, emphasize bodies–notoriously human bodies, 'expose their guts', dissect them, and make them vulnerable to the stimulated gaze of the 'predator.'

In *RINXUI*, the cyborg night-vision the viewer is equipped with, allows them to witness what the protagonists of the film are incapable of seeing, and, more importantly, to see *them* without being seen, bringing into question the ethics and the *politics of witnessing*. Evidence of violence and death 'glows' as an augmented vision immerses the viewer in *translucent darkness*. But this gaze is not only voyeuristic but violent. As the night-vision cameras move closer to the protagonists' bodies, they become more exposed and vulnerable to the viewer's gaze, and the viewer becomes accomplice of the antagonists. This violent transference of violence puts the viewer in an ethical conundrum that can lead to discomfort and to looking away. This discomfort is intentional: a decolonial gesture that forces the viewer to critically consider their position of power, not only within the film, but in regards to any privileged position they might hold in comparison to the reenactors, who, unlike them, are unable to turn away from the violence pictured in the film (Figure 2.8).

In clear contrast to Hollywood's finished, perfectionist, and flawless aesthetic, which usually leaves no space for 'cracks' or for the 'breaking' of verisimilitude, *RINXUI's* rough, loose, and flawed aesthetic, where theatrical or cinematic artifacts are not hidden, continuously 'fractures' the viewer's expectations and throws them off balance. 'Realistic' violent movies rely on non-chronological filming and impeccable editing, which gives them the artificial appearance of being complete and truthful. This completeness detaches and distances the viewer, transforming the representation of violence into passive and uncritical entertainment for profit. The use of sequential real-time filming and unscripted dialogues pulled from memory and experience, challenges the traditional concept of realism (truthful representation) based on verisimilitude (having the appearance of truth). In a loop of unceasing darkness, the episodes of fictionalized reenactment that compose *RINXUI*, incarnate reality to generate an uncomfortable sensorial experience for the audience of the film (comparable to the tourists' experience in *La carminata*). The staging of communal/collective memory that brings the body to the center in the performance, is underscored in the film by the *dissecting glow* of infrared lights. This double corporeal emphasis–through embodiment and forensic

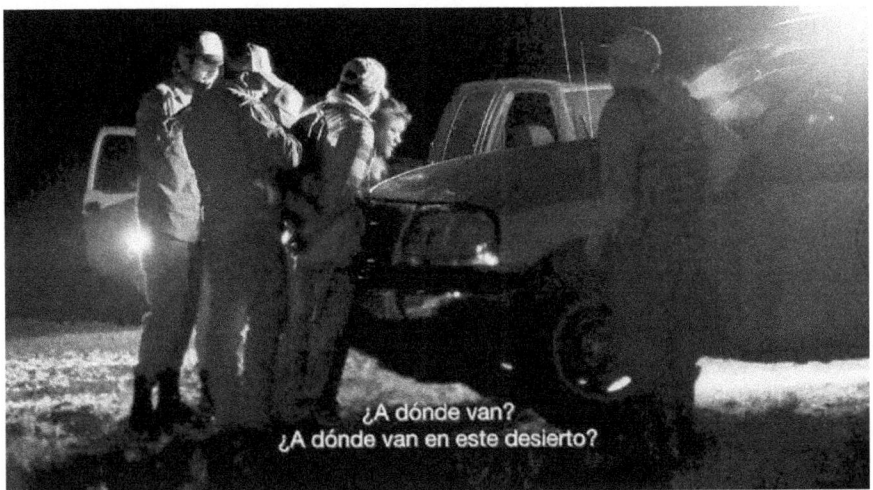

FIGURE 2.8   Still shot from *RINXUI* [*into the night*] by Adela Goldbard, 2019–20

aesthetics–complicitly immerses the audience of the film in the sensorial distress of an endless epic, where the radical use of dramatic violence becomes a mode of decolonial subversion and revenge. And it becomes the audience's choice to either look away or to read the politics between the lines.

References

Alvarez, Natalie (2018) *Immersions in Cultural Difference. Tourism, War, Performance.* Ann Arbor: University of Michigan Press.

Burke, Peter (1997) *Varieties of Cultural History.* New York: Cornell.

De León, Jason (2015) *The Land of Open Graves. Living and Dying on the Migrant Trail.* Oakland: University of California Press.

Gaete Balboa, Pablo G and Monroy Gaytán, José F. (2018) *Economía Social y solidaria hñähñu: Descolonialidad del poder en la comunidad de El Alberto.* Hidalgo. Mexico City: CLAVE Editorial.

Mignolo, Walter D. (2007) Delinking. The rhetoric of modernity, the logic of coloniality and the grammar of de-coloniality. *Cultural Studies* 21 (2–3): 449–514. https://doi.org/10.1080/09502380601162647

Quijano, Anibal (2000) Coloniality and Modernity/Rationality. *Cultural Studies* 21 (2–3): 168–178. http://dx.doi.org/10.1080/09502380601164353

Rivera Cusicanqui, Silvia (2020) *Ch' ixinakax utxiwa. On Practice and Discourses of Decolonization.* Cambridge: Polity Press.

Robinson, Dylan (2020) *Hungry Listening. Resonant Theory for Indigenous Sound Studies*. Minneapolis: University of Minnesota Press.

Taylor, Diana (2003) *The Archive and the Repertoire: Performing Cultural Memory in the Americas*. Durham and London: Duke University Press.

CHAPTER 3

Collecting Crumbs of Lost Knowledge
Learning from Postindustrial and Postsocialist Disruptions

Andrzej W. Nowak

> If it goes up, he, oh yes, it will go up, but I said, it's going to move. Half a pickaxe will be ... you have to put the wheelbarrow here, this way. But ... we'll put a wheelbarrow and put it here, and you'll go on the right flank ... how high the wood is, make a cape, tear off the shelf, and then, chop, chop.
>
> RAKOWSKI 2009, 168

∴

1   Introduction

I come from Konin, a town that experienced its most significant period of development in history during the communist era. From a small shtetl, once on the border between the Russian Empire and Prussia, it transformed into a city of almost 100 thousand inhabitants. After 1989, however, the post-communist transformation was a period of decline rather than development. The story of this city will serve as my starting point. Konin, as a modernist now-topia, concrete Utopia, was first built at the cost of erasing pre-modern, earlier communities. After a brief period of prosperity, it has been the subject of postindustrial erasure. The text points out the layers of knowledge (Nowak 2021b) and forgetfulness that make up the history of the communities in and around this city. The purpose of the text is to teach us two lessons – the first is relatively well-known and recognized today, which is the story of the costs of modernization and the displacement of what is pre-modern, indigenous, and local. This part of the story resonates with posthumanist, postcolonial, feminist, etc. critiques. More complicated and challenging to accept is the second lesson. It is the lesson of what socialist modernization has achieved (Chukhrov 2020), how even this imperfect concrete[1] Utopia, or perhaps it would be better to say a now-topia,[2] was nevertheless an achievement that, in some cases, obtain more than Western Marxists and leftist thinkers had theoretically anticipated. I am referring primarily to Keti Chukhrov's reference to areas freed from direct commodification and the production of social institutions and devices intended to accomplish de-alienation processes (2020, 135).

Since I am aware of the problems that are caused by reckless and hasty processes of modernization, I would like to try to defend modernization and modernity with the above in mind. I would also like to point out what we lose when modernity disintegrates. The concrete modernist utopia of the emerging industrial city was not a perfect one. Moreover, it realized the promise of socialism/communism only vaguely and in a very ambiguous way, but nevertheless embarked on a mission to reclaim it. Thinking about the concrete Konin's now-topia, I would like to follow this indication: *A Utopia is not a happy, ecstatic state but the basis for further struggles and further conquests* (Bernal 1939, 392). The method adopted in this text is "evidence-based storytelling," a combination of autoethnographic observation (Lunceford 2015) and philosophical reflection. I follow here in part the approach developed by Annemarie Mol:

> Philosophers who leave their studies are likely to be surprised. Examining a practice is not a matter of collecting suitable examples but of learning new lessons. Good case studies inspire theory, shape ideas, and shift conceptions. They do not lead to universally valid conclusions, but neither do they claim to do so. Instead, the lessons learned are pretty specific.
> MOL 2008, 9

My autoethnographic experience serves as the starting point of my analysis, allowing me to filter the material and complement the philosophical reflection with a situated starting point. In this approach, as I have advocated, the work of autoethnography supplemented by empirical references should "feed" theoretical reflection, not replace it. It is meant to help reconstruct a

---

1 In this text I deliberately draw on the ambiguity of the word "concrete" meaning a building material and something tangible. It is worth noting that the word "concrete" was also used to describe the most orthodox part of the Communist Party apparatus, that which was most hostile to reform and change (see Wałdoch 2021).
2 I use the phrase to emphasize that utopia does not necessarily mean a detached, effortful process of imagining or dreaming, but rather a concrete forward planning that becomes performative. By embodying utopia, we make it. Here I follow John Desmond Bernal and his understanding of utopia (Bernal 1939, 382).

"small humankind," "a miniature humankind" as the parallel of situated and contextualized universalism (Santos 2015). The purpose of this reconstruction is to highlight the parallel proposal that Путь к Коммунизму (The Road to Communism) gave us in comparison to what Sousa Santos expressed as Nuestra America. This study presents auto-ethnographic observations that come from the author's personal background and research in connection with the artistic project *Holiday in Konin (Wczasy w Koninie)*.[3] This project, in which I am a participant, aims to recontextualize the postindustrial past of Konin. The ironic holiday in the postindustrial city seeks to collect and recover crumbs of disappearing knowledge and archive traces of the communities that created it and were bonded by it.[4] What I particularly want to emphasize in the text is the reflection on a specific form of epistemicide (Santos 2015), which, after 1989, included knowledge related to the socialist and modernist experience of the region. Rapid neoliberal deindustrialization in the 90s (Zysiak 2019) changed Poland's demographic and professional structure and industrial cities like Konin. Former miners retired, often prematurely. Their children, forced to emigrate, either within Poland, to larger cities, or abroad, interrupted the continuity of social development. The collapse of large industrial plants after 1989 resulted in changes that were not only demographic but also economic and cultural. The latter is connected with the fact that during the communist period, large industrial plants sponsored local culture (Stańczyk 2019) and sports and were responsible for maintaining community centers, places of entertainment, and sports for the working population (Markiewicz 1961, 1962; Zawadzka 2019). Their collapse meant cutting off these financial obligations imposed on state enterprises during the People's Republic of Poland. New, mainly commercial and service companies and small industrial enterprises, often foreign, are not bound by such obligations; moreover, they avoid tax burdens in Poland. This results in an accelerated loop of underdevelopment and

---

3 This project continued under a new name, "Trzeci TOR" (Third TRACK). The name refers to the numbering of the platforms (tracks) at Konin Railway Station. During and shortly after the Communist era, the third platform was responsible for train traffic to the industrial sector, particularly transporting workers to mines and power plants. Similar to the previous project, this one aims to preserve the memory of industrial Konin. The focal point of the project is to preserve the large excavator, SRs-1800 "Dolores", as a cultural-historical artifact instead of dismantling it for scrap metal. An interview with Mariusz Harmasz the leader of the Third TOR program and chief foreman Grzegorz Przebieracz of KWB Konin: https://www.youtube.com/watch?v=s6IZrFYLm8s and presentation of the excavator: https://www.youtube.com/watch?v=-LhaOmYODkc (Accessed June 20 2023).
4 Interview with Mariusz Harmasz, local artist – head and initiator of the project *Wczasy w Koninie*, https://kulturaupodstaw.pl/slady-w-miescie/ (Accessed June 15 2023).

urban shrinkage, reminiscent of the American "rust belt" with its flagship city of Detroit (LeDuff 2014).[5]

Population change and population decline also entail a loss of the knowledge that these professionals had. Deindustrialization has disembodied knowledge and skills inscribed in workers' hands. This knowledge that was co-constituted by working collectives also has disappeared. Today, even though we all readily refer to knowledge, we cannot even recognize what we have lost (Rakowski 2009). This is all the more paradoxical because today, in philosophy, we can finally appreciate the knowledge embodied in the labor of hands, contained in the synergy of working collectives, bodies, and machines. Research in cognitive science and science and technology (Hutchins 1996; Varela et al. 2017) draws our attention to the fact that in the laboratory and production of knowledge, not only is the scientist essential, but also the technician blowing glass; and in a factory both the engineer designing cars and the foreman knowing how to "press where it is needed". But it is only now, as it disappears with deindustrialization, that this knowledge embodied in grassroots efforts has started to be appreciated and recognized. The bitter paradox is that the golden age of industrialism, which depended so heavily on the hands and bodies of workers as knowledge deposited and embodied in the labor rhythms of the workers' collective, did not appreciate this knowledge either (Dunn 2010). Currently, knowledge has either been excessively abstracted to the point of losing meaning in an overabundance of printed but empty content, or it is being perceived as specialized knowledge written on behalf of interested parties. Nevertheless, practical knowledge, which is acquired through hands-on experience, embodied skills, and the congruence of mind and body, may have been prevalent in the industrial world's reality. However, such kinds of expertise were underappreciated in the knowledge structures of that era (Sennett 1998). The text points out that we should learn from analyzing the disappearing world of postindustrial postsoviet working-class communities. We should study the process of the loss of knowledge embodied in workers' collectives, in the hands of professionals, and how this world of labor also co-produced outside labor communities and culture.

---

5 It is worth noting that the website (blog), which critically analyzed the reeling and deindustrialization of horse meat was called *Polish Detroit* http://polskiedetroit.blogspot.com/ (Accessed June 20 2023). This comparison to Detroit is very often used also to describe the postindustrial decline of the city of Łódź (Zysiak 2020).

By analyzing the processes of disrupting knowledge circuits, the disintegration of communities, and the disruption of its transmission, we can learn a potential lesson for the future. By learning from the destabilized postsocialist and postindustrial (Nowak 2016, 2019, 2021b) world, we can learn how to build, stabilize, and sustain communities sharing embodied knowledge in the future. Lessons from postindustrial and post-Soviet decay (Golubev 2021; Nadkarni 2020; Nowak 2021a) can prepare us for the challenges that disruption associated with the Anthropocene/Capitalocene (Moore 2016) will bring.

2 Erasing a Map – Establishing a Concrete Utopia

Modernism required the establishment through conquest, often destruction, of what had existed before. Because it was created by destroying what existed before, socialist Konin was very modernist in that sense. At the same time, at least the socialist version of modernity was also an incredible phenomenon of creation (Spufford 2010). Cities were created ad nihilo, blocks of flats, cultural institutions, theatres, cinemas, and cafes. Vibrant cities appeared in place of small, often underdeveloped villages. Also, during the communist period, my hometown of Konin became a city of people with upward mobility, transformed the landscape of the surrounding villages, and created a new town – ultimately with a plan (not fully and successfully implemented) to make new people (Markiewicz 1961, 1962). This promise of "newness" in the case of Konin was realized, for example, in the fact that the new city was built on a different bank of the Warta River than its older existing part of the city (although it is worth adding that logistical considerations were probably the main factor here). The socialist town was built on the site of former villages and, like many other cities in the former Soviet bloc or U.S.S.R., was actually made from scratch.

The phrase "from scratch" is crucial here. The modernistic Konin was only seemingly created in a vacuum. In reality, the purity of the designers' drawing boards had to be obtained thanks to the work of bulldozers (Scott, 1998). The New Town required the destruction of pre-existing villages, orchards, fields, and landscape compositions. Additionally, it is worth mentioning that the town was created and grew thanks to lignite opencast mining, a technology that requires the most radical changes to the landscape (Gilewska and Otremba 2011; Kasztelewicz 2005, 2014). Several of the former opencast pits were incorporated into the developing city. They were gradually recultivated during the communist period, and park areas, recreational plots, and a cemetery were created on their premises. The modernist and industrial Utopia was accomplished thanks to the epistemicide of the rural, peasant, and traditional knowledge.[6]

Moreover, the memory of the town's Jewish past was erased (Richmond, 1996). Epistemicide also applied to knowledge related to the Yiddish culture that had existed here for hundreds of years. The new city required a fresh start, and in this way, socialist modernist ideology was easily intertwined with old nationalist and anti-Semitic demons. What was past was regarded as suspect, doomed to destruction. In this way, constructing a new socialist concrete utopia occurred at the cost of forgetting Atlantis and its annihilation. Atlantis was name, Józef Lewandowski, a Jewish resident of the former shtetl that was Konin, called pre-war Konin and its fate (Lewandowski 1991). The Nazi extermination machine annihilated hundreds of years of co-history of this city, created, often in the majority, by its Jewish inhabitants. The so-called "old Konin" – a part that used to be predominantly Jewish before World War II still haunted me with a specific atmosphere of emptiness in my youth. Thanks to my reading, only later could I discover where it came from. The destruction of the Jewish town by the Nazis, in this ironic way, helped to build the new socialist city.

Also, the settlement of Olenders (Kruczkowski 2019, 2023) religious emigrants who came to these lands (Woźniak 2013) were erased from the modernist-socialist picture. They are still commemorated on the maps of Wielkopolska: the word "Olendry" or "Holendry" can still be found in the names of some towns and villages. These immigrants shared with the people of Wielkopolska their expert knowledge of taming water, draining polders, and building canals and ponds (Wallerstein 2011, 66). When we think of these North German and Dutch settlers, we cannot help but recall the early modern period, Spinoza, and the triumph of reason (Lord 2015). These Protestant settlers transferred their know-how and thus controlled nature. At the same time, they were the pioneers of early capitalist economic and environmental relations.

Yes, it was easier to start designing with a "clean" map. A new city, as I mentioned, requires new people. There was a rapid transfer of the rural population, also known in other areas. The former villagers' customs, habits, and knowledge

---

6 It is worth remembering that the USSR, despite its anti-colonial rhetoric sold to the outside world, was itself a project inheriting imperial and colonial designs and fantasies. Such colonialism was, for example, its attitude towards the indigenous peoples of Siberia. Another problem with the postcolonial reading of Soviet history is Russia's present-day embellishment and appropriation of the heritage of the positive side of the USSR. This erases the fact that Ukraine, for example, can be regarded as an equally legitimate heir to the USSR. For example, the history of the Soviet internet (which ultimately failed) and Soviet cybernetics are largely the achievements of scholars from the Ukrainian city of Kharkiv (see Peters 2016).

were lost. It was no longer applicable in the new setting. The inhabitants maintained a hybrid identity over a prolonged period, potentially throughout, due to the patchwork-like nature of changes. When my family and I moved from the village to the new housing estate, the old rural landscape was still visible between the newly built blocks of flats: the remains of houses, the ruins where we used to play, the wild orchards, and the fields still cultivated in the vicinity. The socialist modernist "right angles" were still negotiating with the entwined baroque forms of self-organization of the past (Law and Ruppert 2016; Santos 2015). Moreover, this strange hybrid creation lasted until the collapse of the communist dream in 1989.

I spent my childhood exploring, on foot and by bicycle, this tangle of baroque expressions of nature, of the future, crossed by modernity in the form of pipes, roads, and railroads.[7] It is worth noting that, significantly for the final sections of my text, this baroque self-organization quickly began to entwine and reclaim what it had been previously lost due to the Cartesian grid of modernity taming it. Disused railroad tracks, old roads, and decaying factory halls quickly became scenes of natural excess, an explosion of recovering vitality in the "baroque" self-organization of matter (Law and Ruppert 2016).

3 Hybrid Modern

Let us now turn our attention to the hybrid modern. This epistemicide of pre-modern knowledge was not a "clear-cut" process; pre-modern knowledge was embedded in the bodies and habits and became part of the construction of modern knowledge, and societies formed it, stuck to it, grew on it. For instance, hobbies dating back to their rural origins were still popular among the working-class male population. Fishing, or angling, was especially popular. It has been carried out in a particular way. It took place in a hybrid world involving both human and posthuman reality, as it would be described today. The fishing grounds were lakes created in place of flooded mine pits and canals near power plants. The latter were special because they were filled with heated water (Hillbricht-Ilkowska and Zdanowski 1988; Najberek and Solarz 2011; Zdanowski et al. 2020). This, in turn, resulted from the fact that the Konin canals and lakes system was connected into one specific industrial and natural

---

7 My memories are similar to those of Marxist Andrii Movchan from Kiev. In his work *Pedagogy of Progress*, he demonstrates how the communist pedagogy of progress, as it was enacted during the construction phase, was intertwined with pre-Soviet and post-Soviet realities (see Movchan 2016).

ecosystem. The water from the lakes was used to cool the furnaces of the power plant, and returning warmer, it heated lakes simultaneously. To prevent the complete eutrophication of their waters, they were stocked with exotic Asian fish species not typically found in Poland: amur and bighead carp. In this way, in the heart of socialist modernity, the workers, the new people of the system, followed their rather traditional reactionary, rural customs, catching Asian fish of considerable size, which benefited from the heated lakes. The warm water also served the development of tourist and recreational resorts on their shores. Crowds were bathing and sunbathing on the beaches from which both Konin power plants were perfectly visible. We perceived it as a natural element of the landscape. We were not surprised by the tangle of pipes, electric wires, chimneys, trains carrying coal, canals, and resting places.

Furthermore, the ability of rural and working-class people today to consider leisure activities by the lake is the outcome of socialist and industrial development that happened not too long ago. In the past, Polish peasants working in semi-slavery conditions in the countryside could not imagine taking time off by the lake (Kalinowski and Wyduba 2021). Yes, real socialism, although it did not deliver what the communist dreams had dreamed of, still remained a "transitional phase" (Chukhrov 2020), but it did much to create bubbles, spheres free of direct commodification, and viable, fulfilled mini-utopias. The hubbub of the voices of working-class children on the beaches of the lakes near Konin is something that, from the perspective of the societal fascism of devastated suburbs (Santos 2015), the slums of the Global South, is still a dream that may one day come to pass.

4 We Step into Modernist Now-topia in "Children's Shoes"

The progress and development of industrial socialism have come at a cost, however. As noted above, the foundation was laid by epistemicide, both deliberate (by repressing the rural past) and passive (by silent accepting the epistemicide committed by others, such as the erasure of the memory of the Jewish people and national minorities exterminated by Nazi Germany during World War II). The socialist-industrialist modernity had made a bargain, perhaps a malevolent one. It is not my place to pass judgment. However, it occurred. I will describe its specifics with an example. Ryszard Kapuściński, before he started, for better or for worse (Wainaina 2007), to be known as a global, anti-colonial but at the same time modernist journalist, was also a chronicler (including a photographer) of the emerging People's Republic of Poland. Interestingly, in 1959, he made a reporter's visit and captured the emergence of this Konin concrete Utopia. Out of many photographs, one is stuck in my memory. It shows a woman, Zdzisława Bobrowska née Walesa (born 1919), and her five children standing on a sandy road with electric wires and railroad tracks in the background. There are at least three children who are barefoot. The photo was taken in Nieslusz, a village near a coal mine, which later lost its autonomy and became part of Konin. This photo has great symbolic importance to me. This modernistic pact (Kochanowicz 2018), yes, it broke with the old, but also in the sense that it broke with the world of barefoot children.[8] The industrial-socialist utopia provided children with access to schools, shoes, medical attention, dry and clean as well as heated and well-lit housing. The epistemicide of pre-modern knowledge was also the partial destruction of knowledge about hunger, cold, and infectious disease (Muraskin 2012). It is the eradication of knowledge about how to survive in the pre-spring, when winter still holds sway, and it is too early to harvest new crops. In this context, we can question whether all knowledge is something to be celebrated, even that created in the humiliation of the conditions of existence to survive? Maybe it is better for it to pass into the area of oblivion?

The industrial new-topia intertwined our lives with life-giving (and death-giving, which was less said about the industry) (Brown 2020; McBrien, 2016). Though partially erased, the rural landscape covered by a layer of new settlements made its presence known, especially as habitus, sets of habits deposited in bodies and minds. I have already written about fishing. It was (and is) a predominantly male hobby, but more gender balance was evident in another custom that shone through from the past – mushrooming. In autumn, it was a holiday; whole families would go to the woods; moreover, mines, power plants, steel mills, and other factories would organize group trips by bus to the woods to pick mushrooms (Tsing 2015). Allotments were another vital sphere of exchange, a transfer between the old and the new (Bellows 2004). This Prussian invention from the times of Bismarck settled well in socialist Poland. Not only did it bolster the budget of family farms, but at the same time, it reduced the tension between the modernist now and the past remembered in the rural body (Movchan 2016). Today, allotment gardens not only allow postindustrial pensioners to enjoy the greenery but, in a strange combination of pre-modern and post-modern, they give a chance to produce healthy, green food.

Yes, socialist now-topia erased the past, however, it also opened up new opportunities. As Boris Groys points out, many Western Marxists were reluctant

---

8   Children's shoes are powerful modernistic symbol, one of the best depictions of them is found in *Children of Heaven* (1997), an Iranian family drama film written and directed by Majid Majidi about a brother and sister and the history of their desire for a pair of shoes.

to thematize the concrete experience of so-called real socialism in the 1960s and 70s. After the death of Stalin in 1953, and especially after the Prague Spring of 1968, there was a great deal of bitterness and disillusionment, a loss of faith in "real socialism," and a search for hope in abstract debates, youth communes, or the exoticism of Mao China (Chukhrov 2020, 11). The concept of real socialism as a transitional stage for building communism has been largely neglected. In Chukrov's opinion, and I agree with her, in the U.S.S.R., in Poland, and in other countries of the so-called East Bloc, a number of non-commodified spheres have been created, spheres that exist without the direct influence of capital and its libidinous economy. Chukhrov emphasizes that real socialism was boring precisely because it allowed people to be free from the pressure of libidinal overaccumulation (2020, 79). Yes, I remember this boredom also from late socialist and early postsocialist Konin. This boredom allowed for endless conversations without any pressure, the so-called P.O.M.s (*powolne obchody miasta* – "slow town walks") – postsocialist flânerie, which we were still indulging in during the transformation years (the 90s). In late-socialist Konin, life went on in the micro-worlds of meetings on the so-called *betony* (concretes), a place behind the city's main cultural center.9 However, this boredom inside the disintegrating concrete Utopia produced specific alternative communities (Yurchak 1999).

> From the point of view of libidinally constructed capitalist consciousness, the modes of non-alienation brought about by the absence of private property and superseded by common wealth would result in boredom and hardship. However, in the framework of socialism, the same conditions might have been experienced as the plenitude of life, as full-fledged activity and production.
> CHUKHROV 2020, 80

Despite our current ease to criticize modernity, we must not forget that Konin was a lively socialist city for several decades, with the highest population it ever had, multiple community centers, cinemas, a stadium, soccer teams, and music festivals were held. Konin was a small, socialist and industrial utopia,

---

9   I was too young to experience this form of counterculture in socialist Konin directly. I gained knowledge thanks to my interlocutors. It should be added that my story should not confuse, I don't want to use the climate of nostalgia and Ostalgie to cover up the repressiveness of the system in PRL. For example, a few years ago I discovered in the archives of the Institute of National Remembrance (IPN) that one of the important figures of counterculture life in Konin, a person I knew, was a secret agent of the security service.

relatively speaking. However, the 1990s neoliberal transformation caused its destruction.

5 Crumbling of Socialist Modernist Utopia and Its Embedded Knowledge

The post-communist transformation of Poland and its aftermath, including the consequences of the shock therapy, are beyond the scope of this text. As stated previously, the following text is partly a response to the disintegration of the industrial, modernist world observed through autoethnography. This is a response to the collapse of the socialist and modernist concrete Utopia, which had seemed unshakeable but crumbled under the pressure of market forces and the neoliberal transition. Nowadays, plants are growing over its ruins.

My biography is characterized by periods of transition, and it may not be up to date. I enrolled in a *technikum*, a vocational school, to become a chemical technician in September 1989. It was a time of rapid change and transformation. (Ponerau 2020) The continent of so-called 'real socialism' is experiencing tectonic shifts and tremors. The process of demodernization (Zysiak 2020) included both the collapse of industry and the dismantling of the enlightenment legacy associated with the modernist-socialist project. As I have already mentioned with regard to Keti Chuckrov's remarks, Real Socialism even if imperfect and entangled with an authoritarian regime, was, however, associated with an attempt to install a modernist Utopia. This was the nature of the universal program to educate society from the elementary school level to the university, where the children of peasants and workers could enter on a large scale for the first time (Zysiak 2015). During my secondary education at the chemical college, I partly experienced this pedagogy of progress (Movchan 2016) and the ideology of socialist modernity, which was still very much in the foreground. We learned about pipes, chemical factories (kombinats), laboratory equipment and wore white coats. In the school corridors stood mockups of factories, classrooms were filled with models of technical equipment on which we were to work in the future. To this day, my imagination is organized by the diagrams of technological processes that hang on the school walls. Similar to the promise of communism, our education became outdated quickly. I prepared myself for a world that is transient and fades away (Yurchak 2013). After finishing school, there were no more chemical technician job opportunities in factories in Konin and its outskirts. My association with capitalism and post-communism was the experience of losing ground and cities that started to fall apart (Adamczak 2021). It is also why I am so dedicated to telling the story of how this second Atlantis – a concrete socialist and modernist utopia – came to fall. One of the ripening symbols of this process was the liquidation over the years of the library in building in Hotel Górnik ("Hotel Miner"), which was once conceived as a resource for industrial Konin. I remember that in high school, I went late to sell off the remains of its book collection. This also corresponds with my family's memories of a vacation center for miners located by the Polish Sea. I remember that on the first day of our stay, we always signed up for the library located there. Today, the resort has been privatized, and the library has been liquidated. I learned from a person who was currently vacationing there that when asked about the library, she was told that the only remnant of it was a bookshelf located in a utility room shared with the cleaners. Brutally literal symbols of epistemicide of modernistic knowledge and ambition of socialist modernity.

The previous examples may have implied a conventional perspective of modernity connected with print media, book knowledge, or, more broadly, the concept described by McLuhan as "the Gutenberg Galaxy". And in this sense, modern knowledge is materially marked by the "ocularcentrism" belonging stereotypically to Western and modern print culture and is knowledge "from above", that is, un-situated and disembodied. However, this is not necessarily true. To begin with, it is essential to remember that modernity is not an incorporeal entity concept that is contrasted with the embodied knowledge of indigenous peoples and traditional ways of knowing (Chmielewska et al. 2021). Modern knowledge and modernity also had their carriers. Those for whom it was indigenous (Holubec and Mrozik 2018; Kohonen 2017). Those for whom modern knowledge, including industrial knowledge, was home. For many male and female workers, the factory was their nature, which they harnessed (Dunn 2010; Rakowski 2005, 2009). Personally, I grew up in the cult of machinery; most of the men in my family worked in an open-pit coal mine. They talked with satisfaction about the excavators, the stackers, the gigantic monstrosities of several dozen feet that they operated on a daily basis. For many of them, it was an incredible sense of accomplishment – considering that in the villages they came from, electrification and electricity were something they only experienced in their teenage years. So, contrary to a certain calque, a stereotype, modernity for them was hyper-corporeal. It was not a Cartesian world of abstraction but rather a strangely transhuman, machine-like corporeality. Also, female workers in Konin's clothing factories participated in the industrial agency of machines, although to a lesser extent.[10] This vital intermingling

---

10   The People's Republic of Poland tried to manage gender-industrial relations, hence the placement of "women's" factories so that women could also work professionally if possible.

with modernity, its technology, its mythology is also confirmed by the already-mentioned Andriy Movchan:

> My father worked with high technology – he was involved in the creation of aircraft prototypes at Antonov A.S.T.C. We have a whole dynasty of Antonov workers on his side – my grandparents actually met when they moved into the workers' dormitory at the aircraft plant during the great wave of urbanization in the 1950s. The cult of aviation in our family was strong back then. I think this also contributed to a certain progressive worldview. My home desktop was decorated with a large-format black-and-white photo of Mriya during the famous flight with the Buran space shuttle on board. The AN aircraft were a real pride of our family ... And in the '90s, my father had to make shovels and hoes from aviation titanium at the factory. For subsistence farming.
> 2016

His description of the collapse of industrial Ukraine and the de-skilling of modern professionals who had to become petty traders, subsistent farmers after the collapse of real socialism was also close, albeit on a different scale to what I myself observed. This is why I propose a hypothesis, perhaps iconoclastic for some: it is deindustrialization that has disembodied knowledge. With the collapse of the industrial-machine concrete Utopia, the skills inscribed, and embedded in workers' hands also disappeared.[11] While we often talk about knowing today, we may fail to realize how much we've lost. This is all the more paradoxical because it is precisely today that scientific knowledge is able to recognize and appreciate the knowledge embodied in the work of the hands, contained in the synergy of the workers' collective and the machines. Recent research in cognitive science (distributed and embodied cognition) focuses on reconstructing the cognitive and knowledge-generating processes taking place precisely through bodies, and teamwork (Clark and Chalmers 1998; Hutchins 1996; Nowakowski and Komendziński 2014; Popova and Rączaszek-Leonardi 2020). But what is the use of the fact that the bottom up, embodied knowledge was finally noticed and appreciated by science, when this happened at the moment of its disappearance along with deindustrialization, and given that science itself, destroyed in the course of neoliberal reforms, is in crisis (Crouch 2016; Mirowski 2011). The bitter paradox is that the golden age of high

---

11 Of course, this story is very local. On a global scale, industrialization has not disappeared, but only shifted geographically according to the neoliberal principle of the "runaway factory".

modernism so deeply rooted in industrialism, which depended so heavily on the hands and bodies of workers, knowledge deposited, embodied in the labour rhythms of the workers' collective, did not appreciate this knowledge either. Concrete knowledge, embodied expertise, and the harmony of mind and hands, which refers to the integration of cognitive and motor abilities, were potentially more prevalent in the industrial world than in today's late postindustrial and digital world. Nevertheless, these knowledges were not highly valued in the knowledge structures of that era. Modern society valued knowledge that was based on "divine points of view" and the power of abstract rationality (Moore 2014), rather than on the situated and practical knowledge of the concrete. While embodied expertise was foundational in practice, it was frequently overlooked (Vasilyeva 2012). This was outstandingly well put in Paolo Bacigalupi's short story *Pump Six* (Bacigalupi 2008). In this story, technology serves as the foundation for the narrative's momentum. The novel's setting is a projection of our current world, situated in the near future. In this forthcoming world, the consumptive, hedonistic, predatory capitalist world has separated itself from what made it possible, what conditioned its existence, that is, from homo faber and the knowledge embodied in the minds, bodies, and hands of workers and engineers. Capitalism, depicted by Bacigalupi as a cannibalistic development driven by the rush to accumulate profit, has devoured modernity and technoscience. The distinction between modernity and capitalism is significant in this text since it indicates the potential for rescuing modernity from capitalism, at least analytically.[12]

The story depicts a catastrophic scenario: New York City is about to be destroyed by flooding caused by rising sea levels due to anthropogenic climate change. The city is sheltered through a handful of old pumps, which the protagonist of the story monitors. Unfortunately, this futuristic world has forgotten the knowledge of building these old pumps. Our protagonist is the only one who still has a certain amount of knowledge about them. The pump maintainer is not an engineer. However, he is one of the few people in town who has direct contact with a real engineer. The protagonist in this story symbolizes the interruption of knowledge transfer. The whole city's future depends on whether there is even one person left in whom the key knowledge – how to fix pump number six – has been deposited.

Let us now shift our focus from the realm of fiction to post-communist Poland. The story aptly describes the process of loss of embodied knowledge

---

12   In this context, it is particularly important to refer to these glimpses of the future embodied by the reality of "real socialism" socialist Utopia, as identified by Chukhrov (2020). This serves as a means to reclaim a modernity that is non-capitalistic.

we have been facing as a result of neoliberal, forcible deindustrialization, and it has also been brilliantly described by Elisabeth Dunn based on her research participating in the Polish juice and preserves factory "Alima Gerber" (in communist times this factory was a part of famous *kombinat* named – Hortex) (Dunn, 2010). Hortex was a widely recognized brand, symbolizing healthy food for children. It was regarded not only as a high-quality product but also trusted as a product resulting from rational and scientifically verified production. However, Elisabeth Dunn's research shows that this socialist and modernist factory was more than just a rational disembodied implementation of instrumental reason. Theoretically, the work organization in this communist-era factory producing juice and preserves was subordinated to Fordism's rational and modernist rules. Nonetheless, Fordism can solely operate in a society and environment that adapts to its requirements (Grandin 2009). A factory operating under the principles of Fordism, which prioritizes rational Taylorian planning, is most effective when its surroundings also adhere to these principles. The impact of the strictness of rational, abstract planning rules should not be overlooked and must be taken into account. However, what happens when Fordism must be implemented in an environment that is not quite modernized and rather chaotic, as in the present case? In this scenario, a hidden actor must perform the tasks necessary to ensure that the ideal plans are executed successfully. This was also present in this scenario. To produce juices suitable for children, high-quality fruit is required. Unfortunately, the factory frequently receives batches of lower-quality fruit due to logistical issues and purchasing conditions in the People's Republic of Poland. What actions were taken as a consequence? The production was relocated. The modernist plan was not as Cartesian as it seems today, when it's criticized as a socialist modernity critique.

> The Plan might have specified apricot baby food, for example, but if no apricots were available, Alima's procurement specialist would obtain tomatoes from making tomato paste or find some cabbage and ground meat to go with the tomato paste and make gołąbki ("stuffed cabbage rolls") for adults. At one time or another, depending on the season and the availability of materials Alima made marmalades, compotes, fruit drinks, mineral waters, and frozen vegetables, all in addition to baby food.
> DUNN 2010: 16–7

How was this correction achievable despite contradicting the modernist Fordism's spirit, which is known to function optimally during long periods of uniform production? The crew's superior proficiency and often underestimated know-how knowledge led to their success. Their bottom-up innovation enabled them to modify previous operating procedures and adapt and repair machines. As the majority of the crew, the female workers endeavoured to produce high-quality products as they knew children would consume these goods. The feminist ethic of care compensated for the shortcomings linked with the modernist factory. In addition, quality control supplemented the official procedures. Female workers possessed numerous ways to inspect product quality, and they acquired this knowledge from their peers. This was also due to their collective identity as they frequently gathered outside the factory to celebrate name days, birthdays, and other social occasions. When Hortex was privatized, most of the crew were laid off, the employment structure changed, and most of the crew started to be contract workers. The knowledge that was previously based on collective resistance and collectively produced innovations within the Fordist factory was forgotten, and dispersed. New methods of control based on external disciplinary mechanisms were introduced. Through conditionally enforced innovation, the crew in the People's Republic of Poland managed to do something astonishing – they produced knowledge that enabled them to make situational adjustments to Fordism. This knowledge was lost. The knowledge of the embodied concrete is therefore doubly excluded: in the industrial period it existed as a silent background, complement and condition for the success of industrialization, although overlooked, often unnoticed by theorists. Today, especially in Poland, due to anti-communist resentment, it is erased and silenced again and treated as associated with the "wrong communist past" (Dean 2019; Golinczak 2019; Moll 2019; Mrozik 2019; Wielgosz 2019).

6 Why Do We Need Modernist Industrial Embodied Knowledge?

Modernity and its accompanying industrialization, as I mentioned above, are ambiguous. Fordist capitalism and its Eastern Bloc rival, state socialist Fordism, on the one hand, have helped to create a powerful, productive potential, which has helped to emancipate millions of people materially. On the other hand, it produced new forms of disciplining and exploiting labor. The ambiguity of industrialization and its end can also be seen when we look at ecology. The People's Republic of Poland was industrialized without regard for natural costs, a feature of capitalism from the very beginning (Moore 2015). This also applies to the city of Konin: mining exploitation caused the drying up of nearby lakes, destroyed water relations, and changed ecosystems (Sobolewski 2008; Stachowski 2006; Stachowski at al. 2016). The deindustrialization that happened after 1989 was disastrous for the factory workers, as experienced in many regions, including Konin, my hometown (Nowak 2019). However, despite the unemployment, retraining, and uncertainty that came with it, deindustrialization positively impacted the environment in Poland. The failure of the national industrial state project led to the loss of not only its negative aspects but also the positive aspects that were, for better or worse, associated with industrialization, which were destroyed and forgotten. Such was the fate of technology and the belief in its Promethean dimension[13] and specific performativity and pedagogy of progress (Movchan 2016). Deindustrialization led to the disappearance of not only the knowledge possessed by male and female workers, the efficiency of professionals, and the technical knowledge of engineers but also the confidence in technology, factories, and knowledge as transformative agents that could change our lives and shape the future (Nowak 2016).

In the present day, uncomplicated modernist optimism is obsolete. The simplistic modernist narrative of science and technology eliminating religion, myth, superstition, inequality, and poverty is no longer believed. The soulless historiosophy of the linear progression has exhausted itself. As Bruno Latour has affirmed, we have never been solely modern. Examining the remains of the factory, now overgrown by bushes, raises the question: is this a positive outcome? The disappearance of factories from the landscape means the decay of 'muscular' modernism and its socio-cultural impact. The empty space created by the absence of the factory reflects an ideological and social void (Nowak 2022). This situation is hazardous because the unfavorable features of modernity and industrialization persist. This becomes evident when examining the unstable employment in Amazon's warehouses. The negative aspects of 'factoryism' are still present, such as the Taylorist management approach, the control over workers' bodies and physiology, confinement, and alienation. What is absent, however, are the positive aspects that were once associated with modernist industrialization, such as the sense of collective agency, the belief in our participation in building the future, and the sense of belonging to a collective. Industrialization has always been an ambiguous process. The question remains whether we can still hold on to at least some of the positive elements it once carried within itself. As we think about the future, we must be able to recall the energy that lay in industrial modernity. The reason is simple. To save the planet and ourselves, we need to act on a global scale. Countering the effects of the industrial era requires an agency equal to, or perhaps even greater than, the one that caused those effects. Rethinking the knowledge embodied by this era

---

13   It is worth remembering that the symbol of the city of Pripyat, which is the backstage of the Chernobyl power plant, was the statue of Prometheus, standing initially in front of the cinema, later moved to the vicinity of the power plant.

is necessary to not only sustain the current world, but to be able to propose a creative utopia to save it. Accelerationism, solar punk, luxury fully automated communism – there are many names for this utopia. It must mean the ability to combine an awareness of our limitations and the limits to growth that we learn from degrowth with a bold vision through which transformation will be possible.

Yes, it seems to be a combination of fire and water. But let us have the courage to dream of the world Richard Brautigan (1967) wrote about in his poem *All Watched Over by Machines of Loving Grace*:

> (...) I like to think
> (it has to be!)
> of a cybernetic ecology
> where we are free of our labors
> and joined back to nature,
> returned to our mammal
> brothers and sisters,
> and all watched over
> by machines of loving grace.

References

Adamczak, Bini (2021) *Yesterday's tomorrow: On the loneliness of communist specters and the reconstruction of the future*. Cambridge, Massachusetts: MIT Press.

Bacigalupi, Paolo (2008) *Pump Six and other stories*, 1st Edition. San Francisco: Night Shade Books.

Bellows, Anne C. (2004) One hundred years of allotment gardens in Poland 1. *Food and Foodways* 12(4): 247–276.

Bernal, John D. (1939) *The social function of science*. London: George Routledge &. Sons Ltd.

Brautigan, Richard (1967) *All Watched Over by Machines of Loving Grace*. Available (consulted June 10 2023) at: http://www.brautigan.net/machines.html

Brown, Kate (2020) *Manual for Survival: A Chernobyl guide to the future*. New York: ww Norton & Company.

Chmielewska, Katarzyna, Mrozik, Agata and Wołowiec, Grzegorz (2021) *Reassessing communism: Concepts, culture, and society in Poland, 1944–1989*. New York: Central European University Press.

Chukhrov, Keti (2020) *Practicing the Good: Desire and Boredom in Soviet Socialism*. Minneapolis: University of Minnesota Press.

Clark, Andy; Chalmers, David (1998), Th Extended Mind. *Analysis* 58(1): 7–19.
Crouch, Colin (2016), *The knowledge corrupters: Hidden consequences of the financial takeover of public life*, Cambridge, UK, Malden, MA: Polity Press.
Dean, Jodi (2019) Anti-communism is All Around Us. *Praktyka Teoretyczna* 31(1): 15–24.
Dunn, Elisabeth C. (2010) *Privatizing Poland: Baby food, big business, and the remaking of labor*. Ithaca, NY: Cornell University Press.
Gilewska, Mirosława and Otremba, Krzysztof (2011) Kształtowanie krajobrazu rolniczego na terenach pogórniczych Kopalni Węgla Brunatnego w rejonie Konina. *Roczniki Gleboznawcze* 62(2): 109–114.
Golinczak, Michalina (2019) Communism as a General Crime: Applying Hegemony Analysis to Anti-Communist Discourse in Contemporary Poland. *Praktyka Teoretyczna* 31(1): 94–117.
Golubev, Alexey (2021) *The things of life: Materiality in late Soviet Russia*. Ithaca: Cornell University Press.
Grandin, Greg (2009) Fordlandia: The rise and fall of Henry Ford's forgotten jungle city. New York: Metropolitan Books.
Hillbricht-Ilkowska, Anna and Zdanowski, Bogdan (1988) Main changes in the Konin lake system (Poland) under the effect of heated-water discharge, pollution, and fishery, *Ekologia Polska* 36(1–2): 23–45.
Hutchins, Edwin (1996) *Cognition in the Wild*, 2nd Edition. Cambridge, Massachusetts: M.I.T. Press.
Kalinowski, Sławomir and Wyduba, Weronika (2021) Rural poverty in Poland between the wars. *Rural History* 32(2): 217–232.
Kasztelewicz, Zbigniew (2005) Wybrane uwarunkowania determinujące rozwój Kopalni Węgla Brunatnego 'Konin'. *Przegląd Górniczy* 61(2): 1–13.
Kasztelewicz, Zbigniew (2014) Approaches to Post-Mining Land Reclamation in Polish Open-Cast Lignite Mining. *Civil And Environmental Engineering Reports* 12(1): 55–67.
Kochanowicz, Jacek (2018) *Backwardness and Modernization Poland and Eastern Europe in the 16th-20th Centuries*. Milton: Taylor & Francis.
Kohonen, Lina (2017) *Picturing the Cosmos: A Visual History of Early Soviet Space Endeavor*. Bristol, UK; Chicago, USA: Intellect.
Korolczuk, Elzbieta (2016) The Vatican and the Birth of Anti-Gender Studies. *Religion and Gender* 6(2): 293–296.
Kruczkowski, Damian, Buziak, Jarosław, Fukowska, Joanna et al., (2019) *Oldrzy wokół Konina*. Konin: Wielkopolskie Stowarzyszenie na Rzecz Ratowania Pamięci FRYDHOF.
Kruczkowski, Damian (2023) *Potomkowie Olendrów Opowiadania o ewangelikach z Konina*. Konin: Setidava.Wydawnictwo Miejskiej Biblioteki Publicznej im. Zofii Urbanowskiej w Koninie.
Law, John and Ruppert, Evelyn (2016) *Modes of Knowing*. Manchester: Mattering Press.

LeDuff, Charlie (2014) *Detroit: An American autopsy*. New York: Penguin Books.
Lewandowski, Józef (1991) *Cztery dni w Atlantydzie*. Uppsala: Ex libris.
Lord, Beth (2015) *Spinoza beyond philosophy*. Edinburgh: Edinburgh University Press.
Lunceford, Brett (2015) Rhetorical Autoethnography. *Journal of Contemporary Rhetoric* 5(1/2): 1–20.
Markiewicz, Władysław (1961) Rekrutacja pracowników i skład społeczny załogi Kopalni Węgla Brunatnego 'Konin'. *Ruch Prawniczy, Ekonomiczny i Socjologiczny* 22(4): 203–229.
Markiewicz, Władysław (1962) *Społeczne procesy uprzemysłowienia. Kształtowanie się zakładów produkcyjnych w konińskim rejonie górniczo-energetycznym*, Poznań: Wydawnictwo Poznańskie.
McBrien, Justin (2016) Accumulating extinction: Planetary catastrophism in the Necrocene. In:.
Mol, Annemarie. (2008) *The logic of care: Health and the problem of patient choice*. London: Routledge.
Mirowski, Philip. (2011) *Science-Mart: Privatizing American Science*. Cambridge, Massachusetts: Harvard University Press.
Moll, Łukasz (2019) Erasure of the Common: From Polish Anti-Communism to Universal Anti-Capitalism. *Praktyka Teoretyczna* 31(1): 118–145.
Moore, Jason W. (2014) The end of cheap nature, or, how I learned to stop worrying about 'the' environment and love the crisis of capitalism. In: Suter Ch. and Chase-Dunn Ch. (eds) *Structures of the world political economy and the future of global conflict and cooperation*, Zurich-London: LIT Verlag, 285–314.
Moore, Jason W. (2015) *Capitalism in the Web of Life: Ecology and the Accumulation of Capital*. New York: Verso Books.
Moore, Jason W. (ed.) (2016) *Anthropocene or Capitalocene?: Nature, History and the Crisis of Capitalism*. Oakland: PM Press: 116–137.
Movchan, Aleksander (2016), Педагогіка Прогресу. Available (consulted June 10 2023) at: https://commons.com.ua/uk/pedagogika-progresu/
Mrozik, Agnieszka and Holubec, Stanislav (eds) (2018) *Historical memory of Central and East European communism*. New York, NY, Milton Park, Abingdon, Oxon: Routledge.
Mrozik, Agnieszka (2019) Anti-Communism: It's High Time to Diagnose and Counteract. *Praktyka Teoretyczna* (31): 178–184.
Muraskin, William (2012) Polio eradication was an ideological project. *BMJ* (Clinical research ed.), 345: e8545.
Nadkarni, Maya (2020) *Remains of socialism: Memory and the futures of the past in post-socialist Hungary*. Ithaca, London: Cornell University Press.
Najberek, Kamil and Solarz, Wojciech (2011) Jeziora Konińskie jako ognisko inwazji gatunków obcych w Polsce. In: Głowaciński Z., Okarma H., Pawłowski J. and Solarz

W. (eds) *Gatunki obce w faunie Polski II*. Kraków: Instytut Ochrony Przyrody PAN, 614–623.
Nowak, Andrzej W. (2016) Dezindustrializacja – wiedza utracona. In: Iwański M. (ed.) *Perfumy: Posłowie do dezindustrializacji*. Szczecin, Bytom: Wydawnictwo Naukowe Akademii Sztuki w Szczecinie; CSW Kronika w Bytomiu, 152–173.
Nowak, Andrzej W. (2019) Poprzemysłowe, posthumanistyczne i postsocjalistyczne sploty – turkusowe jezioro, ciepły kanał i wczasy w Koninie, *Mocak Forum* 15: 10–17.
Nowak, Andrzej W. (2021a) Double death of socialist future. FUTURES & FORESIGHT SCIENCE 3(2).
Nowak, Andrzej W. (2021b) Layers of Recovery. In: Bakke M. (ed.) *Refugia. (Prze)trwanie transgatunkowych wspólnot miejskich* [Refugia: The Survival of Urban Transspecies Communities]. Poznań: Adam Mickiewicz University Press, 42–55.
Nowak, Andrzej W. (2022) Fear, Doubt and Money. War of Ideas, Production of Ignorance and Right-Wing Infrastructures of Knowledge and Hegemony in Poland. In: Gagyi A and Slačálek O (eds). *The Political Economy of Eastern Europe 30 Years into the 'Transition'. New Left Perspectives from the Region*. Cham: Springer International Publishing, 223–249.
Nowakowski, Przemysław and Komendziński, Tomasz (2014) Cognition as shaking hands with the world. Introduction. *Avant*, V (2): 11–6.
Peters, Benjamin (2016) *How not to network a nation: The uneasy history of the Soviet internet*. Cambridge, Massachusetts: The M.I.T. Press.
Ponerau, Florin (2020) The political (auto)biography of a generation. *Left East*, January 2 2020. Available at: https://www.criticatac.ro/lefteast/political-autobiography-generation1989/
Popova, Yanna B. and Rączaszek-Leonardi, Joanna (2020), Enactivism and Ecological Psychology: The Role of Bodily Experience in Agency. *Frontiers in Psychology*, 11: 539841.
Rakowski, Tomasz (2005) Ofiara i oczekiwanie. Badania nad pewnym lokalnym doświadczeniem industrializacji. *Środkowoeuropejskie Studia Polityczne* (2).
Rakowski, Tomasz (2009) *Łowcy, zbieracze, praktycy niemocy: Etnografia człowieka zdegradowanego*. Gdańsk: Wydawnictwo słowo/obraz terytoria.
Richmond, Theo (1996) *Konin: A quest; [one man's quest for a vanished Jewish community]*, 1st Edition. New York, NY: Vintage Books.
Santos Bonaventura de, S. (2015) *Epistemologies of the South: Justice against epistemicide*. London, New York, London: Routledge.
Scott, James C. (1998) *Seeing like a state: How certain schemes to improve the human condition have failed*. New Haven, Conn.: Yale University Press.
Sennett, Richard (1998) *The corrosion of character: The personal consequences of work in the new capitalism*, 1st Edition. New York: Norton.

Sobolewski, Wojciech (2008) The extreme low and high flows of Polish rivers in the years 1986–2005. *Annales U.M.C.S, Geographia, Geologia, Mineralogia et Petrographia* 63(1): 201–212.

Spufford, Francis (2010) *Red plenty*. Minneapolis, Minnesota: Graywolf Press.

Stachowski, Piotr (2006) Kształtowanie środowiska rolniczego na terenach pogórniczych Kopalni Węgla Brunatnego „Konin". *Rocznik Ochrona Środowiska (Annual Set of Environment Protection)* 8: 279–297.

Stachowski, Piotr, Oliskiewicz-Krzywicka Anna and Kupiec Jerzy M. (2016) Naturalne uwarunkowania stanu wód jezior w rejonie Kopalni Węgla Brunatnego „Konin". *Rocznik Ochrona Środowiska* 18 (1): 642–669.

Stańczyk, Xavery (2019) Stalinowska socjogeneza kultury młodzieżowej w PRL. Próba nowego ujęcia [The Stalinist Sociogenesis of Youth Culture in the Polish People's Republic: An Attempt at a New Approach]. *Studia Litteraria et Historica* (8).

Tsing, Anna L. (2015) *The mushroom at the end of the world: On the possibility of life in capitalist ruins*. Princeton: Princeton University Press.

Varela, Francisco J., Rosch, Eleanor, Thompson, Evan (2017) *The embodied mind, revised edition: Cognitive science and human experience.* Cambridge, MA: MIT Press.

Vasilyeva, Zinaida (2012) DO-IT-YOURSELF PRACTICES: Technical knowledge in late Soviet and Post-Soviet Russia. *Tsantsa* (17): 178–181.

Wainaina, Binyavanga (2007) On Kapuscinski's 'gonzo orientalism'. *Mail&Guardian*, 20 Marach 2007. Available at: https://mg.co.za/article/2007-03-20-on-kapuscinskis-gonzo-orientalism/

Wałdoch, Marcin (2021) (rev.): Przemysław Gasztold, Towarzysze z betonu. Dogmatyzm w PZPR 1980–1990. *Świat Idei i Polityki* 20(1): 208–213. Available (consulted June 10 2023) at: https://www.ceeol.com/search/article-detail?id=1011081

Wallerstein, Immanuel (2011) *The modern world-system*. Berkeley, London: University of California Press.

Wielgosz, Przemysław (2019) From the Anti-Communist Consensus to Anti-Communism. *Praktyka Teoretyczna* 31(1).

Woźniak Krzysztof, P. (2013) *Niemieckie osadnictwo wiejskie między Prosną a Pilicą i Wisłą od lat 70. XVIII wieku do 1866 roku: Proces i jego interpretacje*, 1st Edition. Łódź: Wydawnictwo Uniwersytetu Łódzkiego.

Yurchak, Alexei (1999) Gagarin and the rave kids: transforming power, identity, and aesthetics in post-Soviet nightlife. In: Barker AM (ed.) *Consuming Russia: Popular culture, sex, and society since Gorbachev.* Durham, NC: Duke University Press, 76–109.

Yurchak, Alexei (2013) *Everything was forever, until it was no more: The last Soviet generation.* Princeton, NJ: Princeton University Press.

Zawadzka, Anna (2019) Jednostka nowoczesna, człowiek kulturalny. O drukowanym poradnictwie dla młodzieży w latach 70. *Teksty Drugie* 3: 126–147.

Zdanowski, Bogusław, Napiórkowska-Krzebietke, Agnieszka, Stawecki, Konrad et al. (2020) Heated Konin Lakes: Structure, Functioning, and Succession. In: Korzeniewska, E. and Harnisz, M. (eds) *Polish River Basins and Lakes* – Part I. Cham: Springer International Publishing, 321–349.

Zysiak, Agata (2015) Modernizing science: between a liberal, social, and socialistic university--the case of Poland and the. *Science in context* 28 (02): 215–236.

Zysiak, Agata (2019) People will enter the downtown – the postwar ruralisation of the proletarian city of Łódź (1945–55). *Rural History* 30(1): 71–86. Available at: https://www.cambridge.org/core/article/people-will-enter-the-downtown-the-postwar-ruralisation-of-the-proletarian-city-of-lodz-194555/06B7BAC128EBCBBE38433F7AC945ED48.

Zysiak, Agata (2020) "Good" and "Bad" Workers and the Collapse of the Expected Life Course: The Postwar Working Class in Detroit (U.S.A.) and Łódź (Poland), 1940s–1980s. *East European Politics and Societies* 35(1): 3–25.

CHAPTER 4

Borderforms

Grant Leuning and Pepe Rojo

1   **Borderwriting**

At the western edge of North America, halfway down the Californian coast, there is a wall (Figure 4.1). It is eight meters high and twenty-five kilometers long, stretching from a ridge on Otay Mountain out to the Pacific Ocean along the US-Mexico border. This wall, which cuts between the cities of Tijuana and San Diego, expresses the contradictions in this place. One of the first pieces of the US-Mexico border to have a wall built on it, it is also the world's busiest border crossing with one hundred million crossings a year. The cities that it separates are inseparable, economically, ecologically, and culturally, yet families and communities in those cities are separated every day, often brutally. Even the material of the wall is a contradiction. It is not a solid surface, but a series of steel poles placed ten centimeters apart, with open air between. Out where the wall meets the ocean, the poles keep going off the edge of the continent for a dozen or so meters, as if they forgot to stop, as if they could not tell whether the last pole was a period or the end of an ellipsis.

This border, more than most, is a piece of writing. With no natural features to guide it, it did not exist until 1848 when it was written into a legal apparatus by the Treaty of Guadalupe-Hidalgo (1848), which ended the US Intervention in Mexico and cost Mexico more than half of its territory. California too was cut in half. The treaty set the limit separating Upper from Lower California as a straight line drawn from the middle of the Rio Gila, where it unites with the Colorado, to a point on the coast of the Pacific Ocean, distant one marine league due south of the southernmost point of the port of San Diego. As the signatures closed the clauses on that document, interior cities were rewritten into border towns, biospheres were split, and an abstract line was cut through the desert to the ocean, to a place known in Tijuana as 'the corner of the world'.

The modern border wall is an attempt to conjure contradictions that can be held separate and stable. First-world San Diego and third-world Tijuana. San Diego's control economy of 'phones, drones and genomes' (Bratton, 2013) and illegal Tijuana, the most violent city in the world, about which Manú Chao sang: "Welcome to Tijuana: tequila, sexo y marihuana" (1998). As much as it is an instrument of military control, the border wall is also an attempt to make

FIGURE 4.1 *Experimental Subjectivation*, NS channel still.
PHOTO BY GRANT LEUNING

this binary visible and give it tangible weight. But while boundaries and legal texts fantasize about a strictly regulated and well-defined zone, reality escapes this symbolic gesture. The border exists because of the millions of people who rely on their interconnection across this border to survive. Without them performing the inventive but dangerous and sometimes lethal work to side-step the wall's fantasy of closure, there would be no wealth to contain, no threat to keep at bay, no human life at all. In these side-steps, the people of Tijuana and San Diego build a space that is broader than the wall and less distinct. Christopher Brown calls this the *edgelands*: "blurred spaces between different land uses and territories that can be occupied by the invisible, the accidental, and the unofficial" (Brown 2012). The bars of the wall are straight, while the flows of edgelands are chaotic. Hierarchies of class, race, and legal status flip around or muddle each other. The regulation of property, geography, movement, labor, economy, and technology are spread across two massive and incommensurate legal regimes. From the cracks between those regimes flow the darker forces, the forces of weapons, drugs, surveillance, and desire that constantly threaten to tear down the wall and at the same time, justify building it higher.

This chapter takes up two pieces of writing from these edgelands. First, a flag that was once flown over a minor revolution and a short-lived people's republic, bearing the words "Tierra y Libertad". Second, the Comité Magonista, a collectivity that has been written into being by our experiments with that flag's reproduction, writing those same three words in infinite repetition and variation with different techniques, materials, and media. These writings are not those of a treaty, but the working chaos of interpretation, negotiation, and above all, material and collective practice. Through these two pieces, we will focus on three tactics that undermine the wall as the primary representation of the edgelands: the scrambling legibility of the flags parading in the street, the smearing of space in the printing of flags with paint and stencils, and the drawing-out of border time in flags that are sewn-together.

Our program is organized around a concept, *penshacer*, a portmanteau that joins *pensar*, thinking, and *hacer*, doing. Before any interpretation, production is already a thinking through of an ecology of social and material relations. Rather than organizing that material, we are organized through it. Our analysis of the flag reflects that, as we think primarily through our materials and our labor. Penshacer also means undergoing these material and aesthetic practices politically, as collective and improvisatory actions. These actions are speculative, exploratory, and experimental. We use them to make flags, but more importantly, they allow us to explore the demands of the material, to experiment with new arrangements of people within the fluidly composed committee, and to chase the unexpected results as far as they go. These are works of writing as an experimental material process rather than the organization of definable meaning. Through this kind of writing and being written together, we will approach the flag *Tierra y Libertad* as a Borderform, an alternative expression of those forces that are at their most violent and vulgar in the shape of the Wall.

2   The Flag *Tierra y Libertad*

At the beginning of the 20th century, the Californian border was an isolated and untended pocket of tough farmland and inhospitable rocks. As revolution broke out across mainland Mexico, a small band of trade unionists, anarcho-communists, immigrant dock workers, and Indigenous fighters began to take territory in North Baja, capturing small towns along the border between California and Mexico. They were called Magonistas, after Ricardo and Enrique Flores Magón, the Mexican revolutionaries who were exiled to the United States in 1904. By 1911, the brothers Flores Magón were in Los Angeles agitating for armed insurrection through their revolutionary anarchist newspaper, *Regeneración*. It was from *Regeneración* that the fighters took their ideological and rhetorical cues. When the Magonistas captured the coastal city of Tijuana, they raised a flag with the slogan chosen by Ricardo Flores Magón; white letters over a red background, it declared: "Tierra y Libertad". *Land and Freedom* (Figure 4.2).

The Magonista revolution was short-lived. A month later, troops from the successful mainland revolution of Francisco Madero came and wiped out the last lingering Magonistas (Hernández 2022; Lomnitz 2014). It was a failed experiment, a possible future extinguished. But it is during the Baja campaign of the Magonistas that the phrase leaves the pages of newspapers and education campaigns and becomes a revolutionary flag marking a people's self-governing autonomous zone. Though the Magonista experiment was short-lived, the slogan was taken up by the legendary Emiliano Zapata. From there it reverberated beyond the confines of anarchism, showing up variously in the English Georgist Land reformers, the anarchists of the Spanish Civil War, the Kenyan Land and Freedom Army (Parsons 2017), the Zapatistas in contemporary Chiapas (Healey 2021), the Puerto Rican *Popular Democratic Party*, Perú's *Movimiento Tierra y Libertad*, and even as the enthusiastic slogan of Andrés Manuel López Obrador, the current president of Mexico (2019).

FIGURE 4.2 *Raw Assemblage*, detail, part of the *Occupy Thirdspace II/Ocupa Tercer Espacio II* 2022 exhibition at the San Diego City Library, curated by Sara Solaimani.
PHOTO BY VIVIANA GONZÁLEZ GÓMEZ

Despite its international spread, the memory of the Magonistas' time in charge faded in Baja. A few monumental street names, a small centenary celebration, but no flags were left waving. In 2016, the Comité Magonista began experimenting with this flag as a mark of the open edgelands and not the closure of the border zone. We produced thousands of flags with a community of more than one hundred artists, activists, and academics. This community has organized public events around the places where the flag *Tierra y Libertad* was flown, in Tijuana, San Diego, Mexico City, and the Chihuahua Desert. We paraded, staged an historical tour of revolutionary Tijuana, handed out blankets and food, seed-bombed land, forced *Tierra y Libertad* kites to cross the border illegally, and burnt the phrase onto the beach, that other border of Tijuana. We organized a Magonista Party, a festival of flags, art, film, music, and poetry that took place in downtown Tijuana on the anniversary of the Magonista defeat and a procession that took us to Mexico's City Palace of Government, where we handed out books and flags on the anniversary of the Mexican Constitution. In all of these, we were asking a similar question: what happens if we stop leading the message, and follow the flag where it wants to go?

3   Scrambling Legibility

It is not immediately obvious that this particular flag would propose itself to us as a tool for scrambling legibility. The most obvious feature of the flag *Tierra y Libertad* is its exclusive use of text. Territorial flags are almost universally symbolic. In those rare exceptions that these flags do include text, the text is accompanied by non-linguistic symbols or is heavily stylized. But the Magonista flag is only text, white letters on a red background, unadorned and unstyled. The text also has a specific linguistic demand. Legibility, definition, delineation – all of these seem to be more present in a textual flag than one that uses the interpretive openness of the symbolic. Just as the border claims to be a simplification moments before exploding into the complexity of edgelands, the text of the flag *Tierra y Libertad* allows it to expose the contradictions of meaning, both semiotic and political, that are at work in this symbol (López 2022) (Figure 4.3).

Focusing on the form rather than the meaning brings up a design problem specific to flags with text. Unlike flags with color patterns or symbols, a flag with lettering can only be properly read from one side. The back side is inverted, gibberish. But this problem is an instructive one. In the edgelands, misreading is an essential constitutive element of reading. Legibility demands the flag has a right and a wrong side, a side on which one language is privileged

FIGURE 4.3 *Untitled*, found during a flag-making event, 2016.
PHOTO BY GRANT LEUNING

and another denigrated. But the wrong text is not distinct from the right text. These are composed of the same gestures, the same material, the stitches that bind the letters to the base cloth or the paint bleeding through to the other side. In other words, the flag expresses the same matrix of forces as the border, a double-sidedness that is structurally compromised by its separations. The flag's text repeats in its own register many of the features of border language: the mutual entanglements, the linguistic divides, the violence of imbalance and the non-reciprocation of value. Even in the stitches and the work-product of paint, one can see the appearance and obscurity of labor that moves from the invisible maquiladoras to the spectacle of US consumerism.

This physical derangement of the text into non-meaning also appears when we consider the message semiotically. The terms in question, *Tierra* and *Libertad,* are both dangerously empty signifiers. As a demand for land reform, the phrase is anachronistic. The autocratic and feudal regimes that it once addressed are long gone and looming in our near future, leaving the phrase somehow both too late and too early. Even as finance capital consumes residential property, and gentrification and landlordism create crises of homelessness, the slogan doesn't resonate as a popular demand. In this void, the words threaten to invert; "Tierra y Libertad" could just as easily point to the "land" of real estate and the "freedom" of borderless speculative capital. The text threatens to become more Dada self-parody than revolutionary polemic. But self-parody is already the condition of the border. The attempt to stabilize and normalize an arbitrary political division against the flow of life and exchange is absurd. The pressure of those one hundred million crossings means this heavily militarized and imposing border is constantly puncturing itself with new gates and ports of entry. Moments later, some other part of the border apparatus notices and demands that the new opening be closed again with a temporary barrier or a pre-fence fence. The hysteria over the intrusion of the foreign other occurs most intensely at the site of the most crossings.

Another ambiguity arises from the flag's one-sidedness, one that becomes immediately obvious when someone tries to wave the flag. With text on one side, the body of the person waving the flag becomes entwined with the flag's legibility. Wind, architecture, traffic – these shift the space of the audience rapidly and without paying close attention, the parade might quickly become a smear of nonsense or a flutter of pure red flags. For the person waving the flag, legibility is a question of putting their body in the right position, rather than providing the right text. The flag has its own say in this and offers its own unruly corrective. If the winds or the wielder move the flag in particular ways, the fabric can whip around so quickly that its demand can be read on both sides, or neither. The white of the letters fractures and becomes a mix of classic flag color fields and half-readable angles and curves.

These unintelligibilities mean that the unstable meanings of "Tierra y Libertad" are more possibilities than dangers. As Sara Ahmed writes, "when bodies take up spaces that they were not intended to inhabit, something other than the reproduction of the facts of the matter happens" (Ahmed 2006, 62). Parading the flags out on the street allows us to get inside the border machine dividing sense and non-sense, into a carnival of polysemic and embodied responses (Figure 4.4). Sometimes it is the ideologically inappropriate encouragement; "I'll pray for you today, boys," an old woman told us sympathetically. Sometimes it is the murky world of the urban legend; A drugstore attendant told us a story about soldiers, who would say "here is your free land" before they executed someone and dropped them into the open grave that they dug for themselves. We are usually pressed about our party allegiances but have also been confused with fans of a soccer club. These strange apertures of the flag *Tierra y Libertad* and its phrase are that space outside-the-facts where both political and semantic possibility lay.

4   Smear Across

Jean-Luc Godard once described the struggle of politics and art as a tension between the politics of messaging, "making political films" and the politics of

FIGURE 4.4 *Untitled*, part of *We All Sleep Today / Hoy todos dormimos*, 2016.
PHOTO BY OMAR PIMIENTA

production, "making films politically" (1970). The more artwork treats politics as a message to be conveyed, the more it retreats into the idealism of communication rather than the politics of production. One of the corollaries to penshacer is a shift in the interpretive position from observer of the artwork to performer, and therefore shifting the problem of writing from meaning to work. When the flags are paraded through the street, they become our theoretical interlocutors as the one doing the waving becomes self-conscious about their bodily orientations and their effect on their flag and the meaning in flutter and flux. Similarly, the painting and sewing of flags is a chance to think the borders in our flag alongside the stencil and stitch.

Production lines produce a multiplicity of products but also of producers; the Comité's material and theoretical interventions are collective. The flags are produced in what we have elsewhere called an "assembly line of flight" (Leuning and Rojo 2021). This is a writing-formation that scrambles, smears, and scatters the text, but it also foregrounds the question of what constitutes the writing, who composes the text, and what organizes the writer. For painted flags, there are at least five positions; the letterer traces the letters, the stenciler cuts them from a plastic sheet, the cutters measure and cut the red fabric to the correct dimensions, the printer uses a paint roller to spread paint across the stencils, while every spare hand searches the space for empty chair backs and anchor points to hang new clotheslines before the next flags emerge.

Only the letterer writes in a recognizably literate way when drawing the letters on the plastic sheeting, but this writing is not yet capable of making a flag. The stenciler writes, but in negative space, as the letters are carved from the sheet. The person who handles the stencil and presses the letters into the fabric is a printer in the old-fashioned sense, one who operates a machine that installs another's writing. In pieces like *Unassemblaje/Unassemblage* (2021) and *Bearprint* (2022), the Comité Magonista fabricated a large printing press in a public space. The painting is performed as a dance as dozens of meters of white and red fabric unspool in an increasingly intrusive line. In these print runs, the printers are also calligraphers, as their peculiar movements give distinctive variations on their stencils. The paint joins in too. As it clots on the edges of the plastic holes, the residues re-shape the letters into unique edges and create a dynamic one-off typeface through the end of the run.

The spatial smear of these writing positions gives them the work of tempo. The pleasure of the production line is its improvisational choreography, a writing of movement. Hands fall into patterns, looking for shared rhythms, reciprocally determining each other by the speed and slowness of their position painting the phrase. The speed of folding out lengths of fabric to be cut hits the slowness of the cutting table. Both struggle to keep up with the stencil painter, but back up when a tyro is at the painting table. All of them vibrate toward the tone of the clothesline and the timbre of the air that dries.

The speed is not simply about accelerating the production of flags. It is also the force and vector that scatters pieces of *Tierra y Libertad* throughout the room. The stenciller making negative space also creates positive remnants, scattering letters and parts of letters across the floor in a cut-up. As the flags dry on their lines, each shows itself as only a fragment of this *Tierra y Libertad*. The text is not a clause but a slogan. It is multiple and serial in essence, a "forest of flags, a grass of hands" in Mayakovsky's phrase (1929). In their collection, half-flags hanging from clotheslines, letters strewn everywhere, the text leaves its meaning and lands in the act of its expression as a chant by a chorus under banners.

The stencils offer a further set of dispersions. After the main printing, the text lingers around the room on the newsprint or fabric that was used to protect the painting surface. Often, paint has seeped through anyway and another *Tierra y Libertad* has appeared on the table or the floor. The stencils are themselves turned into flags as their open letters are contained within a rectangle of the rolled paint. Finally, even when the production is 'finished', the stencils drying against the wall give material form to the extension of the series. Another set of flags is on the way, just as soon as material and enthusiasm can be gathered.

In each of these instances, it is the spatiality of stenciling that scrambles the legibility, smearing the boundaries of word, writer, and written until they have no definable location. Here, the flag has an echo in the violent dynamics of the border-machine. Living between what Mezzadra and Neilson (2013) call the "proliferation of borders" forces people to navigate them through different privileges, access, enforcements, legalities, and practices. This proliferation, no less than that of our productions, has scattered and scrambled any national coherence. Electronic surveillance has scattered borders across the interior, placing a border wall and an agent of enforcement wherever an undocumented person may be. Which is to say, everywhere and on any target the US government chooses. In one deeply unfunny historical irony, the Border Patrol used their military-grade drones to spy on Indigenous Americans fighting to protect their land from encroachment by foreign oil pipelines (Funes 2020).

This extension in space occurs along the line of the border as well (Figure 4.5). Through a policy called "prevention through deterrence", the wall and its technological extensions have spread the site of crossing across the desert, forcing migrants into more dangerous and unmarked routes to avoid being captured. This has horrific consequences. Since 2014, more than 3,300 migrants have been found dead along the US-Mexico border,[1] in an area Jason de Leon (2015) calls "the land of open graves." The true numbers are a mystery because finding the bodies costs too much money and effort. When migration becomes too expensive to control, the Border Patrol outsources murder to the sun.

5 Sew Between

The spatial identity of sewn flags is different from the stenciled flag. Sewn flags are usually made one at a time (Figure 4.6). The letters are fixed to the backing in the clockwork uniformity of a running stitch. The distributed identity of the letters is also flattened. It is the same object "A" persisting from the cutting to the stitching to the flying. There are fewer operators involved and usually only one person at a time can work on a flag. What scrambles the flag is not space,

---

1 Counted by the UN International Organization for Migration (see Missing Migrant Project 2023).

FIGURE 4.5 *Untitled,* part of *La procesión/Procession* 2016.
PHOTO BY GRANT LEUNING

but time. It can take dozens of hours of work to build from cloth to flag, and those hours are spread across days or weeks. Sewing is a slowness that drags the writing out to dwell within the letter until the meaning "Tierra y Libertad" extends so far that gaps start to appear within it.

To dwell within the cracks of the letters themselves means attending to their production. Sewing does this by writing the edges in an irregular but nonarbitrary order. Unlike the line of embroidery or script, the stitched letter is a block, has width, and meaningfully left and right edges. Letters must first be fixed at certain important anchor points, e.g., the baselines, toplines, and the interior edge of the counters in the letters B, D, and A. Then the remaining edges are completed in whatever order one fancies. These two moments, the hierarchy of letter pieces and the choice of which letters to stitch next, introduce dread and desire, and the distinctions that they bear. The counter in the center of the letter A is easily stitched but is fussy about the relative shifts in the backing fabric. The letters I and L are boring and therefore often have careless mistakes. The curved lobes of the letter B are next to impossible to stitch without a run or rivel and can provoke genuine anger at whoever designed them this way. The technique of writing by thread gives the form of the letters content and characteristics independent of their phonetic indications or graphological descriptions.

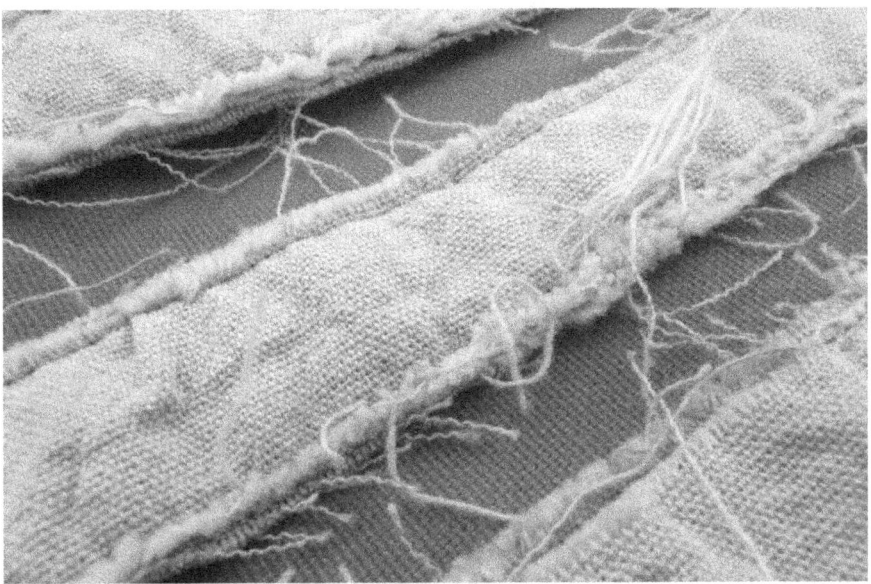

FIGURE 4.6 *String smear*, found during a flag-making event, 2018.
PHOTO BY GRANT LEUNING

Ferdinand de Saussure says that writing has a "complete indifference of the means of production of the sign and of the matter that forms it; we can carve the letters in stone, in wood, write them on black paper in white, on white in black" (1997, 113). By returning to the content of form, the writing of the flag *Tierra y Libertad* asserts the centrality of the means of production of the sign, and therefore the significance of the matter that shapes it. Derrida argues that "[s]ewing betrays, it exhibits what it should hide, dissimulacrums what it signals" (2021, 234). The technique of sewing is a specific meaningful content present in the text. Whatever stability the fabric letterforms have over time is paid for by their fractures as, through sewing, they become visible as collections of angles and differential intensities rather than complete or self-identical shapes.

Displacing the interpretive position into collective production is one side of the coin. Its corollary is a displacement of the thinking of the border into the object being collectively produced. From the beginning, we did not discuss ideology if we were not doing something manual. This was organizationally practical, as we all have different investments in the flag and different claims about what we are doing. Ideologies have the powerful tendency to streamline those differences, to answer questions before being asked, to punctuate. But we came to recognize that while the work of interpreting was in the making, it was the flag that was doing the theorizing. Attending to the practical demands of flag-making offers claims to be evaluated and logics to be grasped.

The stencils have this character. Before the stencils were introduced, the flags were often hand-painted. These flags were not spatially diverse or textually profuse. The writer was the one standing in one place, with one brush, writing the text in script sequence from start to finish. Individual authorship was evident; hand-writing is immediately recognizable as a sign of one's self. This individuality could infect these flags with the element of ownership. When the flags were arranged in preparation for a march, our handwritings would sometimes gleam at us from the pile, raising an awkward question. Do you really want to carry your own personal banner during a performance of authorless collectivity? These handwritten flags weren't deviations or failures. Each belongs fully to the flag *Tierra y Libertad*, its manifold of experiments, its autonomous idea. But we made fewer and fewer of them, and when the production line was introduced for other reasons, we stopped hand-painting them without a discussion. More than the speed and regularity of production, the purpose of the production line showed itself to be this escape from the effects of individuality, identity, authorship, and ownership that aesthetic creations are so susceptible to.

Wanting to be free of the feeling of owning or authoring is not a feeling that is specific to the edgelands of Tijuana and San Diego. The specificity of the flag *Tierra y Libertad* is that the flag makes itself into a claim about this sentiment through its production. Not all collective productions or works of border art need to escape self and ownership. Here the semantics of the texts returns in a different register. The meaning of *Tierra y Libertad* is not held in the message conveyed, but in that message's autonomy, that self-given law for how the slogan is to produce itself. Whatever decay the meaning of the linguistic phrase has undergone, the capacity for radical collectivity is preserved in the phrase's origins in a radical anarcho-communist movement and in a manifesto that called for the abolition of private property and for "el trabajo en común de la tierra y de las demás industrias", the land and industry to be worked-in-common (Flores Magon 1910; Flores Magon, et al. 1911).

Discomforts and relief aside, a flag of mine and a flag of yours introduces the border of ownership into a text that bristles at precisely this relation. Having moved the interpretive trajectory inside production and lost our indifference to the means of production of signs, the making of the flag is not distinct from the flag. The production line is the material form of the slogan's seriality. In this sense, the production line is a flag too, marking the existence of *Tierra y Libertad*, a place where what the thing does in practice is not distinct from what it makes in production: artwork-in-common.

6   Ethnography

The return of meaningful content and its tangled relationship to material brings us back to where this article started, the writing of the line that writes a people into being. What is this line cutting California in two? Some borders rely on geological or hydrodynamic systems to help administer their distinguishing capacity. Pascal laments that borders render "[t]ruth on this side of the Pyrenees, error on the other," (2004, 19) but the Pyrenees are real mountains making exchanges of language and culture difficult. Straight borders, on the other hand, draw from natural conditions their lack, the absence of features that could disrupt the imposition of a straight line or guide it elsewhere. This intensive void makes the administration of straight-line borders both more costly and more overt as the state's material pours in to fill the unmountained air, the unrivered land. But all this material, whether military or aesthetic, needs to draw on real forms of relation present in a space or it will become unstable and collapse. If we return to the material shape of the wall, the repetitions of steel and air manifest the void that is the wall's condition of possibility. Without those voids and openings, the gaps in the fence, the border wall would topple as the coastal winds blow unobstructed down the beach cliffs and over the wide-plain estuary. Without its gates, the entire borderzone would suffocate and die.

The wall expresses the forces of this place as a border zone, which is to say, militarized, colonial, above all racist and capitalist. It presents this expression as monolithic and asserts itself as the constitutive wound from which everything flows, both the law and the life that persists in spite of the law. But the edgelands are here too, a reminder that the logic of this space goes beyond the expression of the wall, showing up in every vital movement and vibrant material.

The flag *Tierra y Libertad* is one such material logic and an acutely powerful expression of this place. Even when it went quiet, sometimes drowned out by its echoes in Zapata's Morelos, Republican Catalunya, and Autonomous Chiapas, those other instances preserved a way back to Tijuana where the phrase continued to linger (Marcos 2002). The writing of the flag and the writing of the relations of this space and the people composed by it are a counter-expression of the forces here in the edgelands. Attending to the contentful forms and formal content of the flag, particularly the work of its production, offers shapes that can be compared to the enactments of the wall, and when there is resonance or inversion, these show how the forces that the wall concretizes are already occurring otherwise.

There is repetition of the politics of language in the way the Borderform shows itself in the one-sided flag, bearing forth the co-constitutive relationship of both sides of the object, the unstable hierarchies of "right" and "wrong" language, and the illegibilities, invisibilities, and underworlds that lurk beneath the surface of the well-defined line. But this linguistic resonance goes further. When the Magonistas crossed the border into Mexico with the phrase and flag in hand, it was not the first border it crossed, nor the last. "Tierra y Libertad" originated as Земля и воля in the 1860s with the Russian Narodniki and Populist movements (Ogarev 1860). Peter Kropotkin brought its specifically anarchist strain with him to Paris, where he started a newspaper *Terre et Liberté* in 1884 (McKinley 26). The slogan stuck to anarchist mastheads in *fin de siècle* France and Spain, before arriving in the Americas in 1910, in Ricardo Flores Magon's *Regeneración*. Its continued trajectories, back to Spain, to England, Puerto Rico, Kenya, Chiapas, Perú, enact the form implicitly embedded in the phrase, the grounding *tierra* with the crossing *libertad*.

The productions and performances also express aspects of the Borderform. The self-conscious awareness of one's orientation as the flag waves the line between signifier and signified around shows up on a massive scale in the shapes of the border cities of Tijuana and San Diego. Just as the waved flag asks the waving body to put itself in right relation to the line, to become aware of how it is positioned relative to the wall of semiotic transmission. The wall illuminates the disparities in how each city is constituted in relation to the border. Tijuana presses against the line, building neighborhoods up against the border. San Diego turns its back and retreats north, leaving the immediate zone of the border as empty hills and a green-washed nature preserve that just happens to preserve the Border Patrol's lines of sight. When the wall separates families, or scatters available labor into the distance, it violently performs the murky smear of spatiality that the flag *Tierra y Libertad* performs in its production line. And just as the temporal fractures of the stitch stretch the phrase and letter until they begin to pull apart, creating openings for new shapes of meaning beyond the meaning of the phrase, the wall too has its torturous separations, the differential syncopated temporality that sparks when a line of people standing for hours waiting to cross hits the line to be crossed, each of these individual threads is given a slightly different speed and trajectory across, both reflective of and reinscribing their particular gradient of identities and legal status.

With the writing of a people, Godard's distinction between making political art and making art political is raised to a higher degree. The apparatus of writing the flag *Tierra y Libertad* is built to make flags politically. But to politicize writing can also mean to write a *polites*, a fellow, a comrade, someone who belongs in this place with you (Plato 1992, 771). With the writing of the flag *Tierra y Libertad*, the product displaced into the process, the interpretive position displaced into the production, and the thinking of the edgelands displaced from wall to flag, it no longer makes sense to say we write flags. The flag *Tierra y Libertad* now has, as one of its instances, the production line that makes flags. With this, it regains the oldest and most obvious role for a flag to have: the designating of a people. The line of the border and the line of the marching flag, the inscribing of a people by the Treaty of Guadalupe Hidalgo and the peopling of the inscription "Tierra y Libertad", the repulsive negation of a border's cut and the dispersive centrality of a red flag at a rally point, each of these is a writing of people in the common difference that enlivens the edgelands (Figure 4.7). In the production line, we are written by the flag. It is an absolute ethnography, the collective writing of our collectivity through an act of writing, one that organizes printers and stitchers and cutters and wavers into Magonistas and edgelanders and makes of them and their flag a writing too.

FIGURE 4.7 *Untitled*, part of *Celebración de la Derrota/Celebration of Defeat*, 2017
PHOTO BY GRANT LEUNING

References

Ahmed, Sara (2006) *Queer Phenomenology: Orientations, Objects, Others.* Duke University Press.

Bratton, Benjamin (2013) "What's Wrong with TED Talks?" *TEDxSanDiego* 2013. Available (consulted May 10 2023) at: https://www.youtube.com/watch?v=Yo5c KRmJafo

Brown, Christopher (2012) Science Fiction in the Edgelands. *The New York Review of Science Fiction* (2012). Available (consulted May 10 2023) at: https://www.nyrsf.com/2012/05/border-closed-network-open-so-reads-the-text-of-an-information-card-handed-out-earlier-this-summer-to-occupants-of-t.html

Chao, Manú (1998) Welcome to Tijuana. *Clandestino.* 1998.

De Leon, Jason. (2015) *The Land of Open Graves: Living and Dying on the Migrant Trail.* UC Press.

Derrida, Jacques (2021) *Clang.* Trans. David Wills and Geoffrey Bennington. University of Minnesota Press.

Flores Magón, Ricardo (1910) "Tierra." *Regeneracion* 1 October 1910: 1. Available (consulted June 12 2023) at: https://archivomagon.net/wp-content/uploads/2022/12/e4n5.pdf

Flores Magon, Ricardo et al. (1911) "Manifiesto" or "Tierra y Libertad Manifesto". *Regeneración* 23 September 1911: 1. Available (consulted June 10 2023) at: https://archivomagon.net/wp-content/uploads/2022/12/e4n56.pdf

Funes, Yessenia (2020) CBP Drones Conducted Flyovers Near Homes of Indigenous Pipeline Activists, Flight Records Show. *Gizmodo* 18 September 2020. Available (consulted June 10 2023) at: https://gizmodo.com/cbp-drones-conducted-flyovers-near-homes-of-indigenous-1845104576

Godard, Jean-Luc (1970) What is to be Done? *Afterimage* (1970): 10–16. Trans. Mo Teitelbaum.

Healey, Sharon (2021) ¡Tierra y libertad! A 100 Year-Old Echo for the Maya of Chiapas. *Human Rights & Human Welfare* 1.2 (2001). Available (consulted June 20 2023) at: https://digitalcommons.du.edu/hrhw/vol1/iss2/3

Hernández, Kelly Lytle (2022) *Bad Mexicans: Race, Empire, and Revolution in the Borderlands.* WW Norton & Co.

Leuning, Grant and Rojo, Pepe (2021) Following Flags: Experimental Mass Production in the Borderlands. *Communicazioni Sociali: Journal of Media, Performing Arts and Cultural Studies* 43.1 (2021): 120–127. Available (consulted June 10 2023) at: http://digital.casalini.it/10.26350/001200_000119

Lomnitz, Claudio (2014) *The Return of Comrade Ricardo Flores Magón.* Zone Books.

López, Marco Antonio Samaniego (2022) Significados diferentes de Tierra y Libertad. *Signos Históricos* 24.47 (2022).

Marcos, Subcomandante (2002) A Storm and a Prophecy. *Our Word is our Weapon.* Seven Stories Press, 22–37.

Mayakovsky, Vladimir (1929) *Conversation with Comrade Lenin.* Trans. Grant Leuning. 22 April 2020. Available (consulted June 10 2023) at: https://cavatropvite.substack.com/p/conversation-with-comrade-lenin

McKinley, Alexander C. (2008) *Illegitimate Children of the Enlightenment: Anarchists and the French Revolution 1880–1914.* P. Lang.

Mezzadra, Sandro and Neilson, Brett (2013) *Border as Method, or, the Multiplication of Labor.* Duke University Press. https://doi.org/10.1215/9780822377542

Missing Migrant Project (2023) Migration within the Americas. Available (consulted June 20 2023) at: https://missingmigrants.iom.int/region/americas

Obrador, Andrés Manuel López. (2019) Declaration of The Year of Zapata. *Conferencia de prensa del presidente Andrés Manuel López Obrador del 11 de enero de 2019.* n.d. Available (consulted June 10 2023) at: https://www.gob.mx/presidencia/prensa/conferencia-de-prensa-del-presidente-andres-manuel-lopez-obrador-del-11-de-enero-de-2019

Ogarev, NP. (1860) "Что нужно народу?" *Колокол* 1860. Available (consulted June 10 2023) at: https://web.archive.org/web/20161104051729/xix-vek.ru/material/item/f00/s00/z0000003/st114.shtml

Parsons, Timothy H. (2017) Mau Mau's Army Of Clerks: Colonial Military Service And The Kenya Land Freedom Army In Kenya's National Imagination. *The Journal of African History* 58.2 (2017): 285–309. www.doi.org/10.1017/S0021853717000044

Pascal, Blaise (2004) *Pensées.* Trans. Roger Ariew. Hackett.

Plato (1992) Protagoras. *Plato: Complete Works.* Trans. Stanley Lombardo and Karen Bell. Hackett, n.d. 746–790.

Saussure, Ferdinand de (1997) *Saussure's Second Course of Lectures on General Linguistics (1908–1909).* Ed. Eisuke Komatsu. Trans. George Wolf. Pergamon.

United States of America; The United Mexican States (1848) Treaty of Guadalupe Hidalgo. 1848. *National Archives.* Available (consulted May 10 2023) at: https://www.archives.gov/milestone-documents/treaty-of-guadalupe-hidalgo

CHAPTER 5

The Networked Public Sphere and the Sectarian Public

Stephen Dersley

1   **Introduction**

"The war replaced the pandemic – which, in turn, had displaced Trump – as the source of all fear and loathing" (Gurri 2022) One of the most daunting aspects of our contemporary public sphere is the sheer speed at which issues appear, demand total attention, necessitate minor adjustments of positions or perhaps major reconfigurations, but then quickly recede from view and become absorbed into the basal layers of our cognitive-affective antagonisms. The first introduction of this text was written in the first weeks of February 2022, and thus when COVID-19 vaccines and Canadian truckers were the source of heated controversy. Back then, a *Guardian* article on Trump supporters who were beginning to distrust Trump due to his persistent praise of the coronavirus vaccines (see Smith 2022) seemed like a good point of entry for exploring Martin Gurri's central thesis – put forward in *The Revolt of the Public, And the Crisis of Authority in the New Millennium* (2014, updated in 2018) – that the 21st century public is structurally disposed to reject and undermine all forms of institutionalized authority – even that of a former president who continually attacked or undermined key institutions at home and abroad, such as the 'fake news' media, the FBI, NATO, WHO, the CDC, the EU, and even the US government (said to be controlled by the 'deep state'). When revising this text today, i.e., 22 March 2022, or Day 28 of Russia's invasion of Ukraine, when the civilian populations in cities like Mariupol and Kharkiv are enduring barbaric treatment, and when military aggression and nuclear threat have replaced COVID-19 as the main sources of collective anxiety, the issue of Trump supporters distrusting Trump now seems to be a rather trivial and quaint example of a public mobilization. Especially as the battle for public opinion has become a crucial front and mode of response in Russia's war. The publics in Ukraine and Europe have primarily responded to Russia's invasion with networked collective action, revealing new potentials of crowdsourcing (for sharing safe routes, for connecting refugees with hosts, for acting on the maps, enemy locations and movements gathered and shared by OSINT; for recording atrocities and establishing war crime accountability etc.) and crowdfunding (for military fundraising, humanitarian aid, pet rescue etc.). In this horrific context, Gurri's model of information driven conflict between the public and authority takes on a new meaning.

Furthermore, the information war also provides confirmation of Gurri's structural model. Russia's media war is conducted on two fronts: firstly, a 20th-century style top-down, one-to-many propaganda war waged against the Russian population, based on restricted and false information, on banning words and social media platforms; and, secondly, a 21st century many-to-many network war that pumps pro-invasion talking points and memes into non-Western regions of the Twittersphere, i.e., BRICS, Africa, and Asia. In contrast, Ukraine's information war is a profoundly 21st-century, many-to-many networked campaign: President Zelensky has demonstrated the galvanizing power of direct address video clips disseminated via social media platforms, Twitter is embraced as a weapon in the war effort (Tidy 2022) and global public opinion is swayed by a flood of dark humour memes and tractor brigade video clips. Thus, in Gurri's terms, Russia's war can be framed as a war between, on the one hand, a neocolonial power that sees Fourth Wave control of mass media as vital to its survival, and on the other hand, a nation that is using all the resources of Fifth Wave media in its decolonial struggle for its survival as a sovereign state (Sheiko 2022; Tokariuk 2022).

At the same time, Russia's invasion has also highlighted another aspect of the 21st century public sphere indicated by Gurri, namely the deeply fractious and sectarian nature of the networked public. The messaging of Ukraine and the Russian Federation is received by a divided public sphere and fed into entrenched partisan conflicts. Particularly in US Twitter discourse, positions previously articulated on Trump, COVID-19 and the culture wars reliably predict positions adopted on Russia's invasion, which range from blaming the war on NATO expansion (Chotiner 2022; Hitchens 2022; Nineham 2022), to parroting Russian talking points and disinformation (see Durden 2022), to attacking Ukraine and Zelensky (Carlson 2022a, 2022b; Owens 2022; Tracey 2022), to America First positions which treat 'the Russian civil war' as irrelevant to American interests (see Yarvin 2022a; 2022b), to treating Putin as the social-conservative saviour who will defeat the 'Globohomo American Empire' (GAE) (Hirsch 2022). These discourses articulate positions that have been subjected to incessant fracturing and recycling over the past decade; thus when Candace Owens declared, on March 17, that "President Zelensky is a very bad character who is working with globalists against the interests of his own people" (Owens

2022) this statement draws on the anti-Semitic connotations that have filled the signifier 'globalist' as it circulated through the meaning systems associated with Brexit, Trump, COVID-19-related scepticism, and the Great Reset theory. In the UK, it took about a month for the divisive issues of Brexit and the transgender controversy to become entangled in the nexus of commentary on the Russian invasion (O'Connor 2022).

Gurri's own commentary on the Russia's invasion reflects his distinctly pessimistic view of the 21st century public expressed in *The Revolt of the Public*. In this book, the public was defined as the transient networked communities that form around issues to express an opinion. When people eventually lose interest in the issue, as they inevitably do, such publics simply cease to exist. In Gurri's characterization, the public is both a powerful force that can bring about revolutionary social transformation and a fickle, fleeting collective that is cursed with a short attention span. In March 2022, after commending the Ukrainian masterclass in seizing control of the narrative and mobilizing public opinion, Gurri concluded that these successes may be short-lived, because the Ukrainian struggle is perceived

> by a restless online public trapped in the twilight shadows of post-truth. A fall from grace in the aftermath of defeat isn't hard to imagine. The world will move on to the next stirring cause. The information sphere will disintegrate into the usual noise and outrage: the return of the Tower of Babel.
> GURRI 2022

In my view, this gloomy depiction of the contemporary public results from Gurri's rather limited conception of collective action, as subsequent sections of this study seek to demonstrate. What follows is an attempt to critically evaluate various conceptions of the public, public opinion, and the public sphere. I attempt to contextualize and problematize Gurri's model of technology waves and his model of conflict between authority and the public: firstly by outlining Gurri's conception of Fifth Wave as a structural transformation; secondly by revisiting the 'cyberutopian' works of Yochai Benkler and Clay Shirky to identify the key elements of the Fifth Wave's structural transformation; thirdly by returning to the conceptions of the public presented by Walter Lippmann and John Dewey in the 1920s to provide a broader context for Gurri's subtractive definition of the public; and lastly by highlighting concepts that are either implicit in Gurri's text or lacking, such as collective action, social practices, and postcollective knowledge production.

2 The Fifth Wave

As befits a former CIA analyst, in *The Revolt of the Public* Gurri provided a very hot take of events in Egypt in 2011 and various protest movements that subsequently erupted between 2011 and 2014 (e.g., the *Indignados*, Occupy, the London Riots, Euromaidan, Anonymous). In the updated version of 2018, Gurri reflected on Brexit and Trump and claimed that these developments confirmed his initial hypotheses. Gurri's analysis hinges on two key concepts: the Fifth Wave, and the conflict between authority and the public. Gurri casts history as a permanent Manichean conflict in which *authority* attempts to exert and maintain power over *the public* through the control of information. While the struggle between the public and authority remains constant, in Gurri's model history is driven and punctuated by unpredictable pulses of innovation in information technology, which trigger waves of social transformation.

2.1 *Waves and Structural Transformations*

The innovations that triggered the five waves suggested by Gurri (2018, 27) can be reconstructed as follows: 1) writing (4th Millennium BCE), 2) the alphabet (8th-5th centuries BCE), 3) the printing press (15th to 19th centuries), 4) mass media (19th and 20th centuries), and 5) personal communication technology (21st century). In this reductive model, a transformation in the means of information production ultimately leads to a transformation of social relations, often triggering long periods of upheaval and military conflict. Some forms of information technology enabled top-down control of the masses (e.g., sacred texts, TV), while others facilitated the kind of bottom-up networking that undermines authority and leads to cultural and political revolution (e.g., the printing press, letters and the postal system in the 18th century, social media).

According to Gurri, we are now being swept up by the Fifth Wave: a cataclysmic tsunami of information triggered by the public's access to personal communication technology. This development freed the public from the top-down, one-way transmission of the mass media, which reduced people to passive consumers of information, knowledge and culture. In the 21st century, due to a conjunction of technological innovation and geopolitical developments, the public began to engage in multidirectional, decentralized communication that lay outside the control of governments and hierarchical organizations guarding their monopolies over fields of professional expertise. For Gurri, the revolt of the public is above all the revolt of an active public that is challenging professional authority and creating its own information, knowledge and culture. This explosion of bottom-up, amateur data production and communication is battering professional authority (journalism, universities, science) and pummelling entire industries (e.g., the music, film and publishing industries, legacy media).

Gurri's waves can be conceived of as triggering structural transformations of the public sphere. In early Habermasian terms, structural transformation indicates that social relations are reshaped by new means of production and forms of economic activity, and the public sphere is conceived of as a general forum of societal communication that is "open to all" (Habermas 1989, 1).[1] When distinguishing between the 20th-century masses and the 21st-century public, Gurri adduces "obvious structural reasons" that condemned the former to reactivity: "members of that public were unable to develop their own TV programs. They couldn't act" (2018, 98). Thus, in Gurri's model, technological functionality and capability are posited as fundamental determinants of the communicative options open to the public. The structural limitations imposed on the 20th-century public as consumers of mass media were also replicated in the political sphere: in liberal democracy, the organization of politics into parties and elections entailed that the public had a narrow window and limited options for communicating its opinions (Gurri 2018, 93).

2.2   The Rise of the Networked Public Sphere

Gurri's conception of the public draws on 'cyber-utopian' works from the heyday of the blogosphere, such as Yochai Benkler's *The Wealth of Networks* (2006) and Clay Shirky's *Here Comes Everybody* (2008), though dispensing with their enthusiasm and optimism. Benkler's contribution is of particular importance, since his analysis of the "networked information economy" provides a more rigorous basis for arguing that the shift from the Fourth Wave mass-mediated public sphere to the Fifth Wave networked public sphere amounts to a structural transformation. In a nutshell, Benkler attributed the emergence of the networked public sphere to a steep decline in costs. In the era of mass media, i.e., from the mid-19th century to the end of the 20th century, the production and communication of information and culture required large outlays of capital (mechanical presses, TV and film studios, cable and satellite infrastructure etc.). Hence the information and culture economies were organized as industries with unidirectional producer-to-consumer transmission models. (Benkler 2006, 3–4) In other words, the means of information, knowledge and culture production were monopolized by states, media barons, the entertainment industry, universities etc. Unless they had vast amounts of capital at their

---

[1] This is Jürgen Habermas's first, 'Republican' model of the public sphere. An account of Habermas's later models of the public sphere, such as that presented in *Between Facts and Norms* (1992), is beyond the scope of these reflections.

disposal, ordinary members of the public were simply unable to start a newspaper or a new TV channel, or to publish a book. However, from the mid-1990s, decreasing costs associated with the means of industrial production (computer hardware, portable communications devices, network infrastructure etc.) entailed the public had increasing access to the means of information production (from an economic perspective, culture and knowledge are forms of information) (Benkler 2006, 36).

The declining price of computation, communication, and storage have, as a practical matter, placed the material means of information and cultural production in the hands of a significant fraction of the world's population – on the order of a billion people around the globe (Benkler 2006, 3–4). By 2022 this number had more than quadrupled, to around 5.3 billion people, or over 60% of the world population (Statista 2023). The physical capital necessary for the production and distribution of information, culture and knowledge has become decentralized and diffused throughout the growing population of users (Benkler 2006, 32). The transition to the networked public sphere is thus defined by a) the transfer of capital and functionalities to the public, and b) the emergence of flexible, decentralized networks that destabilized the industrial information economy.

Crucially, for both Benkler and Shirky, the transformation of the information economy and the public sphere engendered new social practices. Benkler emphasized the rise of nonmarket forms of production, best exemplified by collaborative projects like Wikipedia and photo-sharing sites. In Benkler's account, information is a 'nonrival' good (since my consumption of a piece of information does not prevent you from consuming it) with zero marginal costs (since information, e.g., Tolstoy's *War and Peace*, only needs to be created once) and therefore lends itself to nonmarket production (Benkler 2006, 36). Benkler invoked a utopian future, in which human beings achieve more as social beings than they do as market actors, envisaging that the primary practices of such beings would be the creation and communication of meaning, which would lead to "a more critical and self-reflective culture" and individuals who are "less susceptible to manipulation" by the media (2006, 6–15).

In turn, Shirky focused on the new organizational potential inherent in the networked public sphere and the consequences of 'mass amateurization'. Changes in forms of association and expressivity are downstream of deeper changes in the economic base: the costs associated with creating or joining groups collapsed, giving rise to new communities of practice (Shirky 2008, 100). These communities have self-assembled outside of the traditional institutions and organizations dominated by the state and business, and created a new communicative ecosystem based on sharing, collaborative production and collective action. Shirky identified the emergence of this ecosystem as a fundamental discontinuity: "the largest increase in expressive capability in the history of the human race" (2008, 106). The process is driven by mass amateurization: when information was scarce and publishing was expensive, production and distribution required professionals. The fact that anyone with a smartphone has the ability to produce and publish information entails that expertise is no longer necessary, not that everyone becomes an expert: "this technological story is like literacy, wherein a particular capability moves from a group of professionals to become embedded within society itself, ubiquitously, available to a majority of citizens" (Shirky 2008, 78).

Though Shirky was less optimistic than Benkler – he acknowledged that "the loss of professional control will be bad for many of society's core institutions", and notes that the printing press plunged Europe into centuries of 'intellectual and political chaos" (Shirky 2008, 73), in 2006–2008 both authors viewed the networked public sphere in an overwhelmingly positive light. Particularly in the context of American liberal democracy, the more symmetrical participation made possible by social media and personal communication technology was presented as offering the potential for correcting the excessive power wielded by media owners in the industrial information economy (Benkler 2006, 220).

Gurri basically agreed that a fundamental transformation had occurred in the public sphere, due to the tsunami of user-generated information, but having observed subsequent events unfold – the 2008 financial crisis, the 2011 Arab Spring, the protest movements of 2011–2014, and then the shocks of Brexit and Trump's victory in 2016 – he reframed this transformation in terms of an existential binary conflict between authority and the public. In the second decade of the 21st century, the networked public sphere became a "sociopolitical combat zone" (Gurri 2018, 65).

3 Conceptions of the Public

3.1 *Distrust and the Sectarian Public*

For Gurri, from 2008 onwards the public has been above all an increasingly distrustful public. He attributes this partly to the nature of the Fifth Wave itself, and partly to the very public examples of "Center failure". Firstly, as a result of the Fifth Wave, information is transformed from a scarce commodity to an overwhelming surplus, and the explosion of sources brings about a collapse in previously trusted authority: "Once the monopoly on information is lost, so too is our trust" (Gurri 2018, 20). Public broadcasters and print media came to be increasingly seen as presenting an arbitrary or official version of events rather than unbiased news. The rise of new media repositioned legacy media as the mainstream (MSM), downgrading its status to just one source among "a near-Infinite set of new sources" (Gurri 2018, 20). Secondly, failure has exacerbated the public's distrust of authority. Gurri cites many examples of experts and governments failing to anticipate and respond to crises which had catastrophic effects on people's lives: the debacle of the Iraq War, the 2008 financial crisis, the European sovereign debt crisis of 2009–14, etc. At the same time, Gurri suggests that the public's response to the failures of supposed experts is indicative of the tectonic separation that has opened up between authority and the public since 1961, when the public forgave President Kennedy for the deception and failure of the Bay of Pigs.[2]

Apart from being distrustful and structurally antithetical to authority, expertise and professionalism, Gurri's public is also sectarian and divided: it is a 'heterogeneous beast' involved in "a colossal, many-sided conflict" (Gurri 2018, 59, 86). Any careful reader of *The Revolt of the Public* will probably find Gurri's definitions of this public frustratingly vague. Aside from its structural determinants – amateurism, opposition to authority – Gurri assigns very few defining characteristics to the public; instead, he prefers to use the subtractive method and specify what the public *is not* – it is not the people, the masses, or the crowd. At the most general level, Gurri's conception identifies two key features. First, the public is defined as sharing "common habits of behavior" specific to the Fifth Wave (Gurri 2018, 85). Thus, the various manifestations of the public that Gurri recounts – the Tahrir Square protests, the London riots of 2011, the Indignados, the Occupy movement, Euromaidan, Anonymous – all took advantage of network capabilities, such as social media, to organize collective action against authority. Second, the public is manifested through the communication of opinion. When it communicates, the public does not do so as a homogeneous entity, speaking as a totality of amateur individuals communicating *en masse*, with one voice; instead, opinion is articulated through "*vital communities*: groups of wildly disparate size gathered organically around a shared interest or theme" (Gurri 2018, 23).

---

2   Gurri's somewhat superficial diagnosis is supported by the deeper analysis of Benkler's 2020 essay *A Political Economy of the Origins of Asymmetric Propaganda in American Media*, which traces a steep decline in trust from 1964 to the present. This is attributed to a variety of factors, such as the 1973 oil crisis and the inflation of the 1970s, which 'undermined public confidence in government stewardship of the economy', as well as political movements (feminism, civil rights, decolonization) and intellectual trends that questioned the objectivity of science (Benkler 2020, 60–61).

This conception entails that the public is necessarily heterogeneous, amorphous and unpredictable. At the same time, Gurri provides ample evidence that this protean and sectarian public has the power – through coordinated actions involving crowds, social media networks, and popular mobilizations – to bring about political revolutions (the Arab Spring, Euromaidan, Brexit). In this model of events, vital communities are sometimes able to capture the imagination and support of a critical mass of the public with their theme or focus of interest. Hence the explosive, international popularity of the Black Lives Matter movement following the killing of George Floyd in May 2020, or the support garnered by President Zelenskyy following the Russian invasion of Ukraine in February 2022. In contrast, some vital communities clearly fail to gain support or even antagonize the public, e.g., the Extinction Rebellion and Insulate Britain movements. When he deals with crowds, protests and demonstrations, Gurri attributes the public with great agency. The public is described as turning a crowd "into a form of communication", "an instrument to communicate public opinion" (Gurri 2018, 101). Widespread expressions of support for a demonstration can lead the public to gravitate towards the crowd, which can sometimes lead to a political uprising. There seems to be a positive feedback loop at work: "If the public can be said to re-create the crowd into a form of communication, it is equally true that such a crowd, once convincingly expressed, will create its own public" (Gurri 2018, 101).

The fluid, fickle and fractious networked public presented in Gurri's book both draws on and is distinguished from the images of the public evoked in two classic American works that identified and addressed problems associated with the public in the pre-television era of mass media: Walter Lippmann's *The Phantom Public* (1925) and John Dewey's *The Public and its Problems* (1927). Gurri adopts and reframes Lippmann's image of the public as a phantom, reaffirms Dewey's diagnosis of an amorphous and disorganized public, and contrasts the apathetic and disempowered mass-mediated public of the 20th century with the agency and potential for political efficacy that the 21st century networked public has at its disposal.

Both Lippmann and Dewey responded to a perceived crisis in participatory democracy. In the early 1920s, studies showed that participation in elections was in steep decline, and social scientists cited evidence to claim that people who actually voted did so for emotional reasons, or out of habit, rather than for rational reasons (Westbrook 1991, 284). Such studies, along with Freudian and behaviourist psychologies, undermined the central tenets of democratic theory: that ordinary people were capable of "rational political action", and that "the participation of all citizens in public life" should be maximized (Westbrook 1991, 282). If democrats wanted to counter conservative, racist and nativist tendencies, and hold onto the idea that society should maximize the common good, the concept of the public required urgent reconsideration.

3.2 Lippmann's Phantom Public

Lippmann tackled the crises of public opinion and the public from the perspective of democratic realism. In both cases he stressed limitations – those that prevent ordinary people from forming accurate opinions of the unseen environment, and those that prevent the public from influencing public life. And in both cases his solution was to empower experts: public opinion should be organized by "an independent expert organization"– for the press, not by the press (Lippmann,1993, 30–31); and the common good should be taken care of by well-informed "executive men" (Lippmann 1993, 187).

The basic argument presented in *The Phantom Public* is that the omnipotent public of democratic theory is a harmful illusion. Lippmann mercilessly exposes the limited agency that ordinary individuals have when it comes to influencing public life. According to the democratic ideal, the public is given opportunities to express its will and opinion at elections. From Lippmann's democratic realist perspective, a democratic election is "a sublimated and denatured civil war, a paper mobilization without physical violence" (Lippmann 1993, 48). At an election the public is not asked to express its thoughts on public policy; instead, individuals are merely given the opportunity to align themselves with a candidate who has made a promise (1993, 46–47). Lippmann spells out the extent of the influence exerted by the public when voting: "It is a way of saying: I am lined up with these men, on this side. I enlist with them. I will follow. I will buy. I will boycott. I will strike. I applaud. I jeer. The force I can exert is placed here, not there" (1993, 47). The most that the public can do, as "outsiders" or "bystanders" with no executive power, is make occasional interventions: to influence the agents who are in fact able to take executive action; or to neutralize the use of arbitrary force during periods of crisis (1993, 59–60).

In this resolutely non-idealized depiction, the public is cast as irrational, uninformed, bereft of deliberative opportunities, and prone to manipulation by special interests (1993, 96). In a passage cited by Gurri, Lippmann concludes:

> I hold that this public is a mere phantom. It is an abstraction. ... The public is not, as I see it, a fixed body of individuals. It is merely those persons who are interested in an affair and can affect it only by supporting or opposing the actors.
>
> Lippmann 1993, 67

Lippmann's public is a phantom in the sense that it is an illusory ideal propagated by theories of popular government. For Lippmann, it is precisely this mystical conception of the public that is the source of problems. The democratic image of the public – as a pantheistic power, the people united as a single person with one will, destined to pursue universal and common purposes – either leads to apathy, when individuals sense their lack of real influence over public affairs, or to "outsiders" meddling in matters that they do not understand. The phantom public hides the reality of modern American society in the mid-1920s: characterized by "deep pluralism"; individuals with narrow points of view, expressing localized and relative opinions, pursuing private interests (1993, 87, 137, 188).

Following Lippmann's bleak diagnosis, no reinvigorating remedy is possible: the reality of atomized, self-interested individuals cannot be reintegrated by means of yet another illusory conception of the public; a genuine public sphere cannot be formed when ordinary people do not have the time, access or competence necessary for understanding the complexities of the unseen environment. The ambiguous solution that Lippmann offers in the final sections of his book suggests a form of technocratic elitism: the ideal society is one in which individuals can achieve their purposes with "the least frustration", and this requires some individuals to work for the purposes of others, free from the interference of the "ignorant and meddlesome" public (1993, 188). This has been interpreted as Lippmann recommending "a delegation of authority to specialized, competent experts" (Robbins 1993, VIII) or falling back on "the hope of creating a professionally competent public bureaucracy" (Aronowitz 1993, 79). Thus, in its most brutal formulation, Lippmann's remedy for the illusions bred by the theory of participatory democracy, as well as for the ills generated by industrialized mass culture, is to protect the experts who have real decision-making authority from the encroachments of incompetent outsiders. In other words, the public "must be put in its place" (Lippmann 1993, 145). In contrast to the Jeffersonian tradition of cultural formation through public education, which assumed that individuals had to be "trained for citizenship" before they could participate in democracy (Aronowitz 1993, 76), for Lippmann the role of education should be reduced to making the public aware of its limited role.

3.3 Dewey's Inchoate Public

The central diagnosis of John Dewey's *The Public and its Problems* (1927) is that the public of the machine age is disorganized and confused (Dewey 1927, 30–31, 122). Responding to Lippmann's anti-democratic elitism, Dewey rejects the notion that the conception of the public is the source of problems. The democratic public is apathetic, "inchoate and unorganized" (1927, 109) for structural reasons. When American society was based on local face-to-face communities, which were "homogeneous and static" (1927, 140), the political and legal structures allowed the public to express its interests and participate in the democratic process. However, after industrialisation and communication technology completely transformed American society, eliminating distance and creating "mobile and fluctuating associational forms" (1927, 140), the public was unable to use the inherited political agencies and forms (1927, 31). The vast and remote forces of the machine age – immigration, mass-produced opinion and impersonal relations – disintegrated community life and left the public lost and bewildered (1927, 109–116).

Dewey identifies two basic reasons for the public's epistemic crisis. The first is institutional lag: political and legal forms fail to keep pace with industrial transformation, including technology that facilitates "the rapid and easy circulation of opinions and information" (1927, 114). In Dewey's conception, these structural changes have generated a new public – one that will remain "inchoate and unorganized" as long as it is obstructed by the inherited structures: "To form itself, the public has to break existing political forms" (1927, 31). The second is the increasing complexity involved in managing the infrastructure of modern urban life: the public is excluded from the most pressing issues (e.g., sanitation, public health, housing, urban planning, immigration, education) (1927, 124–25). Such matters are settled by "trained technicians" rather than the decisions of the majority. The public's frustration with existing political structures and the resulting lack of agency led to widespread apathy and decreasing participation in the democratic process.

However, even when frustrated and eclipsed, Dewey's public still has the capacity to influence authority, even if inadvertently. In a key passage that evokes Lippmann's meddlesome phantom public, Dewey depicts the public as an impotent ghost that nevertheless has tangible effects on real-world action:

> Given such considerations, and the public and its organization for political ends is not only a ghost, but a ghost which walks and talks, and obscures, confuses and misleads governmental action in a disastrous way.
> Dewey 1927, 125

Thus, while Lippmann's public is an illusory concept masking the reality of atomized individuals pursuing their own interests, Dewey's public is a real community of confused and unintegrated individuals. Rather than there being no such thing as the public:

> There is too much public, a public too diffused and scattered and too intricate in composition. And there are too many publics, for conjoint actions which have indirect, serious and enduring consequences are multitudinous beyond comparison, and each one of them crosses the others and generates its own group of persons especially affected with little to hold these different publics together in an integrated whole.
>
> Dewey 1927, 137

Instead of abandoning the concept of the public, or reducing it to a bare minimum, Dewey considered ways of reinvigorating this entity. The remedy that Dewey proposes is centred on an imagined restoration of local community life. A reconstituted public must be able recognize itself as a community, be able to define its interests, and inform the experts as to its needs (1927, 146, 208). A central role is assigned to education, since "a community of action saturated and regulated by mutual interest in shared meanings" cannot be created from thin air. The young have to be brought into such a meaningful community through unremitting instruction focused on its "traditions, outlook and interests" (1927, 154). In the ideal transformation of "the Great Society into the Great Community", higher education would be interdisciplinary, and there would be "full publicity" (1927, 167–71), i.e., there would be no censorship of matters that concern the public. In order for the public to participate as an integrated and democratic community, it must be educated, informed, and able to contribute to debate and discussion (1927, 208). Robert Westbrook dismissed Dewey's plans for reintegrating the public through reinvigorating local, face-to-face communities as "wistful in the absence of specific suggestions for doing so" (1991, 315). In other words, Dewey provided a convincing analysis of how industrialisation and mass media culture had disintegrated face-to-face communities and left the public bewildered, but failed to offer an explicit, developed a "politics of knowledge" that could have reintegrated such communities (Westbrook 1991, 316).

The question that can be posed at this point is whether Gurri's conception of the 21st century networked public as "*vital communities*: groups ... gathered organically around a shared interest or theme" (Gurri 2018, 23) can be worked into a theoretical framework that could develop such a "politics of knowledge". In other words, do the digital networks of the 21st century facilitate local, community-based forms of integrated knowledge production, and new collectivities – or postcollectivities – that were simply impossible when Dewey was writing?

3.4 The Rebooted Public

Gurri's *The Revolt of the Public* attempts to reboot the concept of the public for application to the phenomena and events of the 21st century. Though he cites Lippmann's designation of the phantom public, Gurri's treats the public as a real but elusive entity, rather than as an illusory concept or theoretical spectre. On the one hand, Gurri indicates that the public is "composed of private persons welded together by a shared point of reference" (2018, 100). Yet on the other hand, in contrast to a crowd, which is always *manifest* (2018, 101), the public is "dispersed" throughout networks and tends to influence events "from a distance only" (2018, 101). Hence Gurri's public – while composed of real, private persons who form vital communities – is only tangible in its communication, when it voices its opinion in networks. It can be presumed that when a community stops communicating its opinions about an issue, this particular instantiation of the public simply ceases to exist. The private persons that formed such a public withdraw back into privacy until the next issue comes along. News media, polls, referendums and elections do not represent the real public opinion that exists out there as the thing-in-itself, as the sum total of private opinions. This amorphous, ambivalent and fluctuating mass of private cognitive-emotional stances has to oriented to an issue, probed with questions, presented with response options, sampled and subjected to analysis, and reported on. Public opinion is phenomenal in the sense that it is produced as nothing but representation – when journalists, politicians, governments, polling organizations and data analytics firms make it speak.

If Gurri's model is applied, the arrival of the Fifth Wave led to the mass media and the institutions of authority losing their asymmetrical control over the production, representation and shaping of public opinion, since the transfer of functionality that occurred with the spread of networked communication technology gave the public the capability to voice its opinions directly through the networks. Thus, while claims to represent or have the support of public opinion remain central to legitimization strategies, and while political programs and government policy are in an increasingly symbiotic relationship with opinion polls and data analytics, the stream of phenomenality generated by the professional representation of public opinion now has to interact and cope with the streams of data produced by the public, as it posts its nonprofessional images, videos, memes, analyses and opinion.

The media has adapted its Fourth Wave channels and genres to the Fifth Wave, most obviously through the presence and activity of corporate and journalist accounts on social media, but also by adapting old formats so that they capture and incorporate social media content (e.g,. tweets, smartphone videos) into articles and TV reports. Furthermore, as legacy media institutions now publish articles based almost entirely on investigations of social media activity, they have taken upon themselves the function of reporting on – or even policing – the public's unacceptable opinions. There is a distinct tendency for professional journalists and university professors to associate nonprofessional communication on social media platforms as part of a broader "degradation of standards" (Starr 2020, 73) and disruption of "conventional norms of reasonable discourse" (Bennett and Livingston 2020, 12). This is best exemplified by the increasing use of the terms "disinformation" and "misinformation" by journalists and scholars alike to denote the threat posed by unregulated discourse in the public sphere, as evidenced by condemnation of Joe Rogan's podcast by legacy and mainstream media (see Blake 2022; Reality Check Team 2022), or the collection of scholarly essays in *The Disinformation Age, Politics, Technology, and Disruptive Communication in the United States*, which treat 'disinformation' as an unproblematic, neutral term for describing the "intentional falsehoods and distortions" overwhelmingly spread by the conservative partisan media and alt-right social media networks (Bennett and Livingston 2020, 12).

From this US-centric perspective at least, the sectarian public that Gurri identified as emerging with the Fifth Wave and in the networked public sphere had already been polarized and entrenched by partisan Fourth Wave media – due to Limbaugh's radio show, following the abandonment of the fairness doctrine (1988), the emergence of Fox News (1996) and Breitbart News (2007) – long before social media networks took hold (Benkler 2020, 51). Thus, what Gurri refers to as the revolt of the public is framed by the media and scholars as a predominantly right-wing conservative or alt-right phenomenon. The legacy institutions of the Fourth Wave – the media, the democratic party, universities – are aligned with the sections of the Fifth Wave public that continue to place their trust in them, while the "transgressive publics" of the right have broken away from the truth-seeking public sphere and plunged into an "alternative public sphere" based on disinformation disorder (Bennett and Livingston, 2020: 33). If, as Bennett and Livingston assert, "disinformation tilts to the right" (11), the implicit assumption is that trustworthy information tilts to the left, and thus the American public aligned to the centre and the left are neither distrustful of authoritative institutions nor susceptible to discursive manipulations.

It is precisely such naïve views of the information environment that Gurri's model seeks to dispense with. According to his model, whenever we encounter a networked community exercising its agency by contesting information, articulating a position and organizing collective action against authoritative institutions, we can identify an instantiation of the public – irrespective of whether the community can be mapped onto the industrial-era categories of left, right or centre; thus BLM protestors and anti-vaxxers can both be treated as examples of the public, or examples of *publics*, in structural terms – regardless of the ideological gulf between these communities.

4 Conclusion: the Paradoxical Public and New Postcollectives

The networked public sphere does not only coordinate the large-scale uprisings that Gurri tended to focus on: it is involved in a whole ladder of collective action ranging from "tiny acts of participation", such as liking or retweeting a political message, "right up to political violence and armed struggle", as Margetts, John, Hale et al. argue (2015). The public's opposition to the institutions of authority is manifested in practices as diverse as making media consumption choices, producing and disseminating non-professional knowledge, participating in protests and boycotts, refusing to comply with laws and measures, crowdfunding and crowdsourcing during a military invasion etc. Such practices could be adduced as evidence that the publics of the 2020s have gained agency and organisational capabilities that were diagnosed as completely lacking by Lippmann and Dewey in the 1920s. However, these gains in agency come at a cost. The social media platforms through which the public articulates opinions and coordinates collective action are obviously not neutral entities: they inculcate exploitable forms of behaviour and are subject to political influence and control. Nick Couldry and José van Dijck situate social media within a "new techno-economic materiality" (2015, 3). In this conception, the social is defined as *"a site of necessary, and necessarily contested, representation"*, and social media platforms, by constructing "a new and hegemonic *space of social appearances"*, are working to install a specific version of the social. They argue that this is being achieved through encouraging micro-level adjustments of practice, inculcating habits, and continuously extracting value by tracking interactions (2015, 2–4).

In turn, Shoshana Zuboff argues that information capitalism "aims to predict and modify human behavior as a means to produce revenue and market control" (Zuboff 2015, 75). The use of the networked public sphere requires the adoption of entirely new screen-based habits that add to the predictive capacities and extractive potential of surveillance capitalism. Hence, the increase in agency that defines the Fifth Wave is somewhat paradoxical: the price is paid in submission to behavioural manipulation, unheard-of levels of surveillance, and the extraction of value from accumulated data. For surveillance capitalist companies, the non-professional data shared on their platforms is an unlimited source of free "behavioral surplus" that is appropriated and sold on futures markets for prediction purposes (Zuboff 2019, 63–96). Thus, the revolt of Gurri's public is subjected to commodification and monetization by a formally indifferent logic of accumulation.

Firstly, if any vestiges of the norms that governed participation in the bourgeois public sphere survived in the degenerate pseudo-public sphere of the mass media (Habermas 1989, 162), they were utterly obliterated with the arrival of screen-based interaction on social media. The new modes of information production – often accessible to 'Everyone' in the world, frequently anonymized, usually responding emotionally in real-time – incentivize heated interaction and have led to the adoption of new communication norms that are decidedly non-bourgeois and non-academic. Secondly, the increase in agency and expressive power has been accompanied by an explosion of antagonistic and manipulative discourses. Discourses can be defined as articulatory practices that create meaning and positions relationally and differentially (Laclau and Mouffe 1985), and collective identities tend to be formed through the construction of discursive enemies (Mouffe 2005). Hence a key element of the success behind certain mobilisations that have been or could be identified as expressions of the public, such as Brexit, the MAGA movement, QAnon, and the anti-vaxx movement, was the creation of a 'we' defined in opposition to a nefarious 'them'. While 'we' are ordinary folk, the normal, decent people of Britain or America, they – i.e. the remote representatives of authority – are designated as *the political class, globalists, the elites, the experts, the scientists, the laptop class, the cabal* etc. (for example see Farage 2013; Johnson 2016).[3] Grassroots concerns about the effects of immigration, about democratic deficits, about vaccine side effects etc. become entangled in discourses that channel the energy of networked collectives towards specific actions and social practices, including some which affect the outcomes of referendums and elections. Only the most naïve believers in people power would argue that no political manipulation or ulterior interests are at the work in such processes.[4] Of course, discursive manipulation influenced the democratic process before the arrival of the networked public sphere, e.g. the indisputable influence of tabloid newspapers like *The Sun* in the UK, but the functionalities and vulnerabiliies of Facebook

---

3   And conversely, the mainstream media describes such movements with loaded terms that are assumed to designate heinous political positions, e.g. 'populist', 'right-wing'. A case in point is the use of terms like 'rightwing firebrand' in the description of Poland's Law and Justice party (see Shotter and Majos 2019).
4   For an idealized evocation of 'the public' that voted for Brexit but was then silenced by the first COVID-19 lockdown (see O'Neill 2020).

and Twitter, combined with the public's new capacity to generate and disseminate content, have greatly increased the disruptive potential.

Gurri's dualistic conflict between the public and authority falls back on categories inherited from the Third Wave (the print-based public sphere) and reinforced by 20th century scholarship which framed the cultural conflicts of the 18th and 19th centuries in binary terms: the Enlightenment vs. the Counter-Enlightenment, the bourgeois public sphere vs the state authorities. Perhaps the most persuasive reconstructions were those of Reinhart Koselleck and Jürgen Habermas. Koselleck's *Critique and Crisis* (1959) (Koselleck 1988) depicted the Enlightenment as a pathogentetic process whereby philosophical critique became liberated from theological control and turned its corrosive criticism on the church and state. Habermas' *The Structural Transformation of the Public Sphere* (1962) rejected Koselleck's intellectualist and negative depiction and revealed the economic determinants that led to the bourgeois public sphere holding the state authorities to account with the judgement of public opinion. Though opposed, both accounts treated their main protagonists (critique, the public sphere) as structurally homogenous entities. However, more recent scholarship (e.g. Israel 2001, Sauter 2009) has argued that 'the Enlightenment' was a far more heterogeneous historical phenomenon, driven by local, situated and differential conflicts. Thus, if the model of binary conflict between the public and the state brutally simplified the discursive phenomena of the European Third Wave, is there any sense in rebooting this model to grasp the Fifth Wave?

In my view, the concept of the networked public sphere is ultimately more useful than the model of conflict between the public and authority. There are certain actors that are bent on degrading the public sphere and lowering the level of interaction:

> In early 2018, Steve Bannon, publisher of Breitbart News and Donald Trump's former strategist, gave a concise explanation of how to exploit confusion and distrust: the way to deal with the media, he said, is "to flood the zone with shit".
> STARR 2020, 69

When we focus on local and situated knowledge and practice, we cannot afford to lose sight of the general public sphere or space as a general field of contestation. However, when it comes to fine-grained analysis of networked collective action, the public vs. authority model often has limited or crude application. For example, at first sight the phenomenon of open-source intelligence (OSINT) researchers seems to fit the model rather well. Many of these researchers are described as "amateurs" or "hobbyists", who work collaboratively as they sift through satellite images, TikTok videos, and security feeds, sharing findings like troop movements and aircraft models' on Twitter (Schwartz 2022). So this online community could be framed as an instantiation of the public that opposes the authority of actors like the Russian Federation, countering top-down disinformation with grassroots transparency. However, matters are not so simple:

> There has been a divide in the community between more professionalized outfits, like the investigative outlet Bellingcat founded in 2014, and hobbyists such as Intel Crab, who often lack formal training. Bellingcat often incorporates the work of amateurs into its own investigations.
> SCHWARTZ 2022

This divide was immediately underscored by the founder of Bellingcat, Eliot Higgins, whose Twitter thread in response to Schwartz's article emphasized his decade of experience, his networking, the fact that Bellingcat has trained "over 4000 people", and the trust that Bellingcat's MH17 investigation earned in "the accountability community" (Higgins 2022). The attainment of this professionalism was further confirmed a few weeks later, when Bellingcat published the conclusions of its investigations into the murder of Boris Nemtsov, which were conducted with the BBC and the Insider (see Bellingcat 2022; BBC Eye Investigations 2022). However, little is gained by framing this division in the OSINT community as a conflict between authority and the public, that is, as Bellingcat becoming an MSM-aligned authoritative institution opposed to amateur hobbyists. It would perhaps be more fruitful to view the knowledge produced by OSINT researchers on a continuum: while the continuum would be marked by complete anonymity and hobbyism at one extreme, and the trained professionalism of identifiable and vulnerable people at the other, it could be assumed that expertise is demonstrable across the whole range. Thus, rather than a community internally divided by a public vs. authority conflict as it engages in conflicts with external authorities, OSINT researchers can be viewed as forming fluid and heterogeneous collectives that use professional and hobbyist knowledge production to contest the public sphere – as it descends into an information war environment – and hold murderous authorities to account.

In other words, OSINT researchers could be reconceived as one of the new postcollectives postulated in this volume, which "most often arise from a specific situated need, often a crisis or a threat", and are "manifested in the entanglement of the material and the digital" (Jelewska, Krawczak, Reid). As such, they operate at the intersection of digital spectrality and war-torn reality, scouring the simulcra produced via the non-human apertures of phone cameras, satellites, CCTV etc. to reconstruct the operations of actors in material reality and disseminate the findings in the networked public sphere.

References

Aronowitz, Stanley (1993) Is Democracy Possible? The Decline of the Public in the American Debate. In: Robbins B. (ed.) *The Phantom Public Sphere*. Minneapolis: University of Minnesota Press.

BBC Eye Investigations (2022) Boris Nemtsov: Murdered Putin rival 'tailed' by agent linked to FSB hit squad. *BBC News*, 28.03.2022. Available at: https://www.bbc.com/news/world-europe-60878663

Bellingcat (2022) Boris Nemtsov Tailed by FSB Squad prior to 2015 Murder. *Bellingcat*, 28.03.2022. Available at: https://www.bellingcat.com/news/2022/03/28/boris-nemtsov-tailed-by-fsb-squad-prior-to-2015-murder/

Benkler, Yochai (2006) *The Wealth of Networks: How Social Production Transforms Markets and Freedom*. New Haven, Conn.: Yale University Press.

Benkler, Yochai (2020) A Political Economy of the Origins of Asymmetric Propaganda in American Media. In: Bennett, W. Lance and Livingston, Steven (eds) *The Disinformation Age: Politics, Technology, and Disruptive Communication in the United States* (SSRC Anxieties of Democracy). Cambridge: Cambridge University Press, 43–66.

Bennett, W. Lance and Livingston, Steven (2020) A Brief History of the Disinformation Age: Information Wars and the Decline of Institutional Authority. In: Bennett, W. Lance and Livingston, Steven (eds) *The Disinformation Age: Politics, Technology, and Disruptive Communication in the United States* (SSRC Anxieties of Democracy). Cambridge: Cambridge University Press, 3–40.

Blake, Aaron (2022) The coronavirus misinformation on Joe Rogan's show, explained. *Washington Post*, 02.02.2022. Available at: https://www.washingtonpost.com/politics/2022/02/02/actual-joe-rogan-coronavirus-misinformation/

Carlson, Tucker (2022a) Anything Less than Hating Putin is Treason (Fox News). Twitter 23.02.2022. Available (consulted July 12 2023) at: https://twitter.com/TuckerCarlson/status/1496302694088257539

Carlson, Tucker (2022b) Biolabs in Ukraine (Fox News). Twitter 15.03.2022. Available (consulted June 10 2023) at: https://twitter.com/TuckerCarlson/status/1503548039268601864

Chotiner, Isaac (2022) Why John Mearsheimer Blames the U.S. for the Crisis in Ukraine. *New Yorker*, 01.03.2022. Available at: https://www.newyorker.com/news/q-and-a/why-john-mearsheimer-blames-the-us-for-the-crisis-in-ukraine

Couldry, Nick and van Dijck, José (2015) Researching Social Media as if the Social Mattered. *Social Media + Society*. https://doi.org/10.1177/2056305115604174

Dewey, John (1927) *The public and its problems*. New York: H. Holt and Company.

Durden, Tyler (2022) NATO And Russia – Whistling Past Each Other's Graveyards. *ZeroHedge*, 26.03.2022.

Farage, Nigel (2013) Speech to UKIP Conference, September 19. Available (consulted June 10 2023) at: https://www.ukpol.co.uk/nigel-farage-2013-speech-to-ukip-conference/

Gurri, Martin (2018) *The Revolt of the Public and the Crisis of Authority in the New Millennium*. San Francisco: California: Stripe Press.

Gurri, Martin (2022) War and Persuasion. *City Journal*, 6 March. Available at: https://www.city-journal.org/war-and-persuasion

Habermas, Jürgen (1989) *The Structural Transformation of the Public Sphere: an Inquiry into a Category of Bourgeois Society*. Cambridge, Mass. MIT Press.

Higgins, Eliot (2022) Twitter thread, 07.03.2022. Available (consulted June 10 2023) at: https://twitter.com/EliotHiggins/status/1500931858216931333

Hirsch, Loramie (2022) Global American Empire, Getting Woke Going Broke. *Men of The West*, March 4 2022. Available (consulted June 10 2023) at: https://www.menofthewest.net/global-american-empire-getting-woke-going-broke/

Hitchens, Peter (2022) We have pointlessly made an enemy of Russia. *Daily Mail*, 23.03.2022. Available at: https://hitchensblog.mailonsunday.co.uk/2022/02/we-have-pointlessly-made-an-enemy-of-russia-.html

Israel, Jonathan I. (2001) *Radical Enlightenment*. Oxford: Oxford University Press.

Johnson, Boris. (2016) The liberal cosmopolitan case to Vote Leave. *Vote Leave*. May 9. Available (consulted June 10 2023) at: http://www.voteleavetakecontrol.org/boris_johnson_the_liberal_cosmopolitan_case_to_vote_leave.html

Koselleck, Reinhart (1988) *Critique and Crisis: Enlightenment and the Pathogenesis of Modern Society*. Cambridge, Mass: MIT Press.

Laclau, Ernesto and Mouffe, Chantal (1985) *Hegemony and Socialist Strategy: towards a Radical Democratic Politics*. London: Verso.

Leyh, Brianne McGonigle (2020) Imperatives of the Present: Black Lives Matter and the politics of memory and memorialization. *Netherlands Quarterly of Human Rights* 38(4): 239–245. https://doi.org/10.1177/0924051920967541

Lippmann, Walter (1993) *The Phantom Public*. Transaction Publishers.

Margetts, Helen, John, Peter, Hale, Scott and Yasseri, Taha (2015) *Political Turbulence: How Social Media Shape Collective Action*. Princeton University Press. https://doi.org/10.2307/j.ctvc773c7

Mouffe, Chantal (2005) *On the Political*. Abingdon: Routledge.
Nineham, Chris (2022) Responding to the Terrible Events in Ukraine Requires context. Stop the War Coalition website, 21.03.2022. Available (consulted June 10 2023) at: https://www.stopwar.org.uk/article/responding-to-the-terrible-events-in-ukraine-requires-context/
O'Connor, Mary (2022) Ukraine war: Boris Johnson sparks fury after comparison to Brexit. *BBC News*, 20 March 2022. Available at: https://www.bbc.com/news/uk-politics-60809454
O'Neill, Brendan (2020) Unlock the people. *Spiked*, 01.05.2020. Available at: https://www.spiked-online.com/2020/05/01/unlock-the-people/
Owens, Candace (2022) 'President Zelensky is working with the globalists.' Twitter: 17.03.2022. Available (consulted July 12 2023) at: https://twitter.com/RealCandaceO/status/1504529380873318403
Owens, Candace (2022) 'Ukraine wasn't a thing until 1989!' Twitter 17.03.2022. Available (consulted July 12 2023) at: https://twitter.com/RealCandaceO/status/1504273197046321160
Reality Check Team (2022). Joe Rogan: Four claims from his Spotify podcast fact-checked. *BBC News*, 31.01.2022. Available at: https://www.bbc.com/news/60199614
Robbins, Bruce (1993) Rethinking the Public Sphere. In: Robbins B. (ed) *The Phantom Public Sphere*, Minneapolis: University of Minnesota Press.
Sauter, Michael J. (2009) *Visions of the Enlightenment: The Edict on Religion of 1788 and the Politics of the Public Sphere in Eighteenth-Century Prussia*. Boston: Brill.
Schwartz, Leo (2022) Amateur open-source researchers went viral unpacking the war in Ukraine. *Rest of World*, 07.03.2022. Available (consulted May 12 2023) at: https://restofworld.org/2022/osint-viral-ukraine/
Sheiko, Volodymyr (2022) How to respond to the «dialogues of reconciliation» between Russians and Ukrainians. *Chytomo*, 11.03.2022. Available (consulted April 12 2023) at: https://chytomo.com/en/how-to-respond-to-the-dialogues-of-reconciliation-between-russians-and-ukrainians-sheiko/
Shirky, Clay (2008) *Here Comes Everybody: the Power of Organizing without Organizations*. New York: Penguin Books.
Shotter, James and Majos, Agata. (2019) Poland election: the unfinished counter-revolution. *Financial Times*, 09.10.2019. Available at: https://www.ft.com/content/176e701c-e8ec-11e9-85f4-d00e5018f061
Smith, David. (2022) 'Trump is not my God': how the former president's only vaccine victory turned sour." *The Guardian*, 5 February. Available at: https://www.theguardian.com/us-news/2022/feb/05/donald-trump-vaccine-republicans-operation-warp-speed
Starr, Paul (2020) The Flooded Zone: How We Became More Vulnerable to Disinformation in the Digital Era. In: Bennett W. Lance and Livingston Steven (eds)

The Disinformation Age: Politics, Technology, and Disruptive Communication in the United States (SSRC Anxieties of Democracy). Cambridge: Cambridge University Press, 67–92.

Statista (2023) Number of internet users worldwide from 2005 to 2023. Available (consulted at March 20 2024) at: https://www.statista.com/statistics/273018/number-of-internet-users-worldwide/.

Tidy, Joe (2022) Twitter is part of our war effort – Ukraine minister. *BBC News* 07.03.2022. Available at: https://www.bbc.com/news/technology-60608222

Tokariuk, Olga (2022) Twitter thread. Available (consulted July 12 2023) at: https://twitter.com/olgatokariuk/status/1503324243731361806

Tracey, Michael (2022) Ukraine is Trying to Goad the US into World War III. Personal blog, 06.03.2022. Available (consulted April 10 2023) at: https://mtracey.substack.com/p/ukraine-is-trying-to-goad-the-us?s=r

Westbrook, Robert (1991) *John Dewey and American Democracy*. Ithaca, N.Y: Cornell University Press.

Yarvin, Curtis (2022a) A new foreign policy for Europe. *Gray Mirror*, personal blog, 17.01.2022. Available (consulted April 10 2023) at: https://graymirror.substack.com/p/a-new-foreign-policy-for-europe

Yarvin, Curtis (2022b) Enjoying your Russian civil war. *Gray Mirror*, personal blog, 07.03.2022. Available (consulted April 10 2023) at: https://graymirror.substack.com/p/enjoying-your-russian-civil-war?s=r

Zuboff, Shoshana (2015) Big Other: Surveillance Capitalism and the Prospects of an Information Civilization. *Journal of Information Technology* 30(1): 75–89.

Zuboff, Shoshana (2019) *The Age of Surveillance Capitalism: The Fight for a Human Future at the New Frontier of Power*. New York: Public Affairs.

PART 2

Co-existence

∴

CHAPTER 6

Collective Co-existence, Climate Apocalypse, and a Nature-Relational Way Forward

Peter H. Kahn, Jr., Sarena Sabine and Carly E. Gray

1   Introduction

We begin by looking into the future – not too far in years to be too far-fetched, but far enough to point to a critical time in terms of our collective coexistence. 15 years ahead. If we were writing this in the early 1900's, our time frame would have been around 100 years. Our timeframe is shorter now because in technological terms the rate of change has been increasing exponentially. As an example of an exponential function, take a dollar and double it every day. After a week you have 64 dollars, which is a nice amount but nothing too surprising. But after a month you have over a billion dollars. That is part of the experience of exponential functions: They can start out looking rather modest, if not linear, but at some point shoot skyward, at which point it is difficult for the human mind to comprehend even the next iteration. So, it has been in our evolutionary history (Ehrlich and Ehrlich 2008). About 1.6 million years ago, *Homo erectus* is believed to have first controlled fire. About 50,000 years ago, *Homo sapiens* deliberately used bone, ivory, and shell objects to shape projectile points, needles, and awls, and engaged in cave painting and sculpture. About 10,000 years ago, with the rise of agriculture, rudimentary tools were invented to domesticate land and animals. By about the middle of the third millennium B.C., blast furnaces in China were invented to cast iron. By the sixth century there was the iron plow, and by the thirteenth century the spinning wheel. The Western Renaissance emerged in the 1700's, and then after that was the Industrial Revolution. The greatest amount of technological innovation in the shortest period of time has occurred in the last fifty years, and even in the last twenty years, especially with those technologies that build on digital computation. Back in 1965, Moore's (2006) law was that the number of transistors in microchips doubles about every two years, which pretty much continues to this day. In turn, exponential technological growth has spurred equally fast social transformations. It took 70 years for the landline telephone to become pervasive in modern societies and transform modes of communication. It took seven years for the cellphone to do the same thing; and now, more recently, for social media by means of smartphones to create "information echo chambers" where falsehoods are amplified, social life splintered, and democracies threatened.

What we see 15 years from now is not pretty. Currently, most of the world has been experiencing the destructive effects of climate change, such as droughts, water scarcity, rising sea levels, wildfires, famines, once-in-a-hundred year (or thousand year) extreme weather events, and so on. We could say: "well, in 15 years there's going to be more of this," which is true. But what do we mean by "more?" Again, most of us think linearly not exponentially, which especially comes into play when trying to apprehend the predictions from climate scientists, and the interactions of major climate events. For example, we know that as average global temperatures rise, wildfires will increase in their number, intensity, and range. Those will not be isolated events (Phillips 2021), though we tend to think of them as such. Each event could trigger multiple "tipping points" (Armstrong, Staal, Abrams et al. 2022). For example, wildfires of substantial magnitude can reduce snowpack and speed up spring snow melt, increasing droughts, and lead to drier landscapes even more susceptible to fire. Moreover, wildfires release into the atmosphere huge quantities of carbon dioxide and other potent greenhouse gases, such as methane and nitrous oxide. Those pollutants then not only become a further driver of global warming but cause increasing harms to air quality across regions and nations globally. Over eight million deaths each year are attributed to air pollution (Lelieveld, Klingmüller, Pozzer et al. 2019). Currently 99% of the world population breathes air with harmful levels of pollutants (World Health Organization 2022). Yet emissions continue to rise, fueling what the United Nation's Secretary-General calls humanity's "war on nature" (Guterres 2023).

People need to breathe air. People need to drink water. People need to eat food. If we do not change course, the most basic elements of biological functioning will be undermined for billions of people, and there will be human deaths at a scale we have never seen before on this planet. As this unfolds, there will also be social upheaval on a scale we have never seen. Massive class, political, regional, and nation-state conflict and warfare, with increasingly destructive technological weapons. Jackson and Jenson (2022) refer to something like our scenario as *An Inconvenient Apocalypse*, the title of their book.

It is not 100 years out, or even 50. People who think so are not understanding the exponentially-driven magnitude and pervasiveness of coming harms due to climate change – coupled with other ecologically damaging human activity, including resource over-extraction and toxic pollutants, the extinction of species, pandemics of new and untreatable diseases, and weapons of mass destruction.

Will humanity be able to change course? We do not know. No one does. And in that sense perhaps it is no longer the important question. What is important is that we need to act as if it is possible because that is the only way it will be prevented, if it is possible. And if it is not possible, then we need to help set the groundwork for the collective coexistence of people who make it through. Because if in 15 years (or some other near timeframe that seems right to you) some version of this apocalypse bears out, obviously the planet will still be here, and human life will still exist, compromised, yet seeking a new way forward. We have heard it said of a famous artist, and perhaps it is apocryphal, so we won't mention his name, that he was not interested in participating in the revolution in his midst; rather, he was seeking to paint the peace for after the revolution. That is another way of understanding why we need to act. To set in motion the conditions for collective coexistence for later, if it is too late for now. Thus, in this chapter we would like to offer five transformational ideas to help shape the work we need to be doing now – individually and collectively – this month, this year, this decade.

2 From Domination to Relation

It is sometimes said, as if it is truth, that back in the Paleolithic era – say 30,000 to 100,000 years ago – that we were brutish and organized around principles such as "might makes right," "winner takes all," and "red in tooth and claw." In *Leviathan*, for example, Thomas Hobbes (2005) argued in 1651 that the natural state of *Homo sapiens* before governments and laws, before civilization, was one of continual warfare, and "continuall feare and danger of violent death; And the life of man, solitary, poore, nasty, brutish, and short" (102). But based on anthropological scholarship, this account is surely wrong. For example, short lifespans? Based on analyses of mortality profiles obtained from small-scale hunter-gatherer and horticultural populations from around the world, Gurven and Kaplan (2007) argue for an adaptive life span of 68–78 years. Continual warfare? Our Paleolithic hunter-gatherer kin were commonly organized in small bands and tribes of 2–4 dozen people wherein organized warfare was not practiced (Diamond 1997), as it was not adaptive insofar as all members of the group were important for group survival (Thomas 2006). Indeed, perhaps most remarkable from the anthropological record of our hunter-gatherer kin in Africa is their egalitarian forms of relationship (Eisler 1987; Thomas 2006). Women were valued for their life-giving and life-sustaining abilities, and men valued for their strength and hunting abilities. Both had equal (though different) powers. The social structure was flat, without chiefs. Patriarchy was non-existent.

These social systems began to change with the rise of agriculture about 10,000 years ago. As agriculture took hold, food production increased, which mostly ended nomadic life and allowed for larger families. Populations increased, and then people migrated outward, onward. At that junction, as discussed by Kahn and Hasbach (2013), two social structures were then open for the development of human culture. The first, the village, comprised "voluntary co-operation, mutual commendation, wider communication and understanding" (Mumford 1961, 89). According to Eisler (1987), such a social system was "primarily based on the principle of linking rather than ranking" (XVII). Eisler proposes that the original direction for mainstream culture was toward partnership but that, following a period of chaos and almost total cultural disruption, there occurred a fundamental social shift. She ties the dawn of patriarchy to the appearance of the nomadic bands of pastoral herders who worshipped a warrior god and who ushered in this second form of social organization some 7,000 years ago. These bands then solidified into what Diamond (1997) calls chiefdoms, which involved a hierarchical social structure that monopolized force in a centralized agency to establish its rule. In chiefdoms, for the first time in human history, religions emerged that justified kleptocracy: the transfer of net wealth from commoners to upper classes. In chiefdoms, chiefs were men.

We want to emphasize three points here. One is that this domination orientation is a root cause of many of the problems not only dating back to our Neolithic past but currently in the world today. It is domination when authoritarian regimes use hurtful if not vicious language and policy to divide people by in-group and out-group, often by class and race, political or professional affiliation, or even intellectual commitments. It is domination when countries wage war. It is domination when countries colonize other (often indigenous) people, and destroy their culture, and enact genocide. Patriarchy is domination. Racism and sexism are, too. This domination orientation is central to many people, groups, and authoritarian governments the world over. Our second point is that this same domination orientation characterizes much of how the modern world understands and enacts their relationship with nature. Here nature is understood and treated as a resource to be extracted, used, mined, fracked, logged, dumped in, dumped on, polluted, and killed. Are there consequences? Yes. We face them now. They are the climate crises we are in, and the impending climate apocalypse. Our third point, as discussed above, is that this domination orientation is not part of our essential nature insofar as it does not go that far back in our evolutionary history. It is not a deep part of our genetic code. Thus, it is within reason, and within our capability, to change directions.

Where to? We suggest that individually and collectively we need to move to a relational orientation. It was foundational to us surviving as a species for large parts of our evolutionary history and can light our way forward still today.

In a relational orientation, one seeks at a minimum to coexist and cohabitate with the Other, always to respect the Other, and when possible to engage reciprocally, and to promote equality, and to minimize, when possible, hierarchical systems, or at least their harmful and unjust expressions (Diamond 1997; Eisler 1987; Topa and Narváez 2022). Jordan's (2017) relational-cultural theory provides further specificity by delineating three core processes of building relation with others. One is engagement: we have to care about the situation and the Other, and demonstrate it. The second is mutual empathy: we attune ourselves to the Other, and respond and relate to their lived experience; in turn, we feel as though we are understood, that we matter. The third is mutual empowerment: mutual relationships foster growth for all involved in five areas outlined by Miller (1986): zest, creativity, worth, clarity, and desire for more connection.

In terms of our relationship with nature, relational ways of being have been central to many indigenous cultures. In her opening to a chapter in *Braiding Sweetgrass*, Kimmerer (2013) writes:

> I once heard Evon Peter – A Gwich'in man, a father, a husband, an environmental activist, and Chief of Arctic Village, a small village in northeastern Alaska – introduce himself simply as 'a boy who was raised by a river.' A description as smooth and slippery as a river rock. Did he mean only that he grew up near its banks? Or was the river responsible for rearing him, for teaching him the things he needed to live? Did it feed him, body and soul? Raised by a river: I suppose both meanings are true – you can hardly have one without the other.
> 22

And so it is from the perspective of many indigenous relational worldviews. Nelson (1989) writes, for example, that according to Koyukon elders all are part of a living community, which includes not only humans and animals, and not only plants, but mountains, rivers, lakes, storms – the earth itself. This indigenous relational orientation often involves metaphysical beliefs in an animate world. Nelson writes, for example, that according to Koyukon teachers, "the tree I lean against *feels* me, hears what I say about it, and engages me in a moral reciprocity based on responsible use ... There is no emptiness in the forest, no unwatched solitude, no wilderness where a person moves outside moral judgment and law" (13). This orientation is one of interrelationship and partnership, where nature can be as responsive to us, in its own way, as we are to it, in our own way.

3   Seeking Ethical Community for All

In the Book of Exodus 5:1, it is written that Moses goes to the Pharaoh and tells him: "Let my people go" (New International Version 2011/1978). The Jews seek their freedom. The Pharaoh says no. This situation is archetypal. Oppressed people the world over seek their freedom. The issue we want to focus on here is how oppressed people seek it, as the answer bears on how people respond to the emerging climate catastrophe ahead.

Two types of responses can be characterized by drawing on the positions of two Black social activists from the United States in the 1960s: Malcolm X and Martin Luther King, Jr. Both men were seeking the liberation of Black Americans from the racist social structures, and racist attitudes and behaviors, of White America. Malcolm X argued vehemently for Black nationalism, a separatist movement for Black people to gain economic and political power. While Malcolm X did not directly advocate for initiating violence against White Americans, he argued that Blacks had the moral right if not obligation to respond to White violence with violence. In a speech titled *The Ballot or the Bullet,* Malcolm X (1965) said:

> Any time you demonstrate against segregation and a man has the audacity to put a police dog on you, kill that dog, kill him, I'm telling you, kill that dog … I'm nonviolent with those who are nonviolent with me. But when you go drop that violence on me, then you've made me go insane, and I'm not responsible for what I do.
>
> 33–34

According to Malcolm X, it was politically foolish and ethically shameful for Black people to try to reconcile with their oppressors.

In contrast, Martin Luther King, Jr. believed just the opposite. Politically and pragmatically, King (1967) believed that no political movement of a minority group can succeed as a separatist movement, and that it needs "constructive alliances with the majority group" (50). He also believed that "[p]robably the most destructive feature of Black Power is its unconscious and often conscious call for retaliatory violence" (54). King wrote that "power and morality must go together, implementing, fulfilling and ennobling each other" (59). For King, nonviolence was the way to both. For example, in his 1966 speech at Southern Methodist University, King said:

> First, I'd like to say that nonviolence, I am convinced, is the most potent weapon available to oppressed people in that struggle for freedom and human dignity. It has a way of disarming the opponent. It exposes his moral defenses; it weakens his morale and at the same time it works on his conscience and he just doesn't know what to do. If he doesn't beat you, wonderful. If he beats you, you develop a quiet courage of accepting blows without retaliating. If he doesn't put you in jail, wonderful. Nobody with any sense loves to go to jail. But if he puts you in jail, you go in that jail and transform it from a dungeon of shame into a haven of freedom and human dignity. Even if he tries to kill you, you develop the inner conviction that there are some things are so precious, some things so eternally true, some things so right that they are worth dying for.
> Southern Methodist University Archives 2014

In this way, King (1967) as a leader sought to be a "molder of consensus" (63) for an ethical community of all, including the oppressors. From our perspective, these two choices – one separatist and retaliatory, the other seeking a universal ethical community – are always at hand for those facing oppression, and who are victims of unjust and uncaring social structures. As climate catastrophe takes hold of our planet, and continues to unhinge social structures, the forces oriented toward violence will understandably increase among those subjected to its worsening effects.

We suggest, however, in line with Martin Luther King, Jr., that violence and retaliation are not the way forward. They do not lead to tenable solutions, practically or ethically, as has been shown repeatedly across time and culture, as in Russia with the Bolshevik revolution, in China with the Cultural Revolution, and in some partial ways in America, with the American Revolution. As Freire (2014) says, "the oppressed must not ... become in turn oppressors of the oppressors, but rather restorers of the humanity of both" (44).

4   Nature Interaction, Health, and Human Flourishing

Over the last several decades, it has become increasingly clear from the research literature that interacting with nature, including exercising in nature, is good for people's physical and mental health (Bratman, Anderson, Berman et al. 2019; Frumkin, Bratman, Breslow et al. 2017). Interaction with nature can reduce stress (Berto 2014), depression (Korpela et al. 2016), aggression (Younan, Tuvblad, Li et al. 2016), crime (Kuo and Sullivan 2001), and ADHD symptoms (Kuo and Taylor, 2004). Interaction with nature can also improve immune function (Rook 2013), , mental health (Bratman et al. 2012), positive affect (McMahan and Estes, 2015), life satisfaction (Biedenweg et al. 2017), vitality (Ryan et al. 2010), and social connectedness (Holtan et al. 2014). There is also research on how interaction with nature contributes to the science of positive psychology (Seligman, 2002), including eudemonic wellbeing (Bratman et al. 2019; Capaldi et al. 2015): a sense of purpose, meaning, and fulfillment, and of human flourishing.

Experiences with wild forms of nature, and sometimes dangerous forms, can lead to some of the deepest experiences in life. For example, the mountaineer Dean Potter explains here why he sought to climb one of the more difficult peaks in South America, the Fitz Roy:

> I went to Patagonia to cultivate my intuition – to listen to the Voice. When I'm really in tune with it, really deep in the zone, I get to a place where I disappear completely, where I merge with the rock, when time slows down, my senses are unbelievably heightened, and I feel that oneness, that full-body psychic connection to the universe. It took risking my life to get there, but mission accomplished. And that's why I climb. I crave these experiences. I certainly don't climb to get on top of rocks.
> KOTLER 2014, 47

Sometimes the depth of experience in nature seems engendered by awareness itself (Passmore, Yang and Sabine, 2022). For example, Edward Abbey (1988) writes in *Desert Solitaire*:

> But for the time being, around my place at least, the air is untroubled, and I become aware for the first time today of the immense silence in which I am lost. Not a silence so much as a great still-ness – for there are a few sounds: a creak of some bird in a juniper tree, an eddy of wind which passes and fades like a sigh, the ticking of the watch on my wrist – slight noises which break the sensation of absolute silence but at the same time exaggerate my sense of the surrounding, overwhelming peace. A suspension of time, a continuous present.
> 12–13

And interacting with nature buffers the hardness of the world, and heals. As Ralph Waldo Emerson writes in his poem *Musketaquid* (1915)

> All my hurts
> My garden spade can heal. A woodland walk,
> A quest of river-grapes, a mocking thrush,
> A wild-rose, or rock-loving columbine,
> Salve my worst wounds. (122)

This is all fabulous news. Climate catastrophe is not an endearing topic. It is neither nourishing nor enlivening. And it can overwhelm the psyche, manifesting as climate grief, climate anxiety, and solastalgia. Moreover, it can lead to inaction at the very moment in time when maximum action is needed. Because interacting with nature assists us in so many ways to be physically and psychologically healthy, it provides us with a mechanism to stay strong during the hard years ahead. It also provides us with yet another reason to protect nature: not only to prevent (if possible) climate catastrophe, but to protect that which nourishes us – body, mind, and being.

5 Environmental Generational Amnesia

Even as nature heals, sustains, and revitalizes us, there is a problem. People are forgetting that it does. The "forgetting" happens across generations, and has been referred to in the literature as environmental generational amnesia (Kahn 2002, 2011, 2017; Hartig and Kahn 2016). One of us (the first author) first identified this phenomenon more than 25 years ago in a study with children in an inner-city Black community in Houston, Texas, on their environmental views and values (Kahn and Friedman 1995). The majority of children interviewed understood the concept of air pollution, but significantly fewer children believed that Houston had air pollution, even though Houston was, at the time, one of the most polluted cities in the United States. How could this be? Our explanation then, and now, is that to understand the idea of pollution one needs to compare existing polluted states to those that are less polluted. But if one's only experience is with a certain amount of pollution, then that becomes not pollution, but the norm against which more polluted states are measured.

The psychology of what happened with these children in Houston is happening this very moment on a worldwide level. All of us have grown up in a world environmentally degraded and diminished compared to generations past; yet as children we constructed an environmental baseline that our environment was relatively normal. As we get older, we begin to experience the destruction of places and landscapes from our childhood and feel a loss; and sometimes we intellectually understand that our baseline of what counts as healthy nature was never accurate. But neither form of insight comes close to correcting our original misperception. This psychological phenomenon helps explain how cities continue to lose nature, and why people do not really see it happening. And to the extent they do, they do not think it is too much of a problem. Environmental generational amnesia also prevents people from understanding how interacting with diverse and abundant nature can help them to be physically and psychologically healthier: to not just survive but to flourish.

People do not know what they are missing. Imagine a person who has never experienced love. You can suggest to them that they have missed out on one of the most beautiful and meaningful forms of human experiences. And they can respond by saying "I don't feel like I've missed that much; my life has been fine the way it is." But even if their life has been fine, you know that they have missed out. Similarly, imagine a person – and it may be you, and if so we do not mean to offend – who has never been beyond the city lights and thus never had the opportunity to perhaps lay on a meadow knoll looking up into the night sky, with a million stars overhead, endless distance into space and time, where one feels very small and simultaneously very large, as if one is a part of the cosmos itself. It is one thing to know intellectually "we are part of nature," and another thing to experience it. If we are to come out of climate catastrophe with the tools to re-envision, rebuild, and rebound, it will be enormously helpful if we have enough abundant and diverse nature still left to experience.

6 A Nature-Relational Way Forward

We have been suggesting that one key solution to climate catastrophe is to move from a domination worldview to a relational worldview. Another solution is to interact with nature, so as to benefit from its healing properties, which can lead people to care more for nature and thus increase motivation to address climate problems (Jax et al. 2018). But there is a tension between these two solutions insofar as the idea of "nature for human health" in a sense treats nature as a means (for human benefit) rather than as an end in itself. From Kohlberg's (1984) account of moral development, this form of moral reasoning would be characterized as Stage 2, the second-to-lowest form of 6 forms of moral reasoning, a form of transactional ethics: you help someone only because you want them to help you. It might go a little too far to say that there is a domination strand that runs through the field of nature for human health. But there is certainly a "control" strand, where nature can be "viewed merely as a 'service provider' from which humans can continue to extract health benefits" (Varanasi 2020, 188). Such a perspective is not relational.

One way to increase a nature-relational orientation is to interact with more wild forms of nature, because such forms tend to engender it (Lam et al. 2023; Weiss et al. 2022). For example, if you are swimming in the ocean with modest-to big-waves, you usually do best by moving with, rather than against, their dynamic motion and energy. When you are in their midst, the very power and motion of the waves help bring you into the present moment, moving with them, by them, through them. This is a form of a nature relation. Or if you are in the mountains and encounter a black bear, there can be a moment when you stop and he stops and you both look into one another's eyes. You recognize his bear consciousness from the standpoint of human consciousness. He recognizes your human consciousness from the standpoint of bear consciousness. To know and to be known by an Other is a beautiful experience. Then likely enough, especially if there is room to do so, you both move sidewise to gain distance from one another. There is no need for conflict. There is plenty of room for both of you to coexist. These, too, are forms of nature relations.

Elsewhere we have put forward an urban design methodology – Interaction Pattern Design – to deepen people's relationships with nature in urban environments (Kahn et al. 2010, 2012, 2018; Lev et al., 2020). There are multiple ideas here. (a) One is to identify forms of human-nature interaction that have phylogenetic and ontogenetic significance. By phylogenetic we mean those forms of interaction that likely were central in our Paleolithic lives, and have a genetic legacy today (Shepard 1996, 1998; Wilson 1984). By ontogenetic we mean those forms of interaction that are important for children and adults to develop and enact for their physical and psychological health, and to flourish. (b) Once these forms of interaction – interaction patterns – are identified, then we can seek to find ways, through design, to instantiate them in urban settings. And (c) ask how these interaction patterns, through design, can be instantiated in slightly more wild forms. The reason is that, as discussed, increased relative wildness can help engender a relational orientation. Interacting with increased relative wildness can also help solve the problem of environmental generational amnesia by increasing people's baseline nature experiences.

As a case in point, consider the interaction pattern of *walking to a desired destination in nature*. This interaction pattern has been enacted ever since we have been a species and was central to the hunter-gatherer nomadic life. Some researchers say that if there is a single best exercise for human health and well-being, it is walking (Morris and Hardman 1997). In cities today, how can one design for this interaction pattern? For one thing, it helps to have sidewalks. For another, it helps to have walkable neighborhoods where there are shops to walk to. In the United States, New York City is a good example of where one can; and Los Angeles of where it is difficult (Speck 2013). Now we ask: How can one design a city for more wild forms of this interaction pattern? One way is to design large urban parks with walkways and trails through them. Central Park in New York City, for example, comprises over 800 acres, and 58 miles of walking trails. Some of the trails have steep inclines and bumpy pathways that are frequently unpaved, and with many compelling "special spots" to walk to. Another way is to create long walking and biking corridors in urban areas. In and around Seattle, Washington, for example, a 19-mile section of an old railroad line that had traversed along Lake Washington and through many communities was repurposed as a wide public pathway. It allows urban residents to walk and bike long distances (or short) to get to many special spots, such as small beaches along the lake, places with a big view of downtown Seattle, and to their places of work. And one more example: *Tending a garden* can be instantiated in shared urban garden plots, or in a relatively more wild form through permaculture that invites wildlife to share the land being tended.

At this time, around 500 interaction patterns have been characterized. Some of these have been discussed in terms of their phylogenetic and ontogenetic significance (Kahn et al. 2017; 2018; 2020), and others more with an eye toward urban sustainability (Kahn et al. 2010; 2012; 2018; Lev, Kahn, Chen et al. 2020). Our suggestion here is that Interaction Pattern Design can be used to help people be resilient during times of climate havoc, and to help revision and rebuild after climate catastrophe.

7   Conclusion

In this chapter we have offered five transformational ideas to position us for hard years to come. The first was that a domination worldview has largely led to the climate crisis we are in, and that the solution is to move to a relational orientation. This means, as we wrote earlier, that we seek at a minimum to coexist and cohabitate with the Other, always to respect the Other, and when possible to engage reciprocally, and to promote equality, and to minimize, when possible, hierarchical systems, or at least their harmful and unjust expressions. Second, we suggested that even as climate havoc will lead to victims of hardship at a scale larger than we may have ever experienced, that violence and retaliation are not the way forward, as they will not succeed and are not ethical. Thus, in line with a relational orientation, we need to be seeking ethical community for all. Third, interacting with nature assists us physically and psychologically, and in terms of the human spirit. Human nature interaction thus provides us with a mechanism to stay strong during and through the hard years ahead. Fourth, the problem of environmental generational amnesia constitutes one of the most difficult psychological problems of our lifetime because we are not aware of how much we have already lost, of what we are missing in terms of life and love with nature, and even how much we are suffering, because we have normalized impoverished conditions from our childhood. And fifth, we need a nature-relational way forward, which includes deeper interaction not only with nature, but more wild forms of nature, even in urban areas.

We asked earlier whether climate catastrophe is inevitable, and said that we did not know, and that no one really knows. If it happens, we also said that it is not the end. Much life, including human life, will survive, albeit in dire circumstances. But even if that happens – and we must try with all of our might to prevent it – a catastrophe can offer opportunity. We have heard an account that likens our times to the transition of a caterpillar to a butterfly. At some point in the metamorphosis between the caterpillar to chrysalis, the caterpillar's basic way of being in the world becomes increasingly dysfunctional, and then ends. It has to, for its unfolding. Similarly, it may be that certain dominant lifeways of our species need to end for a new unfolding to occur. But if this is true, we do not believe it can happen unless the nature-relational foundation is laid now. That is our time's mandate and our gift.

References

Abbey, Edward (1988) *Desert Solitaire*. Tucson: University of Arizona Press.

Armstrong McKay, David I., Staal, Arie, Abrams, Jesse F. et al. (2022) Exceeding 1.5°C global warming could trigger multiple climate tipping points. *Science* 377(6611): 1–10 (eabn7950).

Berto, Rita (2014) The role of nature in coping with psycho-physiological stress: A literature review on restorativeness. *Behavioral Sciences* 4(4): 394–409.

Biedenweg, Kelly, Scott, Ryan P. and Scott, Tyler A. (2017). How does engaging with nature relate to life satisfaction? Demonstrating the link between environment-specific social experiences and life satisfaction. *Journal of Environmental Psychology* 50: 112–124.

Bratman, Gregory N., Anderson, Christopher B., Berman, Marc G. et al. (2019). Nature and mental health: An ecosystem service perspective. *Science Advances* 5(7): eaax0903.

Bratman, Gregory N., Hamilton, Paul J., Daily, Gretchen C. (2012) The impacts of nature experience on human cognitive function and mental health. *Annals of the New York Academy of Sciences* 1249(1): 118–136.

Capaldi, Colin A., Passmore, Holli-Anne, Nisbet, Elisabeth K. et al. (2015) Flourishing in nature: A review of the benefits of connecting with nature and its application as a wellbeing intervention. *International Journal of Wellbeing* 5(4): 1–16.

Diamond, Jared M. (1997). *Guns, Germs, and Steel: The Fates of Human Societies.* New York: W. W. Norton & Company.

Ehrlich, Paul R. and Ehrlich, Anne H. (2008) *The Dominant Animal: Human Evolution and the Environment.* Washington, DC: Island Press.

Eisler, Riane T. (1987) *The Chalice and the Blade: Our History, Our Future.* Mass: Harper & Row.

Emerson, Ralph W. (1915) *Poems, by Ralph Waldo Emerson.* England: J. M. Dent & Sons, Ltd.; E. P. Dutton & Co.

Freire, Paolo (2014) Chapter 1. In: Ramos MB (Trans.), *Pedagogy of the Oppressed* (30th anniversary). London: Bloomsbury Academic & Professional, 43–69.

Frumkin, Howard, Bratman, Gregory N., Breslow, Sara J. et al. (2017) Nature contact and human health: A research agenda. *Environmental Health Perspectives* 125(7): 075001.

Gurven, Michael and Kaplan, Hillard (2007) Longevity among hunter-gatherers: A cross-cultural examination. *Population and Development Review* 33(2): 321–365.

Guterres, António (2023) Secretary-General's Remarks to Launch the Special Edition of the Sustainable Development Goals Progress Report [Speech Transcript]. United Nations, 25 April.

Hartig, Terry and Kahn, Peter H. Jr. (2016) Living in cities, naturally. *Science* 352(6288): 938–940.

Holtan, Meghan T., Dieterlen, Susan L. and Sullivan, William C. (2014) Social life under cover: Tree canopy and social capital in Baltimore, Maryland. *Environment and Behavior* 47(5): 502–525.

Hobbes, Thomas, Rogers, Graham A. J. and Schuhmann, Karl (2005). *Thomas Hobbes: Leviathan. A critical edition by Rogers GAJ. and Schuhmann K.* London: Continuum.

Jackson, Wes and Jenson, Robert (2022) *An Inconvenient Apocalypse: Environmental Collapse, Climate Crisis, and the Fate of Humanity.* Indiana: University of Notre Dame Press.

Jax, Kurt, Calestani, Melania, Chan, Kai M. et al. (2018) Caring for nature matters: a relational approach for understanding nature's contributions to human well-being. *Current Opinion in Environmental Sustainability* 35: 22–29.

Jordan, Judith V. (2017) Relational-cultural theory: The power of connection to transform our lives. *The Journal of Humanistic Counseling* 56(3): 228–243.

Kahn, Peter H. Jr. (2002) Children's affiliations with nature: Structure, development, and the problem of environmental generational amnesia. In: Kahn PH Jr. and Kellert SR (eds) *Children and Nature: Psychological, Sociocultural, and Evolutionary Investigations.* Cambridge, Mass: MIT Press, 93–116.

Kahn, Peter H. Jr. (2011) *Technological Nature: Adaptation and the Future of Human Life.* Cambridge, Mass: MIT Press.

Kahn, Peter H. Jr. (2017) Environmental generational amnesia. In: Fleischner TL (ed.) *Nature, Love, Medicine: Essays on Wildness and Wellness.* Salt Lake City: Torrey House Press, 189–199.

Kahn, Peter H. Jr. and Friedman B. (1995) Environmental views and values of children in an inner-city Black community. *Child Development* 66(5): 1403–1417.

Kahn, Peter H. Jr. and Hasbach, PH (2013) The rewilding of the human species. In: Kahn PH Jr. and Hasbach PH (eds) *The Rediscovery of the Wild.* Cambridge, Mass: MIT Press, 207–232.

Kahn, Peter H. Jr. and Weiss, T (2017) The importance of children interacting with big nature. *Children, Youth, and Environments* 27(2): 7–24.

Kahn, Peter H. Jr., Lev, EM, Perrins, SP, Weiss, T, Ehrlich, and Feinberg, DS (2018). Human-nature interaction patterns: Constituents of a nature language for environmental sustainability. *Journal of Biourbanism* 1&2(17): 41–57.

Kahn, Peter H. Jr., Ruckert, JH and Hasbach, PH (2012) A nature language. In: Kahn PH Jr. and Hasbach PH (eds) *Ecopsychology: Science, Totems, and the Technological Species.* Cambridge, Mass: MIT Press, 55–77.

Kahn, Peter H. Jr., Ruckert, JH, Severson, RL, Reichert, AL and Fowler, E. (2010) A nature language: An agenda to catalog, save, and recover patterns of human-nature interaction. *Ecopsychology* 2(2): 59–66.

Kahn, Peter H. Jr., Weiss, T and Harrington, K. (2018) Modeling child-nature interaction in a nature preschool: A proof of concept. *Frontiers in Psychology* 9: 835.

Kahn, Peter H. Jr., Weiss, T and Harrington, K (2020) Child-nature interaction in a forest preschool. In: Cutter-Mackenzie, A, Malone, K and Hacking, EB (eds) *Research Handbook on Childhoodnature: Assemblages of Childhood and Nature Research.* Cham: Springer International Publishing, 469–492.

Kimmerer, Robin W. (2013) *Braiding Sweetgrass: Indigenous Wisdom, Scientific Knowledge, and the Teachings of Plants.* Minneapolis: Milkweed.

King, Martin L. Jr. (1967) *Where Do We Go From Here: Chaos or Community?* Mass: Beacon Press.

Kohlberg, Lawrence (1984) *Essays in Moral Development: Vol. II. The Psychology of Moral Development.* San Francisco: Harper & Row.

Korpela, Kalevi M., Stengård, Elija, Jussila, Pia (2016) Nature walks as a part of therapeutic intervention for depression. *Ecopsychology* 8(1): 8–15.

Kotler, Steven (2014) *The Rise of Superman: Decoding the Science of Ultimate Human Performance.* Seattle: Amazon Publishing.

Kuo, Frances E. and Taylor, Andrea F. (2004) A potential natural treatment for Attention-Deficit/Hyperactivity Disorder: Evidence from a national study. *American Journal of Public Health* 94(9): 1580–1586.

Kuo, Ming and Sullivan, William C. (2001) Environment and crime in the inner city: Does vegetation reduce crime? *Environment & Behavior* 33(3): 343–367.

Lam, Ling-Wai, Kahn, Peter H. Jr, Weiss, Thea (2023) Children in Hong Kong interacting with relatively wild nature (vs. Domestic nature) engage in less dominating and more relational behaviors. *Environmental Education Research* 0(0): 1–16.

Lelieveld, Johannes, Klingmüller, Klaus, Pozzer, Andrea et al. (2019) Effects of fossil fuel and total anthropogenic emission removal on public health and climate. *Proceedings of the National Academy of Sciences* 116(15): 7192–7197.

Lev, Elisabeth, Kahn, Peter H. Jr., Chen, Hanzi et al. (2020) Relatively wild urban parks can promote human resilience and flourishing: A case study of Discovery Park, Seattle, Washington. *Frontiers in Sustainable Cities* 2: 2.

McMahan, Ethan A. and Estes, David (2015) The effect of contact with natural environments on positive and negative affect: A meta-analysis. *The Journal of Positive Psychology* 10(6): 507–519.

Malcolm X (1965) *Malcolm X speaks: Selected speeches and statements*. New York: Grove Press.

Miller, Jean B. (1986) What do we mean by relationships? *Work in Progress, No. 12. Stone Center Working Papers Series*: 1–13.

Moore, Gordon E. (2006) Cramming more components onto integrated circuits, Reprinted from Electronics, volume 38, number 8, April 19, 1965, pp.114 ff. *IEEE Solid-State Circuits Society Newsletter* 11(3): 33–35.

Morris, Jeremy N. and Hardman, Adrianne E. (1997) Walking to health. *Sports Medicine* 23(5): 306–332.

Mumford, Lewis (1961) *The City in History: Its Origins, Its Transformations, and Its Prospects*. New York: Harcourt, Brace & World, Inc.

Nelson, Richard (1989) *The Island Within*. San Francisco: North Point Press.

New International Version of the Bible (2011) Available (consulted September 22 2022) at: https://www.biblegateway.com/verse/en/Exodus%205%3A1

Passmore, Holli-Anne, Yang Ying and Sabine Sarena (2022) An extended replication study of the well-being intervention, the Noticing Nature Intervention (NNI). *Journal of Happiness Studies* 23(6): 2663–2683.

Phillips, Carly (2021) *How Wildfires Affect Climate Change – and Vice Versa* (May 18, 2021). The conversation. Available (consulted September 22 2022) at: https://theconversation.com/how-wildfires-affect-climate-change-and-vice-versa-158688

Rook, Graham A. (2013) Regulation of the immune system by biodiversity from the natural environment: An ecosystem service essential to health. *Proceedings of the National Academy of Sciences* 110(46): 18360–18367.

Ryan, Richard M., Weinstein, Netta, Bernstein, Jessey et al. (2010) Vitalizing effects of being outdoors and in nature. *Journal of Environmental Psychology* 30(2): 159–168.

Speck, Jeff (2013) *Walkable City: How Downtown Can Save America, One Step at a Time*. New York: North Point Press, A division of Farrar, Straus and Giroux.

Shepard, Paul (1996) *The Others: How Animals Made Us Human*. Washington, DC: Island Press.

Shepard, Paul (1998) *Coming Home to the Pleistocene*. Washington, DC: Island Press.

Seligman, Martin E. P. (2002) *Authentic Happiness: Using the New Positive Psychology to Realize Your Potential for Lasting Fulfillment*. New York: Free Press.

Southern Methodist University Archives (2014) *Transcript of Dr. Martin Luther King's speech at SMU on March 17, 1966* Available (consulted September 22 2022) at: https://www.smu.edu/News/2014/mlk-at-smu-transcript-17march1966

Thomas, Elisabeth M. (2006) *The Old Way: A Story of the First People*. New York: Farrar, Straus, & Giroux.

Topa, Wahinkpe and Narváez, Darcia (2022) *Restoring the Kinship Worldview: Indigenous Voices Introduce 28 Precepts for Rebalancing Life on Planet Earth*. Berkeley, CA: North Atlantic Books.

Varanasi, Usha (2020) Focusing attention on reciprocity between nature and humans can be the key to reinvigorating planetary health. *Ecopsychology* 12(3): 188–194.

World Health Organization (2022) *Billions of People Still Breathe Unhealthy Air: New WHO Data*. Available (consulted September 22 2022) at: https://www.who.int/news/item/04-04-2022-billions-of-people-still-breathe-unhealthy-air-new-who-data

Weiss, Thea, Kahn, Peter H. Jr., Lam, Ling-Wai (2022) Children's interactions with relatively wild nature associated with more relational behavior: A model of child-nature interaction in a forest preschool. *Journal of Environmental Psychology*, 101941.

Wilson, Edward O. (1984) *Biophilia*. New York: Farrar, Mass: Harvard University Press.

Younan, Diana, Tuvblad, Catherine, Li, Lianfa et al. (2016). Environmental determinants of aggression in adolescents: Role of urban neighborhood greenspace. *Journal of the American Academy of Child & Adolescent Psychiatry* 55(7): 591–601.

CHAPTER 7

As I Sit Down to Write a Monsoon Story without Cloud Bands

Harshavardhan Bhat

Meanderings stick. Doodles of reflection fade. This work scribbled through the winter of twenty eighteen, I explored some of the anxieties of writing about monsoon airs. New Delhi, which was the assigned city as part of my doctoral work funded by the Monsoon Assemblages project, was a primary material interlocutor. It provided me with a wealth of stories, notes and observations. These hyphenated notes, feelings, and arguments below are among other things associated with breezing(s) of mucus, confrontation and a humming low. Their temporal affiliations in the articulation of an air of the monsoon, are not necessarily pedagogic attempts at writing co-existence, as data or knowing, but rather as pulse of presence produced through the process of research. Seasons die. Time disorients. Matter laterals. People hurt. When asked for a methodology, these airs collaborate in the versioning and dreaming of what a note could sketch as a methodology.

1   Mucus as Some Kind of Methodology

Places stay with you, even after you depart. You stay in places. You move to places. And places find ways to move with you. My research fieldwork in Delhi had taught me many things. One of those things is that certain matters stick with you (literally) and change (materially) as you leave – clinging on, evolving, changing, mixing and becoming. The winter airs of Delhi, in their toxic form, for breathing human and more-than-humans, in the air – offer to me an analytic through the transdisciplinary transformation of mucus. An inflammation. Inflammatory in the broadest solidarity of collectives. Breathing. The air, read through the mucus of one's body's metabolism and histamine interactivity, clings on to this theoretical and lived field (the city of Delhi) as a material that is inherently vital, living and fluidly cellular. Leaving Delhi, I enter a series of stages, typically travelling through cough, wet cough, and a gradual exit of phlegm through my nose and mouth. In transit to/from Delhi, air travel makes me conscious of the power that this thick liquidity has over the region around my eyes and nose, as pain ruptures in synchronization with changes in cabin pressure as the aircraft descends to land.

Like Delhi's air, which changes texture, density and colour (amongst other things) through the year and during the day, phlegm makes a journey, as it plays its part, in my bodily system and gradually changes characteristics too. As part of this process, I have learnt to cough with care, wipe with care, sneeze with care and interact with wash basins with care. I observe the airs of Delhi and their particular becomings, slowly leave in parts out into the water supply network. When you have an episode of rupture or perhaps an thick elasticity of the feeling of rupture which takes over your body's time, you hold the basin with the fragility of breakdown. Rest. And. Again. Rest. And, break. As the inner tunnels of my wind system become sensitive to the dances of new-aerosols, ruptures perform a solitary event – as repetition. Respiration is solidarity. I am okay. I am okay. I am doing okay. We are still here. Things are. Breath is. There are still birds in the sky.

Researching and writing about a city in/with the airs of the monsoon demands a conscious un-othering of the air. This means that the airs of the monsoon are not just seasonal forms that change an experience of time but airs that form "us" and every possible composition that forms the living. As some spoken theories of *Kali Yuga* (time of the demon, *Kali*) inform me, time itself has changed – and therefore the air. As Gail Omvedt reminds us, even the terror of this oppressive time was historically theorized as a way to maintain an oppressive casteist hold on a theory of time (Omvedt 1995). If the air is wrecked, so is everything. These architectures of difference hold violence. For the air flows – not as choice but as an air of life that lives within, together with and because of the air. It is a becoming-with (Haraway 2007 Wright 2014) in some sense, becoming-inside-of, becoming-because-of-the-air. As Neimanis and Walker observe, "we are thick with climatic intra-actions" (Neimanis and Walker 2014, 558) and the weather etches bodies and bodies make and carry the weather too. The air as the grand living site of all disposability is the active interpretation of most methodologies and methods of development (i.e., the discipline and what follows). For example, most air pollution policies require that the city comprehend air as a jurisdictional space with boundaries. Of course, boundaries politically drawn in the air allow for the performance of power, control and regulation. However, I wonder if methodologies for the study of the air were not subject to the framework of territorial maps, then what kind of airs would we see – inhabiting a world of their own transformation? If Delhi manages to escape in a million other ways outside the bounds of Delhi as we know it, where and how does Delhi crawl, swirl and become entangled as matter that is constantly alive? Stories of the air help us recognise that the site is a transdisciplinary figure, offering the widest range of analytic possibilities.

Back in London, as the Piccadilly line from Heathrow Terminal 4 rattled to Finsbury Park, I felt the airs of Delhi doing their bidding again as my sinus took my hearing through the stages of breath and fold. Mucus methodologies and the management of mucus interacting worlds teaches me that toxicity privileges some more than others. Othering the air as the waste site of growth and economic-life in India in the twenty-first century, forces breath-life to become sinus aware, tear skin, inundate vulnerability Srigyan (2016). points out that not everybody gets to breathe the same air in Delhi. For people, architectures determined by capitalism, class, caste, gender and other socio-political-economic energies determine materials and technologies that envelop some and exclude others. As different forms of expertise propose cuts in how, why and where air should be identified and managed, I find that the airs of the monsoon, for example, find themselves flourishing and exchanging far beyond the perceived season of the monsoon. Storying with the monsoon allows for atmosphere and air to enter a very different kind of storytelling. The airs of the monsoon materialize methodology.

2   Really? You've Come to Delhi to See the Monsoon?

A response that I have repeatedly received from middle and upper-class folk living in Delhi when I tell them that I am researching New Delhi in/under/with the airs of the monsoon is the awkward gesture of a question mark. To paraphrase their response: "Really? You've come to Delhi to see the monsoon?" The monsoon as a rain figure transforms itself as a lived knowledge in and with the matters of the ground. So, for motorists stuck on the highway between Delhi and Gurgaon on weeks where the clouds overwhelm them with generosity, the monsoon becomes a flood figure and the highway becomes a river. In an otherwise dry Delhi, their response continues: "It hardly rains here, *Harsh*. What about air pollution? That seems like a topic relevant to the air." For a city that has been called a seasonal gas chamber by its own government and Supreme Court, anxieties of toxicity thread well as an analytic of understanding the air. People told me that the monsoon wash away pollutants from the air. It is a cleaner of anthropogenic emissions, a 'service provider' for the toxic air, they say. As we now know from the research legacy of the work on atmospheric brown clouds in the subcontinent (UNEP 2008; Ramanathan et al. 2002) by Veerabhadran Ramanathan's team, and others: anthropogenic aerosols and the winter haze disrupt monsoonal metabolism in unpredictable ways. Here I was, at a friend's place, watching his child puff an inhaler to breathe. What assaults his breath is also what assaults monsoonal life. As the air conditioner operated in filtering and sucking out moisture from the air, one notices that even an elite interior performs a fantasy of monsoonal expulsion – against humidity, against wetness, against life – all for a transformed breath, for a different kind of life.

That winter, the Ministry of Environment, Forest and Climate Change proposed cloud seeding exercises to create rain in the New Delhi National Capital Region (NCR) to bring down rates of pollution. The still foggy air of winter in the Delhi region, and the patchy distributed scarce cloud bands above it, did not, interestingly, offer the scientists and technocrats the conditions for rain to be invented in a display of planes, salts and clouds. As it turned out, they needed clouds to cloud seed. I wondered, if they were successful, what kinds of rains would these be? The rain after all was never just the rain. There were stories of good rains, bad rains, heavy rains, joyful rains, violent rains, rains of the snakes, rains that elephants love, rains that some plants love and other don't. There were as many different kinds of rains as the air itself, its matter and condition were different, in different times and at different speeds/patterns/densities. In a conversation with a leading scientist at one of India's eminent agencies pertaining to weather concerns, he casually remarked that cloud seeding after all was "scientifically proven" and if done in the right conditions can produce "adequate results", although more experimentation and research was required to improve "precision".

The monsoon, after all, is often just read as a movement of energy and material. The so-called inter-tropical convergence zone that meets lower pressures in the Indian subcontinent in the summer feeds off the south-east trade winds that carry with them a tremendous amount of moisture. The spin of the earth, enacting the Coriolis force, performs a movement of air, carrying the oceans into the sky, deflecting and drifting finally towards the Himalayas. The air meets Delhi from both the east and the west as an energy of dust, water and other matters, which encompasses a cloudy ground above our ground, one that is bluer than the other. It creates a divide between the sky and the earth. All that is life draws from the air of the monsoon. Can you hear the sound of this force? And here they continued to ask: "Really? You've come to Delhi to see the monsoon?" Please leave the air-conditioned car. The monsoon is in the stickiness. It paraphrases the construct and precedes the theory of it.

I remember a scene from that summer: a vegetable seller selling greens, left their produce open to the air as it started to drizzle. They told me that it was okay because it was raining from the past few days and the rain wasn't dirty. It would keep the greens fresh. A theory of filtration and time brackets seemed to operate. The first rains were meant to be toxic, I was told by an aunty who advised against me wandering around when it rained. I've heard this story before – its many versions. It repeats, in different ways. Outside the methodological bracket of toxicity, I found myself in the corridors of liquid dynamics and meteorology, where folks told me that the monsoon could be perceived as a mathematical problem, a problem of liquid metabolism – upon and in different kinds of masses. It was a movement, a flow, and a phenomenon of complexity, which can be analyzed in scales. Dense numerical datasets that fed into parallel computing machines produced speculative lines of present and future, in turn based on speculative data columns of the past negotiated by careful modelling. I was told that the air had a history, and its predictability was no different from the prediction of financial markets, earthquakes and the general economy.

Listening to stories of communities bathing in mud, worshipping the deity of thunder by submerging in water and preparing for monsoon clouds, I was confronted by the intersectionality of several different histories meeting this force. Each culture had its own science of this air, its behaviour and their becoming-with-this-monsoon. As I opened the bottle of *mitti attar* (the essential oil of the soil) at a leading perfumery in Delhi, I was struck by how evocative it was and how I could not stop thinking of the first rain on grounds covered by construction dust. That was not the way it was described on the bottle and the perfumer assured me that they had kept to the original recipe from ancient times. This was the perfume of the first rains. He showed me a cheaper synthetic variant, to demonstrate that there were others on the market but not of the same quality. With the scent of sandalwood oil, wet mud and mild floral notes in the air, I was told that it was a popular summer perfume. It obviously did not smell like construction dust, but the monsoon had a way to manufacture airs in a plurality of possible flows, with anything that interacts with it. Rain changes the earth, even before it touches it.

I walked around the central market that day enjoying the range of smells it had to offer. Perceiving the world through a monsoon lens, it becomes very hard to spot produce that does not have contemporary monsoonal origins. The expanse of commodities, laterally, historically, spatially, socio-economically, geographically and in every catalogue of meaning making is sheltered by monsoonal possibility and its many forms. The commodity is a suffix for the offering of the monsoon. Hyphenated through its presence and alienated without. The monsoon was unlikely to be theorised as a site, as it is a highly distributed one, and it is not a singular form despite the hubris of the word, but if one was to detach and attach, with monsoonal materialities, constantly in movement, monsoonal figures come alive and these attachment sites (Haraway 2018) distribute, sticky. Monsoonal attachments can be empowering. Monsoonal attachments relationally can also be debilitating. They hold potential for political work (and always have) because these attachments help expose the wider logics of how the monsoon cultivates the living. Even Indian finance ministers (and presidents, governors and academics) have followed the tradition of acknowledging the monsoon as the true finance minister of India.

3   The Ghats Will Accept Your Depression

Writing about the airs of the monsoons is a very peculiar kind of privilege. With regard to Delhi, it pushed me in developing a heightened sense of love for a city that I did not like very much. It encouraged me to look again, ask again, and think again about matters that I would otherwise have ignored. As the temperature, carbon and toxic condition of life worlds across spaces accentuate and change, the monsoon as a thermodynamic, physical, biochemical and ecological being also changes in the way it relates to the life world it has sustained. In describing airs literally, such as the air you are in by the Ghats of the Yamuna in New Delhi where open cremations take place, everything comes together, disintegrates. A woman shared with me her woes of possibly losing her house in the Ghats because of a court battle. A little boy clears the sludge for boats to park. College students with DSLR cameras, accompanied by a local boatman, throw crumbs into the water to attract migratory seagulls to circulate around them. Bodies burn at the Ghats. Ash rises in the air. Every few minutes you can see the Delhi metro pass by on the bridge. The river, like oil, reflects the evening sun through the Delhi haze. Some plastics float.

The lifting away of life by the monsoon through its changing behaviour – sometimes extreme dryness, and at other times extreme wetness – confronts us (Narain et al. 2017). The disappearance of water from our mountains and the killing of our rivers confronts non-human and human communities across the subcontinent to negotiate ways of finding water and re-dealing with it, as dry air takes it away. Breathing in the Ghats, as anywhere, one is keenly reintroduced to the fact that the air is material and as bodies burn, other bodies breathe those matters. All this as the water moves in the Yamuna, devoid of air, polluted and contaminated with every possible inheritance of violence and its historical reproduction. Still, water is water. Still, water is sky and earth. Still, water is here, and there, and will be. Still, water is you and me. Still, water will move – even as oppressive communities, industries and colonialisms attempt to cement it to abyssal excess. Still, water is reaching us, to still stay alive, still keep each other alive. A monsoon air methodology, amongst other things, gives the researcher an insight into how the air is writing its own stories,

FIGURE 7.1   Image of the cloud, by Harshavardhan Bhat

despite its treatment as a technology. Following those disciplines invested in the matter of these airs takes the research to different places where we get to see how monsoon airs mingle with, and create, new conditions and circumstances. Navigating the hazy air, Siberian seagulls circle in celebration of being fed industrial crumbs by the Ghats of the Yamuna – they take us through a different story of a winter air mingling with a monsoon air. The richness of keeping analysis slightly suspended above the ground exposes the work to possibilities of a politics of monsoon air: a methodological reframing of air matters by the monsoon. The monsoon read through this political figuration is more-than-cloud, more-than-water and is definitely more-than-a-fluid-measure. The air enacts its politics for 'us' to see. Methodology in some sense, is indeed inherited from the monsoon. The monsoon becomes more than a volumetric measure. By thinking with its aerial entangled complexity, it becomes more-than-a-season. It becomes a force that ends up doing so much more than what we give it credit for. Like the "seven-hundred-year-old rain" that swirls through the "bottomless chasm." saving "the village from a terrible flood" in the Easterine Kire, Nagaland-inspired novel *Son of the Thundercloud* (2016), the air, older than all of us, has been in a long conversation with the ocean and the ground and is thus older than methodology itself (Figure 7.1).

Acknowledgements

Thanks to the Hyphen team and co-organisers of the Hyphen Exhibition in 2019, particularly Matthias Kispert (for editing), Arne Sjögren (for feedback) and Monika Jaeckel (for connecting) from CREAM, University of Westminster for hosting this conversation in P3 Ambika. This work was funded by Monsoon Assemblages, a research project funded by the European Research Council (ER) under the European Union's Horizon 2020 research and innovation programme (Grant Agreement No. 679873). Thanks to Lindsay Bremner and David Chandler for supervising my work and nurturing the process of study and writing. Thanks to Agnieszka Jelewska and Michal Krawczak of hearing my silent rage on that bleak white enveloped conference day, and sheltering us in the rain.[1]

References

Haraway, Donna (2018) Unblocking Attachment Sites. Rubber Boots Methods for the Anthropocene. A Node-based Conference, Moesgaard Museum, Aarhus University, Aarhus, 26–27 November.
Haraway, Donna (2007) *When Species Meet*. Minneapolis: University Of Minnesota Press.
Kire, Easterine (2016) *Son of the Thundercloud*. New Delhi: Speaking Tiger.
Narain, Sunita, Sengupta, Rajt and Mahapatra, Richard (2017) *An 8-Million-Year-Old Mysterious Date with Monsoon*. New Delhi: Centre for Science and Environment. Available (consulted May 3 2023) at: http://www.downtoearth.org.in/reviews/monsoon-55459
Neimanis, Astrida and Loewen Walker, Rachel (2014) Weathering: Climate Change and the 'Thick Time' of Transcorporeality. *Hypatia* 29, 3: 558–575. https://doi.org/10.1111/hypa.12064

---

1   This chapter was published in Issue 1 of *Hyphen Journal* [as part of the *Hyphen* Exhibition at the University of Westminster] "As I sit down to write a monsoon story without cloud bands – some mucus, confrontation and sadness" as of 1st March 2019, accessible here: https://hy-phen.space/journal/issue-1/bhat-as-i-sit-down-to-write-a-monsoon-story/. Full copyright retained by the author and republished here with permission.

Omvedt, Gail (1995) *Violence Against Women: New Movements and New Theories In India*, New Del: Kali for Women.

Ramanathan, Veerabhadran, Crutzen, Paul J., Mitra, Ashesh P. et al. (2002) The Indian Ocean Experiment and the Asian brown cloud. *Current Science* 83: 947–955.

Srigyan, Prerna (2016) *Delhi's Air: Histories, Technologies, Futures*, MA thesis, School of Human Ecology, Ambedkar University, Delhi.

UNEP (2008) *Atmospheric Brown Clouds – Regional Assessment Report with Focus on Asia*. Nairobi and Bangkok: UNEP.

Wright, Kate (2014) Becoming-with. *Environmental Humanities* 5 (1): 277–281. https://doi.org/10.1215/22011919-3615514

CHAPTER 8

A Meteorology of Media

Brett Zehner

The wild embodied wind of the prairies is like a presence among the fields.
MERIDEL LE SUEUR (1940, 8)

∴

1

Tornado impacts tend toward the surreal. Cars wrapped around trees stripped bare of their bark, school buses thrown through the air like toys, toothpicks driven through engine blocks. People impacted directly by tornadoes report a sudden drop in air pressure; eardrums explode, the lungs are stripped of air just before impact. The body's atmosphere becomes attuned to the radical change around it, undermining any simple division between human and environment. The sheer force of a tornado can be staggering. Tornadoes can move laterally at speeds of 100 feet per second, while the internal wind speeds of the worst storms may exceed 200 miles per hour, enough to rip skin from bone. In one instant, normality; in the next instant–an explosion of debris. Violent winds disarticulate the architectures of the everyday, turning nearly every mundane object into a deadly missile. The split second of a tornado's impact acts as a threshold between altered states. In its vortex, seemingly solid things become things in flux. Some will remain, while others vanish. But for a fleeting moment, what remains and what disappears are held together in catastrophic coherence. Everything is up in the air.

Encounters between earth and air, at the point of a vortex, highlight the strange singularity of tornadoes, troubling distinctions between subjects and objects, scale and movement, culture and nature. Tornadic encounters – touching down, piercing, and transgressing the liminal boundary between earth and sky – thus pronounce the entanglement between earth systems and social processes. The weather event exemplifies the earth, not as a passive receiver of human impact, but as a continually changing set of physical dynamics.

This chapter presents a media theory for tornadic encounters: a meteorology of media. This project is inspired by Jussi Parikka's *Geology of Media* (2015), which translates the methods of geological science to analyze the stratified, nonlinear layers of media history. Parikka expands media theory to include the raw minerality of technological environments. I, however, turn to meteorology, a science reliant on probabilistic prediction, as a methodological lens. As a source for media theory, I argue that meteorology draws our attention to local singularities and events-in-the-making that fall outside the grand scope of media history. In this manner, it is important to make a distinction between climatology and meteorology, two epistemologies that are often conflated. Paul Edwards writes that

> meteorological data systems are built for real-time forecasting. Their priority is speed, not precision, and they absorb new instrumentation, standards, and models quite quickly. In contrast, climatology requires high precision and long-term stability – almost the opposite of the rapidly changing weather observing system.
> 2010, 14

It is also here that a meteorology of media operates at the micro scale, the scale of individual experience. It is a phenomenology of affective weathers, beyond a collective experience. Or, perhaps, it is a pre-collective, pre-individual state of gathering the weather.

As well, it is within the technological assemblage of meteorological knowledge production that the storm chaser's act of citizen science is a necessary supplement to the temporal gap of computational weather predictions. The speed and rhythm of the storm chaser's movements are what make them unique. Chasers fuse real-time data flows with embodied environmental awareness as they navigate gridded road networks to intercept erratic tornadic paths.

In this chapter, I follow the artist Francis Alÿs through his project *Tornado, Milpa Alta 2000–2010*. My response to these artistic performances is informed by my ethnographic fieldwork with storm chasers through the Tornado Videos Network, who I read as practitioners of what Deleuze and Guattari call "nomad science." Through these figures, I explore the aesthetics of tornadic encounters and their capacity for troubling meteorological modes of knowledge production and opening environmental experience to other possibilities of shared risk. With Alÿs, I find the rupture of the tornado productive in disrupting discourses of hubris around climate risk and mediation. I ultimately ask, as a theorist of environmental media – what do we gain by considering storm chasing as a form of art?

2

To begin, we must consider the centrality of art to Parikka's paradigmatic use of environmental science as a model for media studies. Parikka's elaboration of a geological imaginary for media studies builds upon the work of Robert Smithson. Smithson's artistic practices throughout the 1970s engage technological landscapes from the perspective of geologic time. Smithson's critical essays and artworks such as *Spiral Jetty* (1970) enact the technological milieu not as an extension of humanity, but as fundamentally made up of the raw materials of the earth (Smithson 1996). Parikka reads Smithson's experimentation with the given materiality of the earth as an elaboration of non-human timescales. Smithson ultimately decenters the classical humanist perspective of aesthetics and replaces it with something akin to a psycho-geophysics. Writing over three decades after Smithson, Parikka theorizes what he calls the "earth media arts," which experiment with premediated materials and the afterlives of dead technologies. The geology of media attends to "notions of temporality that escape any human obsessed vocabulary and enter into closer proximity with the fossil" (2015, 7). The materiality of the fossil is essential to deep time perspectives. However, if we focus, rather, on the motion of the spiral, we return to the scale and temporality of the individual. Here, Smithson muses on the construction of *Spiral Jetty*:

> On the horizon – a horizon is an impossible point to locate. Even though it is right there in front of you, it is constantly evading your grasp. It is only a mirage that can't be fixed, arrested or stopped, or transferred into an abstract condition, and that is the arrested moment. Those moments constantly change and are giving way to other moments; so you can get into a kind of vertigo situation. A point is like a whirlpool or central vortex. The piece in Salt Lake will be built on a meandering zone, that is unstable, and the idea is to stabilize something that is unstable.
> 1996, 12

The spiral form in Smithson's work supervenes on its material substrate and concatenates deep time with embodied experience via vortical motion. The vortex of *Spiral Jetty* offers a break from the temporal norm, sending viewers into the vertigo of an a-temporal drift. The vortex opens an interval and triggers a network of responses that create a general attitude and set of alienated relations to the environment. The vortex highlights the difference between the geology of media and the meteorological approach I propose. The shift between the geologic and the meteorological register occurs in the temporal scale of the individual subject. What the geology of media cannot account for is the event, the immediate experience of the vast time scale of environmental risk. And the emergency of severe weather occurs at the immediate human scale. It is precisely where the deep time accumulated effects of climate shifts will come into contact with the individual, and perhaps more aptly – the pre-individual.

3

Tornado Alley, spanning the central plains of the United States, is an area in which conditions have historically been ripe for tornadoes. Today it is migrating further east, into more densely populated areas. This geographic shift is brought on by a generally warming climate and, in turn, a wider area of atmospheric instability (Agee et al. 2016). In this region, a tornado is an explicit effect of human activity, if not of direct intentions. It is a ricochet of human endeavor, not a relation emerging from direct causality, but a haunting, intense (re)turn of cultural (re)production.

For a hurricane, preparations can begin a week or more in advance. For tornadoes, by contrast, the average warning time is less than 15 minutes. As the temporality of preparation is compressed, anticipation heightens. The tornado siren is the first aesthetic cue to rapidly changing weather. In their haunting pitch and tone, tornado sirens articulate an atmosphere of foreboding, anticipation and doom. At many sites, Cold War air raid sirens remain as the public address system for tornado warnings.[1] The warning itself is a system of imperatives, organized around a structure of command and control: *be warned!* The state enacts sirens, messages, maps with trajectories, an entire communications network externalizing the responsibility of environmental protection to the individual. During the Super Tornado Outbreak of 2011, for instance, local weather presenters across the South shepherded their respective publics through the catastrophe in firm but calm voices. Phrases such as "unsurvivable above ground" and "guaranteed catastrophic damage" mixed with the weather broadcaster's calm, (usually) masculine voice, in a live play by play – "if you are in the path of this tornado, take your tornado precautions."[2] The role of the weather presenter is that of a conductor, translating between machines, and between human and non-human. The forecast creates a cartography of isobars and isotherms – the weather map wrapping together air and subjects. The

---

[1] For more on meteorological infrastructure and communication systems see Edwards 2010.
[2] I am referencing here Gary England's *Breaking News Weather Emergency* broadcast in Oklahoma, City in May of 2011.

raging atmosphere can be known, up to a point, but not fully controlled. The subject is directed away from harm. As the weather presenter choreographs the viewers' self-protective pattern of response to an orchestrated threat, there is a breakdown of the division between the television studio, the weather station, and the theater.

In reaction, the citizen turns away from an outside threat and toward *home*. In Sara Ahmed's analysis of the cultural aftermath of 9/11, home becomes a symbol of the nation. Ahmed argues that emotions are not solely located within the subject, they circulate and stick to objects, infusing them with a charged tension. Under the threat of the tornado warning, the midwestern family home similarly becomes a 'sticky' symbol of American identity under attack, in this case from arbitrary forces of nature (Ahmed 2013, 70–74). The individual is thereby bound to the retrenched material cultures of home via the emotional attachments brought on by the dual relationship of threat and security. After the tornado has passed, once the family has emerged from their bunker, and homes have been destroyed, we see countless photos of the flag, battered, yet still flying. The basement rec room doubles as a setting for a certain wistful longing. There is a temporal drag of Cold War anxiety, of the collective sense of a threat from above. There is a nostalgia for the air raid shelter where families endlessly practiced resilience in the face of the end of the world. The storm shelter, in turn, becomes a refuge from the tornado menacing the countryside. Sirens blare a generic call, atmospheric in their own right. The dressage of the citizen subject passes through all of its disciplinary training. The senses are trained to recoil; a heavy book protecting the head in the school hallway, a public safety lecture, emergency protocols at work, family emergency plans. These are not at all insignificant moments in shaping a national identity.[3] Bleating their shrill warning, the sirens recall nuclear war simulations, hailing national subjects. The tornado bunker, qua home, becomes the space of the family, under threat, yet protected. Importantly, this sequence shifts individuality away from any form of collective response, as in other disaster responses. Instead, the disaster turns individuals inward, toward their home, to interior spaces, the outside has intruded and reformulates a post-collective society as one shaped by media networks, bunkers, and the protection of interior comforts.

When one hears the sirens, the performative command and control message is activated: citizens should take cover, turn toward safety. Terranova refers to this as 'soft control,' a form of control that need not necessarily emanate from

---

3   For more on dressage as an embodied training paradigm see Lefebvre 2004, 39.

a central authority. (see 2004, 98–131) It is more banal, more automated. The siren is an infrastructural language, directed toward the pre-individual, aimed at moderating flows of affect, sensation, and desire–relations on their way to becoming subject. Here, following Maurizio Lazzarato, we can comprehend the production of subjectivity as *both* a pre-individuated process operating at the level of affect *and* an individuating process operating through authority and social connection.[4] The subject is produced within a socio-technical assemblage made up of urban infrastructures, earth forces, communication systems, and bodily capacities, at once individuated and dividuated by forces that exceed language (Lazzarato 2014).

In her analysis of Hurricane Katrina, Marita Sturken draws our attention to the public service campaigns of ready.gov, which were produced to warn citizens of the dangers of severe weather events. In its appeal to middle-class suburban families, the government agency displays a blatant refusal to imagine any citizen subject that does not fit within the bounds of the nuclear family, linking the state, environment, and normative social structures (Sturken 2006). This meteorological communication network primarily views the weather from satellites and Doppler radar stations. The typical vantage point is a depopulated one. Giant swirling storms are seen from above rather than felt from below. This de-bodied perspective converges with urban planning discourse and architectural models. A generic subject is implied by a structured landscape. FEMA response plans, scripted for the idealized, middle-class family, will prove catastrophic for the majority of the population. Meteorological media is a global system of information wielded to externalize the responsibility of environmental risk to the level of the individual. Again, the imagination of the meteorological apparatus never speaks of collectivity, it targets you, your family, as the victim of global systems. By both ignoring the on-the-ground reality of the citizens affected by the storms, and the fine-grained movement of the storms themselves, pressing social concerns appear in the gaps of state knowledge. The ability of the state to control natural threats to its sovereignty breaks down. The storm is not entirely predictable. Engineering systems can only hold so much force. And these shortcomings converge with an unevenly distributed disregard for the realities of people affected on the ground.

---

4   Lazzarato claims that the contemporary condition under late capitalism is characterized by the simultaneous individuation of subjects as marked by the state as well as the disintegration of the subject via capitalist trajectories of affect and desire.

4

In an artwork titled *Tornado, Milpa Alta 2000–2010*, Francis Alÿs opens himself to non-human resistance by willingly throwing himself into tornadoes – albeit very week "dust devils" – in the Mexican countryside. Alÿs sees the dust storm as a symbol of the imminent collapse of all systems of order. In the description of his installation at the Tate Modern, we can read Alÿs's attraction to the tornadic vortex:

> The act of running into the storm, which we see repeated over and over, also invites interpretation: is the artist no longer able to combat the chaos he encounters? Or is it only within the chaos that he can challenge the turmoil around him? Reaching the epicentre of the storm, the artist is breathless and almost blinded, yet he encounters a furtive moment of peace that could hint at a new moment of possibility.
> 2010

In the work of Alÿs, it is too simple to imagine leaping into a tornado as a nihilistic impulse. The artist sees the tornado as a positive force. Through the chaos of the vortex, through its excessive noise, its blinding debris, its sheer physical force, the vortex becomes a symbol of regeneration, an imperceptible, but open future. The indeterminate act of Alÿs flies in the face of a seemingly overdetermined world of big data.

From the artistic gesture of abandonment through storm chasing, to the citizen science of meteorological storm chasing, we can track an openness to the radically indeterminate. The globalized atmospheric sensing systems which underpin the meteorological apparatus seem omnipresent in the planetary scope of their infrastructures.[5] However, there is still a great need for citizen science to fill in the particulate gaps in local environmental knowledge.[6] The storm chaser, in the context of the tornado, is the eyes and ears that are necessary to confirm the existence of a "tornado on the ground." The storm chaser's role in detection and warning is central in defining the exact path a tornado is taking. Even though Doppler radar has become an important tool for meteorologists in tracking tornado development, it still has a broad range

---

5   See Gabrys 2016 and Edwards 2010 for the necessity of planetary scale computation in the prediction of atmospheric phenomena.
6   For a key text on citizen science and environmental knowledge see Irwin 1995.

of error, and it cannot calculate the infinite complexity of atmospheric data.[7] The storm chaser has the advantage of the haptic, close-up experience of the tornado, whose path is often erratic. The chaser follows singular fluid dynamic developments in supercell storms, often by sight or sound, only and using an innate sense of timing to intercept tornado paths.

Much of my interaction with the storm chasing community occurred through the now defunct Tornado Videos Network of storm chasers. TVN was an online platform which provided live streams of chasers in the field along with chat interaction features. These networks of chasers, of course, have access to mobile Doppler radars and the latest mobile technologies, but their immediate senses are what allow them to follow the singular flows of storm morphology. Chasers are often forced into situations that require sophisticated navigation. Their choices for movement are constrained typically to north-south or east-west movements on the gridded road networks of the Midwest. The timing has to be perfect to intercept a tornado's path, which pays no heed to the grid, but cuts diagonally across this striated space. For the chaser, the experience of the tornado chase is an aesthetic one, a dance of contradictory timing between the wind and the built environment. The chaser operates between two atmospheres – "one of meteorology and one of aesthetics – straddling the uneasy division between nature and humanity, materiality and the sensory, the cosmic and the affective" (Ingold 2015, 76). The split between the meteorological materiality of the atmosphere and its cultural production runs through much of the burgeoning field of air studies. I follow Tim Ingold who argues in the *Life of Lines* (2015) that these two bodies of knowledge are intimately intertwined. It is the concatenation between the built and the atmospheric, the following of singular atmospheric flows, and not overdetermining the tornado, which offers the chaser insight.

The epistemic form of the chaser is akin to what Deleuze and Guattari call "nomad science." The nomad scientist is defined through specific attention to materiality, not by representation, but by working with and making connections between material singularities and irregularities (Deleuze and Guattari 1987, 360–362). They offer the example of a woodworker using the singular flaws and knots in the material they manipulate. Instead of merely cutting a pre-designed pattern onto the wood, the woodworker works with the wood to find singular intensities. Nomad science refuses top-down representations of matter that smooth difference into easily standardized coordinates. The key

---

7   For the tension between the instrumental knowledge of meteorology i.e. – "meteorologists are at the mercy of their machines" – and the need for trained and embodied verification of severe weather, see Fine 2006.

aspect of nomad science is its mode of assessment, not of quantification, but an interpretation and practice of affective intensity, aesthetics, and singularities. The chaser, working as a nomad scientist, begins their work where quantification and information leave off. The chaser's work also begins where the collective imagination and institutions end. Radar and computational models generalize an area of tornadic development, yet an attunement of the senses to rapidly changing conditions allow the chasers to enact a much finer-grained environmental awareness.

The successful storm chaser requires an organization of affect, labor, and social space. The process of following intensities and affects requires a particular form of embodiment in the storm chaser apart from the flattened view of computer screens and televisual machinery. The chaser, as opposed to the television weather forecaster, is out in the open, exposed to the elements. They join with the populace in a live, shared risk. In many instances, the storm chaser is also the first responder on the scene once a tornado has done damage, making their primary role one of care, protection, and repair. In the context of environmental media, borrowing from Michel De Certeau's distinction between strategy and tactics, perhaps the state issuance of meteorological warnings is the overall strategy of infrastructural adjustment to environmental threat, while the chaser provides the short-term tactics of everyday analysis (De Certeau 1984).

Chasers engage what Elizabeth Grosz calls *geopower*, where the non-human forces of the earth make their mark on human expression (Grosz 2008). This non-subjective form of power, through its temporality and destructive force, script the chaser's movements. Aesthetics here is not merely a 'distribution of the sensible' (cf. Rancière 2003), but a process of experimenting with the material forces of the earth. Art, then, may be construed not merely as a cultural achievement, nor a solely human endeavor per se, but as a repurposing of the forces of geography and time for elaboration and experimentation. The chaser's act of citizen science, then, is not far off from that of Francis Alÿs, in directly engaging the material forces of the earth to experiment with indeterminacy. In moments of environmental disaster, both Alÿs and the storm chaser harness the vast forces of the earth as processes that radically re-orient the personal. It is only that the storm chaser ventures further, using a larger toolset in hopes of a shared survival and a future otherwise.

Both Alÿs and the storm chaser remind us that a monolithic object of nature does not exist. The environment resists prediction. It is erratic, chaotic, and without a subjective will. Environmental change always shirks an external ordering by idealizing forces. Thus, it will not suffice to overcode a closed human interiority onto every nook and cranny of nature. Instead, storm chasers risk themselves for the survival of communities unknown to them. Yet they are not of those collectives, they stand outside of the collective, the collective itself has disintegrated when the theory of protection has become libertarian in and of itself. However, rather than turning within in response to the threat of outside force, the chaser joins with the forces of the earth. As such, the non-human substrate is not merely a passive background for the projection of human knowledge; it is fundamentally constitutive of the pre-personal and the postcollective. Thus, the chaser performs the meteorology of media as an ongoing attunement to hybrid ways of knowing personal timescales within climate systems.

The tornadic vortex is a strange bending of time and space which does not easily fit into periods, monoliths, archives or maps. The vortex disrupts and breaks normative modes of epistemology; perhaps this is why, in its metaphoric usage across diverse theoretical fields, it is implied as an outside, an excess, something chaotic or unthinkable. The tornado forces an immediate response from the scientific mediation apparatus that requires a complex interaction between computation, communication, postcollectivity, and individual citizen scientists. A close reading of the tornadic suggests an approach to environmental media that follows the short-term breaks and disruptions in the changing weather in search of new relational trajectories between the individual and the environment.[8]

References

Agee, Ernest et al. (2016) Spatial Redistribution of USA Tornado Activity Between 1954 and 2013. *Journal of Applied Meteorology and Climatology*, 55(8): 8–22. https://doi.org/10.1175/JAMC-D-15-0342.1

Ahmed, Sara (2013) *The Cultural Politics of Emotion*. London, New York: Routledge.

Alÿs, Francis (2010) A Story of Deception, Tate Modern, room guide online. Available (consulted January 3 2023) at: http://www.tate.org.uk/whats-on/tate-modern/exhibition/francis-alys/francis-alys-story-deception-room-guide/francis-alys-6

De Certeau, Michel (1984) *The Practice of Everyday Life*. Berkeley: University of California Press.

Deleuze, Gilles and Guattari, Felix (1987) *A Thousand Plateaus: Capitalism and Schizophrenia*. Minneapolis: University of Minnesota Press.

---

8 A version of this chapter has been published in the *Routledge Handbook on Art, Science, and Technology* (2021). Copyright for *A Meteorology of Media* held by the author.

Edwards, Paul N. (2010) *A Vast Machine: Computer Models, Climate Data, and the Politics of Global Warming*. Cambridge: MIT Press.

Fine, Gary Alan (2006) Ground Truth: Verification games in operational meteorology. *Journal of Contemporary Ethnography*, 35(1): 3–23. https://doi.org/10.1177/0891241605282241

Gabrys, Jennifer (2016) *Program Earth. Environmental Sensing Technology and the Making of a Computational Planet*, Minneapolis: University of Minnesota Press.

Grosz, Elizabeth (2008) *Chaos, Territory, Art: Deleuze and the Framing of the Earth*. New York: Columbia University Press.

Ingold, Tim (2015) *The Life of Lines*. London, New York: Routledge.

Irwin, Alan (1995) *Citizen Science. A Study of People, Expertise and Sustainable Development*, London, New York: Routledge.

Lazzarato, Maurizio (2014) *Signs and Machines: Capitalism and the Production of Subjectivity*. Los Angeles: Semiotext(e).

Lefebvre, Henri (2004) *Rhythmanalysis: Space, Time and Everyday Life*. Paris: A&C Black.

Le Sueur, Meridel (1940) *Salute to Spring*. New York: International Publishers.

Parikka, Jussi (2015) *A Geology of Media*. Minneapolis: University of Minnesota Press.

Rancière, Jacques (2003) *The Politics of Aesthetics*. New York: Bloomsbury Press.

Smithson, Robert (1996) *Robert Smithson, the Collected Writings*. Berkeley: University of California Press.

Sturken, Marita (2006) Weather Media and Homeland Security: Selling Preparedness in a Volatile World. *Understanding Katrina*. Social Science Research Council, October 5, 2006. Available (consulted Jaanuary 3 2023) at: https://items.ssrc.org/understanding-katrina/weather-media-and-homeland-security-selling-preparedness-in-a-volatile-world/

Terranova, Tiziana (2004) *Network Culture: Cultural Politics for the Information Age*. London: Pluto Press.

CHAPTER 9

Not-Only-Human-Habitat, or Pedagogies of Vulnerable Collectives in the Age of Extractivist Fantasies

Anna Nacher

A great necessity to constantly move between two kinds of drone became a good reminder of the precariousness, vulnerability and fragility of life throughout all 2021. One type of drone was a hum emitted by the flickering screen of a machine that became the only connection with the outside world many time zones apart. Another was a whir buzzing in entirely different tonalities and frequencies all over a sizeable bush of hyssop sitting on the edge of a flowerbed in my garden. Two years into the pandemic of COVID-19, my everyday world more than ever seemed to be filled with many agencies beyond my control. Not only the virus itself, but a multitude of agents spanning the whole spectrum of lifeforms: both organic and inorganic as well as carbon-and silicon-based. An academic life run by the usual mix of administrative regulations and a newly acquired corporate identity in a business-as-usual manner amidst all of the chaos of the first year of the pandemic was a frightening experience. Nothing demonstrated a general sense of self-congratulatory pride of belonging to the world of corporations better than the increasingly toxic dependence of the university on software systems, conceived, designed, and developed primarily to meet the needs of corporate clients. Repurposed for higher education and for the university setting, software platforms immediately revealed their flaws: a top-down rigid structure based on the idea of a corporate project falsely touted as "flexible", and difficulties with inviting participants from outside of the organization. The very language that positioned guest speakers as participants "from outside of the organization" suddenly became an exercise in self-reflexive irony of a university-turned-corporation.

I would like to use my specific vantage point of a subject crystallizing at the crossroads of two types of drone, university pedagogy carried out with a computer humming with its internal communicating processes and a hyssop humming with insects, to explore uncertainty, vulnerability, and precariousness as necessary effects of sympoietic arrangements of digital pedagogy in the pandemics, based on assemblages seen as "polytemporal, polyspatial knottings", capable of engaging other lifeforms in "complex patternings" (Haraway

2016, 60). The spatial-aural effect of this movement made me think about confluences and parallelisms inscribed into the fact of transitioning between the plot of land undergoing a messy process of turning a once long-neglected family farm, typical for this part of the Carpathians, into a resilient and self-organizing permaculture on the one hand, and a highly platformized digital pedagogy in the time of the pandemics, on the other. A place that – after it had been acquired by me and my husband in 2014 – was to evolve into a Not-Only-Human-Habitat and a community space to run permaculture workshops, and it quickly became a laboratory in bridging two seemingly disparate worlds. To some extent, my chapter is a field report from the messy process of cross-pollination and the confluence of permacultural design and academic digital pedagogy grounded in efforts to make a creative and somewhat anarchic use of platforms.

Building on Rebecca Solnit's apt observation that "hope locates itself in the premises that we don't know what will happen and that in the spaciousness of uncertainty is room to act" (Solnit 2016), mirrored by Anna Tsing's observation that "only appreciation of current precarity as an earthwide condition allows us to notice this – the situation of our world" (2015, 5), I propose that the appreciation of such precarity – exemplified by the COVID-19 pandemics – will help us make better use of the transitional cultural moment, where the necessity to protect life is necessarily foregrounded in countering the paradigms of neoliberal extractivism. I am primarily interested in tracing how the possibility of counter-extractivist practices located at the very core of permacultural design can be transplanted into digital pedagogy. In my chapter, I would like to bridge them with a gesture to ground my digital pedagogy in the ideas of epistemic cooperation and participatory sense-making (Candiotto 2019) rather than efforts at neoliberal efficiency in acquiring digital literacy skills in response to capricious job markets. This endeavor – modest in scope and range – is grounded in an attempt described best by another researcher. Hence, I am borrowing from Macarena Gómez-Barris, who based her insightful book on an art-inspired idea to "see differently and to question what lies beneath the visible world of the extractive zone and to seek out less perceivable worlds, life forms, and the organization of relations within them, while creating new methods that allow for this tracking" (Gómez-Barris 2017, XIV). This quote signals at the same time that I subscribe to a theoretical attempt at broadening the category of extractivism into the realm of representation and ideology, in order to be able to better trace its impact and to more poignantly address the worldviews that resulted in ecological disaster. At the same time, I aim at contributing to instigating necessary shifts both in imaginations and academic practice.

1   Pedagogies of Extractivism?

Contemporary digital pedagogy, due to its heavy reliance on internet platforms and cloud computing, inevitably subscribes to the logics of extractivism. The notion of extractivism has evolved within the orbit of Latin American development studies and was meant as a counterpart to the other already circulating environmental humanities concepts such as Anthropocene (and the whole range of other –cenes) (Svampa 2019; Arboleda 2020; Riofrancos 2020; Parks 2021). Extractivism, however, in contrast to its better-known counterparts, from the very beginning emphasized the colonialist character of Western modernity. Inevitably capitalist policy was based on the fact that "some regions specialised in the extraction and production of raw materials – primary commodities – while others took on the role of producing manufactured goods" (Acosta 2013, 62). The processes are, however, more complex, as demonstrated by the term "extractive zone" proposed by Macarena Gómez-Barris, who refers in this way to "the colonial paradigm, worldview, and technologies that mark out regions of "high biodiversity" in order to reduce life to capitalist resource conversion" (2017, XVI). Being able to trace the whole continuum is then of key importance: from the actual material practices and policies of removal "of large quantities of natural resources that are not processed (or processed only to a limited degree), especially for export" (Acosta 2013, 62) to more subtle and sophisticated discursive technologies of meaning-making. Although extractivism most often came to refer to "large-scale, profit-driven operations for the removal and processing of natural resources such as hydrocarbons, minerals, lumber, and other materials" (Parks 2021), it also signifies much broader processes where "resources serve a means-ends function, becoming commodities to be extrapolated and turned to profit" (Parks 2021). The term may also be described as "the history of the human concentration of wealth through making both humans and nonhumans into resources for investments" (Tsing 2015, 5).

A good point to start an analysis of the extractivist aspects of digital pedagogy is an obvious bigger (and still insufficiently acknowledged) picture of the raw material-dependent consumer IT market, driven by electric power and water-hungry data centers and server farms, constituting the very backbone of our everyday digital reality, misleadingly dubbed cloud computing. The term is indeed ironic, considering how its association with lightness and immateriality obfuscates a heavy dependence on very tangible energetic resources – from high electric power to huge amounts of water needed for cooling. We encounter consumer goods that seemingly "have no history: no mines, no manufacture, no freighting, and no waste" (Cubitt 2017, 13), which has recently been painfully (nomen omen) undermined by the pandemic-related global shortages in supply chains, as demonstrated by the semiconductor global shortage which has affected a number of industries, including automakers (Campbell 2022). As Pold and Andersen remind us, the notion of "cloud computing" was popularized by Eric Schmidt, Google CEO, in 2006, hence it can function "both as a canny metaphor, business plan, and somewhat loosely confined technological paradigm." (Andersen and Pold 2018, loc.3516). Already back in 2008 the production and use of information technologies constituted 2% of global carbon emissions, outstripping the airline industry in this regard while growing by 15% per year (Cubitt, 2017). Fast forward to a decade later, and in a report "Lean ICT. Towards Digital Sobriety" issued by the Shift Project, a think-tank on energy transition based in Paris, we read that between 2013 and 2019 the share of digital technologies in global CO_2 emission increased from 2.5% in 2013 to 3.7% (Ferreboeuf et al. 2019). Notice that all these estimates come from before COVID-19 hit in 2020. During the pandemic, the scale of operation increased exponentially, with such a massive online shift – even though in the meantime the notion of Green IT has been implemented and is quickly gaining traction (although its real impact has yet to be assessed). Such prominent growth has kickstarted a tremendous boom in specific sectors of real estate in some parts of the world, like Northern Virginia in the U.S. More often than not, these are previously underdeveloped regions suffering from limited employment options yet having access to sufficient energy infrastructure. What also is a factor in the case of Loudoun County – where numerous data centers are located in one county, that has already gained its nickname of Data Center Alley – is its relative proximity to Washington DC (White 2020; Schweitzer 2021).

Yet, academic pedagogy's reliance on cloud computing and internet platforms is far from being one-dimensional. In many cases, we need to account for the complex socioeconomic circumstances of our students' families. The possibility to acquire expensive equipment for each member of a family individually is often outweighed by the need to invest in a broadband internet, which has become such a crucial resource. Hence, cloud computing with its architecture based on free or inexpensive cloud software, available for relatively simple mobile devices, such as cheaper tablets and smartphones, quickly became the basic educational equipment in online education. Universities in my country do not provide students with computers, as often is the case at American universities, even in public education. Neither were we able to teach at our computer lab, where the machines are available. Considering, however, the exponential increase in electric power consumption, cloud computing seems to be a Faustian contract, where less digital waste produced by the end users (less hard drives, CDs or even USB drives) is replaced with higher levels of consumption of electric power that is necessary for the functioning and maintenance of the complex infrastructure of cloud computing, especially in the light of the exponential increase in the carbon footprint of live video streaming – as illustrated by the insightful quip that "there is no cloud computing, there is only someone else's computer". According to Greenspector, in October 2021, 1 min of scrolling TikTok newsfeed had the exponentially biggest carbon impact out of all social media platforms and equalled 2.63 gEqCO2, with the same value for Facebook estimated at 0.79 gEqCO2, for Twitter – 0.60 gEqCO2. Surprisingly, YouTube seems to contribute to a much lesser extent with 0.46 gEqCO2 per 1 minute of scrolling (Derudder 2021). It has also driven an increase in IT consumption: according to industry's own estimates, the number of devices connected to the internet has grown from 2.1 in 2013 to 3.3 in 2020 per person, and video streaming has risen at the rate of 25% per year (Networking 2021). Therefore, requiring your students to have their cameras on – although understandable regarding the quality of pandemic social relations – comes with a hefty price tag for the environment. As estimated by researchers at Utility Bidder, a weekly one-hour video meeting with 6 participants is equivalent to driving almost 10 miles in a petrol car, and simply turning off your camera while in the meeting could reduce the footprint by 96% (Suciu 2021; Obringer et al. 2021).

Energy consumption is just one of the (environmentally costly) dimensions of the extractivist logics that inevitably pull digital pedagogy into its orbit. The availability of rare minerals used for the production of smartphones and tablets is also a significant factor, directly related to the most obvious definitions of extractivism and relatively often brought to our attention, both in scholarship and socially engaged digital art. The latter is demonstrated by a number of art projects. *Rare Earthenware* from 2018 by Liam Young of Unknown Fields Division (in collaboration with a ceramics artist, Kevin Callaghan) is symptomatic of the whole range of endeavors. The artists traced the global supply chain of rare minerals used in electronics, starting with the mining sites in Chinese Inner Mongolia (also known for persistent persecution of Uighur minority by the Chinese authorities). The toxic mud taken from the radioactive lake, where refining of the materials takes place, was used by Callaghan to produce three vases, modelled after Ming dynasty porcelain, with the size of each of them representing the amount of waste resulting from the production of a smartphone, a lightweight laptop, and the cell of a smart car battery (Unknown Fields 2018). A digitally enhanced video, developed with a photographer Toby Smith, documents the research on which this project was based and is an integral part of the presentation.

Pondering the relationships linking digital pedagogy with the logics of extractivism, one cannot also escape uncomfortable transformations instigated by digital capitalism and succinctly demonstrated by all the complexity accompanying parallelisms between data mining and earth minerals mining. In other words, I am interested in tracing colonial extractivist capitalism and its neoliberal afterlives within a digital domain. As Nick Srnicek aptly points out, "in the twenty-first century, the advanced capitalism came to be centered upon extracting and using a particular kind of raw material: data" (2017, 21), the process which on a very basic level is both enabled by all the policies and environmental abuses of extractivism, and at the same time symptomatic of its tendency to transform all phenomena into resources. What on some level can be seen as social interactions, in the extractivist terms of platform capitalism acquires a hefty market value as a treasure trove of massive data sets describing human behavior – to be mined and capitalized on. In this light, we can see social media platforms as mediators or switches between two different modes of extractivism: one that is possible thanks to its traditional forms based on harvesting natural resources such as timber or fossil fuels, and the other that transforms social relations into a minable (in terms of data processing) resource. For the itinerary I propose in my analysis, it is important to keep in mind that extractivism also functions as a potent discursive apparatus shaping imageries, language and ways of thinking, where the extraction of natural resources is "transformed into a system or ideology, a representational and symbolic space linked to the use (and abuse) of nature-as-resource" (Szeman and Wenzel 2021, 516).

2 Permacultural Design: Forging Vulnerable Interspecies Communities as a Counter-Extractivist Practice (and Staying with Troubles)

As I have already revealed, my pandemic digital pedagogies were evolving in a constant movement between the screen and the garden. The garden, however, is far from a highly monitored plot of land, heavily cultivated and confined to the set of rules established by landscape architecture and usually submitted to a heavily chemical pest control. Ours is a garden of transformation, regeneration, and a community place of collaborative educational efforts of different scopes and methods; anarchic, unruly and abundant – following the guidelines of permacultural design, based on the observation of natural patterns in different scales (short-, middle-, and long-term). In a nutshell, not only is permaculture a kind of practice aimed simultaneously at cultivating land in a sustainable way and giving priority to creating an abundance of crops, but it also accounts for regenerative forestry, soil-making and agricultural practices based on the forms of inquiry often inspired by Indigenous knowledge. In some regards, permaculture can be seen as a transdisciplinary practice, understood as "research that is driven by solving the real world problems" (Haddorn et al. 2010, 433). However, it seems that it has not yet become a proper object of study for environmentally oriented humanities, including social anthropology – as noticed by the authors of a few publications in the field of anthropology (Lockyer and Veteto 2013). This may come as a surprise, especially considering the global scale and the persistence of the permacultural movement, which was kickstarted at the end of the 1970s with the pioneering guidebooks of Bill Mollison and David Holmgren and later refined by each of them in further publications, often self-published (Mollison and Holmgren 1978; Mollison 1988; Holmgren 1996; Holmgren 2002). Mollison and Holmgren started experimenting with the principles of the practice that at the time they had called "permanent agriculture", and which eventually came to get abbreviated and entered the mainstream environmentalism as "permaculture". Hence, the fact that it was not even mentioned by Timothy Morton in his otherwise brilliant (and highly influential) book on dark ecology may also be surprising. For permaculture can be seen as a practice efficiently and successfully countering, as Morton puts it, the "agrilogistics" of industrial farming and agriculture, which he understands as a generative hyperobject of modern, industrial agriculture, "the granddaddy hyperobject" and "a machine that predates Industrial Age machinery" (Morton 2016, 43).

Since its very beginning, permacultural design was based on system ecology, landscape geography and ethnobiology, and was performed as an endeavor that often blurred the boundaries separating theory from practice. Even though it started as a practice aimed at designing resilient and sustainable agroecosystems, where human activity was grounded in the deep knowledge of natural processes based on close observation and in collaboration with those processes, permacultural practice today exceeds the domain of gardening or agriculture. It often ventures into social activism, urban regeneration, migration crises, education, and socially engaged art. It seems that what enables such a versatility is its ethical program foregrounding the whole set of practices aimed at creating efficient and pragmatic scenarios for sustainable living; the one that can also be easily transplanted into other areas of life. Three main ethical principles constitute its core: earthcare, peoplecare and fair share. The second principle signals an emphasis on meeting human needs in a sustainable way, which always is based on self-limitation, simplifying and favoring community and collaborative systems, at the expense of consumerism and individual needs. The idea of fair share had initially been articulated as "limiting consumption and population growth" but later, following the critique pointing out the dangers of Eurocentric interpretations, was transformed into the set of principles advocating "redistribution" and "living within limits" (Long 2017). According to another popular guidebook, permacultural ethical principles are based on creating the conditions favoring abundance, which is defined in ecological terms as the sign of healthy ecosystems – hence the key emphasis is on developing communities incorporating non-human actors and on limiting the consumption of mass-produced goods (Macnamara 2012).

In practical terms, the transformation of our plot of land started with careful and diligent observation which was aimed at learning the natural patterns and cycles from the land itself. The key questions concerned the water circulation and distribution, the patterns of sun activity throughout the year, and the quality of soil available for gardening. Learning from the land, we quickly discovered that we are far from being alone on the patch of land located in the village of Lechnica, inhabiting a Havka brook valley tucked between the hills in a scenic area of rocky limestone mountains called the Pieniny. It stretches along the Polish-Slovak borderland that for centuries had been one region, eventually separated by the borders of the modern national states (not unlike other transnational regions in the European mountains, for example Tirol). This is how the idea of Biotope Lechnica as Not-Only-Human-Habitat was born. At its very core lies the principle of accommodating all non-human inhabitants of our plot of land and transforming it into a thriving multispecies community, open to all human beings who want to learn along the same lines. Soon it turned out that this community is quite numerous, including rare and protected species, like *Coronella austriaca* (a snake that has been living with us ever since we acquired the land, in a pile of stones just a few meters from the main house, and extremely rarely making itself visible to anyone) or *Salamandra salamandra* (that apparently breeds here). The beginnings were not easy, as the place had its own history that could also be read directly from the land – the soil proved to be of poor quality, with high concentration of nitrogen as a consequence of big quantities of hog manure released directly into the ground. The previous owners – a big, multigenerational family – for decades were living off a small-scale pig farm and the meat they were able to transform into a produce attractive to their neighbours (an assumption we made based on tools and devices found at the spot upon moving in). The activity probably was not entirely legal, considering the political situation in former Czechoslovakia in the 70s and some of the arrangements that could be found in the buildings (like storage spaces placed in a secluded areas and constituted by a double floor).

Soon it also turned out that creating circumstances allowing for a multispecies community and a true Not-Only-Human-Habitat requires a good deal of patience and perseverance, especially with large mammals, like the deers that quickly became fond of fresh produce from our garden. It became a real problem in a situation, where due to the fact that our occupations still kept us city-bound for most of the week, we were only able to spend weekends at our farm. We had also come to terms with the necessity to be open to all kinds of non-human agencies, from adverse weather patterns (the climate crisis in our region has been manifesting mostly as severe imbalance in water supply, with structural drought and lack of snow in wintertime, becoming increasingly a problem during heavy thunderstorms and torrential rains in summer, with the soil unable to absorb large quantities of precipitation happening in a very short time) to pests activity (with the most acute destruction being instigated by a plague of snails and rodents). We have never, however, resorted to any means of chemical intervention, "staying with the trouble" in a proactive way, constantly seeking to collaborate with the multispecies multitude rather than eliminate the factors that we saw as destructive. Eight years into our Not-Only-Human-Habitat, we see a gradual but clearly perceptible change. The plot of land is thriving, with ever increasing biodiversity comes less and less snail-induced damage (and a much bigger birdfeeder – of the size we had ever expected). Some natural ways of water management were restored, thanks to which the 1-acre plot proved resilient to torrential rains and other water extremities. Permacultural design teaches us to indeed look for the solution precisely where the crisis is and see every crisis as an opportunity. The phrase proved to be confirmed by our practice – regardless of its banality and neoliberal deployment in entirely different contexts of disruptive business models. But it becomes true only when we are able to learn from the land and a particular situation, which also means opening up to agencies beyond our control and a willingness to make do with less than ideal solutions, unexpected outcomes, change of plans and initial ideas, a good deal of detachment from thinking in terms of one-solution-fits-all, and switching to being sensitive to the larger context (or multiple contexts) instead. Throughout the process, I learnt that it is all of the above which constitutes a real collaborative effort and sustainable change.

3 Counter-Extractivist Digital Pedagogies and Vulnerable Communities of Practice after the End of World

Just when the COVID-19 pandemic seemed to near its end, the news of the war in Ukraine broke, kickstarting months of fear, anxiety, and trauma across the whole Central Europe. We inhabit the region which for generations has been impacted by wars, pogroms, and social upheaval, so February 24th triggered many levels of trauma, including intergenerational trauma of war survivors. It also led to relativizing the recent (and still fresh) traumas of the pandemic, as reflected by a popular joke (a clear example of a dry humor) saying that we wish we could go back to the time when there was only COVID-19 to handle. And yet, the question of how to approach digital pedagogies was still firmly in place, as it still seems to continue to loom on the horizon in the light of equally persisting crises. The question proved to be inspiring to other as demonstrated by a nascent idea of the Post-Digital Perma-Library (Jones 2023) or the ideas of tactical publishing and distributed archiving (Ludovico 2024). The lessons learnt in my permacultural endeavor prompted an extensive pondering of what constitutes collaborative practice, how the digital pedagogies' communities of practice are enacted and performed. It is worth remembering that the notion of communities of practice was coined by anthropologists studying the processes of informal sharing of knowledge, techniques, and skills, including in Indigenous cultures (Lave and Wenger 1991; Wenger 1998). Practice in this case is described as a form of focusing the group's energy and activity around a common goal related to knowledge and skill sharing.

The humming of my permacultural community of Not-Only-Human-Habitat inspired another dimension to consider while deciding upon the form of my online digital pedagogy in the pandemics: the possibility of accounting for the contribution of digital culture to the paradigm of extractivism. Yet, the permacultural predilection for flexibility, pragmatism and non-dogmatic approaches prompted practical interrogation of internet platforms with a specific creative practice and checking the boundaries of collaborative efforts within their limits. Inspired by the bouts of creative energy proliferating on the platforms in the first round of the pandemic (a perfect example of which was establishing "A group where we all pretend to be ants in an ant colony" on Facebook), for the fall semester of 2020/21 I chose to get my students engaged in collaborative e-literary writing effort known as netprov. Invented by an e-literature practitioner and scholar, Rob Wittig, and a fluid team of collaborators, netprov is, according to its creator, "networked improv: networked, improvised literature. Netprov is collaborative fiction-making in available media. Netprov is role-playing in writing and images. Netprov is storytelling in real time. Netprov is a great game for students and friends. Netprov is an emerging art form for digital media." (Wittig 2022, 1). To Wittig, netprov is located between internet literature (any endeavor that introduces a bit of fiction into predefined communication infrastructure, like for example, "silly reviews of products and services, using exaggerated voices"), games, and improv theatre. Netprov may sometimes spill out to real life, blurring the distinction between fiction and everyday life like Alternate Reality Games. One of the unexpected examples of spontaneous netprov happened in September of 2022, as a part of the Polish-Czech meme campaign known as #Kralovec, in a kind of chain-reaction, networked and distributed response to illegitimate referendums held by Russian on the occupied Ukrainian territory, and I reported on it elsewhere (Nacher 2022). Some netprovs use multiple media platforms simultaneously – they are experienced both as performances (when they are happening) and as literature (when they get published as an archive of actual enactment). Like any role-playing endeavor, netprov is "a safe, cultural space to play out aspects of our personalities" (Wittig 2022, 3).

In the fall of 2020, Rob Wittig and the team offered a netprov experience under the banner of Moody Locales. It was designed for Reddit, hence the subReddit r/MoodyLocales was created as a hub of the activity meant as "an emotional atlas of the globe". Started on October 16th, it seemed a perfect opportunity to test a new pedagogic approach with the group of students in the class on digital literature in the Literary Criticism master's program. It would allow for developing the distributed, online, off-camera pedagogical experience, where my students could meet their colleagues from American universities online (the groups taught by Rob Wittig at the University of Minnesota Duluth and by Mark Marino at the University of Southern California among others), while working together as a group, but at the same time developing micro-narratives in their respective teams (or individually). Since the very beginning I experienced a mixture of lukewarm indifference at best and outright refusal and hostility at worst. Inviting both of the creators of the netprov for a guest talk followed by a discussion did not help much, neither did any attempts at broadening the range of examples of electronic literature. The main line of critique was surprising: a significant number of students in the group represented the overwhelmingly consistent opinion that what they are encountering does not count as 'real' literature, and that it caters to the lowest common denominator – therefore it does not deserve their attention as future literary critics. I was in a state of constant shock, listening every week to the whole range of very conservative interpretations of what counts as 'real literature', the 'worth' of which was extremely narrowly defined as praised by the experts in the field. We quarrelled a lot – directly and indirectly. Frictions multiplied. I forced my students to experience some of the newest works in the field, distributed reading assignments, required them to read the texts and was as frank with them as they were frank with me. I questioned their conservative convictions and worldviews; they questioned my optimism about vernacular digital forms and sincere fascination with avant-garde forms of digital art. We spent the whole semester fighting. Yet week after week they participated in Moody Locales as their critique of the whole experience was becoming more accurate (and sometimes succinct). I could not deny that some of it was really convincing. I made them learn Twine – a primary open source and free creative platform for anyone interested in text-based games, interactive novels or anything in the vicinity – and develop their first experiments in digital writing (they did not like it, seeing the platform as "primitive"). At the end of the semester, as their final projects, they could choose to either write an essay of literary criticism related to any piece of electronic literature or ... to create a piece of electronic literature on their own, using Twine. After the whole semester I was exhausted, disheartened, prone to questioning my own choices and on the brink of giving up. Just as when in our fourth year on the farm, deers devoured (again) most of the seedlings of the fruit trees that were meant to become our food forest.

In the process, I was observing how, inside of a shaky moment of a crisis, we developed a vulnerable community of practice. Talking to faceless squares on the screen was anything but faceless or meaningless. On the contrary, each time we connected, there was a range of emotions, expectations, and affects to account for. Every week my ability to "stay with the trouble" was deepened and my students' awareness of the logics of platforms was slightly refined. What had started as potentially creative and experimental project, at some point seemingly doomed to fail, gradually evolved into a multifaceted critique of platform capitalism via comparison of the still anarchic and ambiguous Reddit with the "primitive" Twine. The meanings were also evolving – what does a grassroots, self-organised, "primitive platform" mean in a world saturated with sophisticated and advanced corporate platforms that constitute the primary machines of the New Industrial Revolution based on data mining? Created in 2009 by Chris Klimas, an independent software developer, Twine is primarily a community effort, as exemplified by its own website (Twine 2022) and some accounts of its co-creators (Videlais 2021; Salter and Moulthrop 2021). Its counter-extractivist nature is also shared among practitioners and educators: "Using Twine and Bitsy for remote coursework allowed us not to worry about the power of any student's computer: even students with Chromebooks or long-outdated machines could still load a web browser on even a limited internet connection and easily make, and play, the works these tools create" (Salter and Moulthrop 2021:12).

4 Towards Digital Pedagogies as Counter-Extractivist Epistemic Cooperation

It is difficult to fully disengage from the framework of extractivism, which is inherent to the very core of IT technologies and the paradigm of cloud computing. Yet, addressing it as an ever looming on the horizon responsibility is fully within our reach. In fact, properly addressing extractivist histories and the situatedness of the digital exponentially broadens the perspective and may naturally result in increased responsibility when it comes to consumption of born-digital content or frantic purchases of digital devices. It also allows us to mobilize multiple contexts when replying to the challenges of online teaching: should I require students to have their cameras on? At what stake? What platform should I choose as a main tool for remote, distributed and networked learning? How about incorporating information on the carbon footprint of particular digital tools into the curricula? These are all questions exceeding traditional points of interest. They may deeply change the way we teach and the way we forge our communities of practice, previously known as teacher-student relationships. Vulnerability is an inherent affective dimension of this relationship that has not only been insufficiently addressed so far, but has actually been widely underappreciated, suppressed or relegated to the margins. The permacultural disposition to learn from the situation in crisis has prepared me to appreciate vulnerability and precarity, a "good enough" situation prone to change and in a constant flux. Like nothing else, it allows for participatory sense-making which may eventually lead both to a change of paradigm and to an increased sense of cooperation, invited by injecting more authenticity into the process – even if it is less comfortable. According to Laura Candiotto, who ascribes emotions a positive role in the social-cognitive processes, "epistemic cooperation is what brings about the generation of a shared meaning in a participatory sense-making and thus, being emotions socially extended motivations, they boost the relationships among the agents, colouring them with affective dimension" (Candiotto 2019, 237). Hence our vulnerable community of practice does not necessarily need to focus on achieving emotional harmony – as long as we agree to remain in the same epistemic space and agree on the continuity of exchange, not on its specific emotional tone or the outcome.

Then the end of the fall semester finally came. The only remaining part of my task was to fully delve into the catastrophe that the course on digital literature was in that semester. I was reluctant to even open the .html files exported by students from Twine so I could access their content, let alone to diligently trace the offered narratives and check to what extent they follow the guidelines and meet the criteria to get passed as final projects. Yet, I was so wrong. Having finally gathered all my courage, I opened one of the projects, then next, then yet another. I spent the whole evening barely understanding what has happened. Every project was a clear and convincing demonstration of significant effort to express a creative impulse. Most of them offered a captivating narrative or interesting concept, or an aesthetically pleasing story. The best of all, however, was a sophisticated, elaborate, and humorous story where a central plot evolved around a writer-turned-digital artist. I was stunned by the intelligent use of the tool at the students' disposal and their mature, conscious and critical use of multimodal, digital writing. I checked the names (it was a team effort) and found the group of my most fierce opponents, whom I remembered as seemingly detached voices often at the brink of cancelling me, electronic literature in its particular instances and in general, and digital culture as such. Well done, tricksters. You were my trouble. And "staying with the trouble requires learning to be truly present, not as a vanishing point between awful and Edenic pasts and apocalyptic or salvific futures, but as mortal critters entwined in myriad unfinished configurations of places, times, matters, meanings" (Haraway 2016, 2). This is how we traced those less visible forms of organizations that may open up a chance to transform extractive zones (including those of neoliberal academia).

References

Acosta, Alberto (2013) Extractivism and neoextractivism: two sides of the same curse. In: Lang, M. and Mokrani, D. (eds) *Beyond Development. Alternative visions from Latin America*. Quito – Amsterdam: Fundacion Rosa Luxembourg – Transnational Institute, 61–87.

Andersen, Christian U. and Pold, Søren B. (2018) *The Metainterface. The Art of Platforms, Cities, and Clouds*. Cambridge, MA: MIT Press.

Arboleda, Martín (2020) Planetary Mine: Territories of Extraction under Late Capitalism. New York: Verso.

Campbell, Peter (2022) UK car production driven down by global chip shortage. *Financial Times*, July 18. Available at: https://www.ft.com/content/a422455a-8f7b-417f-a540-5fdedee2a2ef

Candiotto, Laura (2019) Emotions In-Between: The Affective Dimension of Participatory Sense-Making. In: Candiotto, L. (ed.) *The Value of Emotions for Knowledge*. Cham: Palgrave Macmillan, 235–260.

Cubitt, Sean (2017) *Finite Media. Environmental Implications of Digital Technologies*. Durham: Duke University Press.

Derudder, Kimberly (2021) What is the environmental footprint for social media applications? 2021 Edition. Available (consulted August 30 2022) at: https://greenspector.com/en/social-media-2021/

Ferreboeuf, Hugues, Berthoud, Françoise, Bihouix, Philippe et al. (2019) *Lean ICT. Towards Digital Sobriety*. Available (consulted August 30 2022) at: https://theshiftproject.org/wp-content/uploads/2019/03/Lean-ICT-Report_The-Shift-Project_2019.pdf

Gómez-Barris, Macarena (2017) *The Extractive Zone. Social Ecologies and Decolonial Perspectives*. Durham and London: Duke University Press.

Hadorn, Hardon G., Pohl, Christian and Bammer, Gabriele (2010) Solving Problems Through Transdisciplinary Research. In: Frodeman, R., Thompson Klein, J., Mitcham, C. (eds) *The Oxford Handbook of Interdisciplinarity*. Oxford: Oxford University Press, 431–452.

Haraway, Donna (2016) *Staying with the Trouble. Making Kin in the Chthulucene*. Durham and London: Duke University Press.

Haraway, Donna (2017) Symbiogenesis, Sympoiesis, and Art Science Activisms for Staying with the Trouble. In: Tsing, A., Swanson, H., Gan, E. and Bubandt, N. (eds) *Arts of Living on a Damaged Planet*. Minneapolis and London: University of Minnesota Press, 25–50.

Holmgren, David (1996) *Meliodora (Hepburn Permaculture Gardens): Ten Years of Sustainable Living* Hepburn: Holmgren Design Services.

Holmgren, David (2002) *Permaculture: Principles & Pathways Beyond Sustainability* Hepburn: Holmgren Design Services.

Jones, Natalie (2023) The Post-Digital Perma-Library: Cultivating Ecosystems of Cosmogonic Knowledge, unpublished manuscript shared in private email exchange with me, following the discussion at the Electronic Literature Conference 2023: Overoming Divides: Electronic Literature and Social Change, Coimbra 2023.

Lave, Jean and Wenger, Etienne (1991) *Situated Learning. Legitimate Peripheral Participation* Cambridge: Cambridge University Press.

Lockyer, Joshua and Veteto, James R. (2013) Environmental Anthropology Engaging Permaculture. Moving Theory and Practice Towards Sustainability. In: Lockyer, J. and Veteto, J. R. (eds) *Environmental Anthropology Engaging Ecotopia. Bioregionalism, Permaculture, and Ecovillages*. New York – Oxford: Berghahn Books. PAGES.

Long, Tobias (2017) The Controversial Third Ethic of Permaculture. *Permaculture News* April 3, 2017.

Ludovico, Alessandro (2024) *Tactical Publishing. Using Senses, Software and Archives in Twenty-First Century*. Cambridge, MA: MIT Press.

Macnamara, Looby (2012) *People & Permaculture. Caring and designing for ourselves, each other and the planet*. Hampshire: Permanent Publications.

Mollison, Bill (1988) *Permaculture: A Designer's Manual*. Tagari Publications.

Mollison, Bill and Holmgren, David (1978) *Permaculture One*. Tagari Publications.

Morton, Timothy (2016) *Dark Ecology. For a Logic of Future Coexistence*. New York: Columbia University Press.

Nacher, Anna (2022) United Forces of Meme in Spontaneous Netprov (or how many tweets it takes to transform #Kaliningrad into #Kralovec). *Electronic Book Review*, November 6, 2022.

Networking, C.V. Cisco Global Cloud Index: White Paper. (2021) Available (consulted August 30 2022) at: http://www.cisco.com/en/US/solutions/collateral/ns341/ns525/ns537/ns705/ns1175/Cloud_Index_White_Paper.html.

Obringer, Renee, Rachunok, Benjamin, Maia-Silva, Debora et al. (2021) The overlooked environmental footprint of increasing Internet use. *Resources, Conservation and Recycling*, Volume 167. https://doi.org/10.1016/j.resconrec.2020.105389

Parks, Justin (2021) The poetics of extractivism and the politics of visibility. *Textual Practice* vol. 35 no. 3 353–362. https://doi.org/10.1080/0950236X.2021.1886708

Riofrancos, Thea (2020) *Resource Radicals: From Petro-Nationalism to Post-Extractivism in Ecuador*. Durham: Duke University Press.

Salter, Anastasia and Moulthorp, Stuart (2021) *Twining*. Amherst MA: Amherst College Press.

Schweitzer, A (2021) The Pandemic Is Driving a Data Center Boom in Northern Virginia, DCist. Available (consulted August 30 2022) at: https://dcist.com/story/21/03/25/the-pandemic-is-driving-a-data-center-boom-in-northern-virginia/

Solnit, Rebecca (2016) *Hope in the Dark. Untold Histories, Wild Possibilities*. Chicago: Haymarket Books.

Srnicek, Nick (2017) *Platform Capitalism*. Cambridge, UK: Polity Press.

Suciu, Peter (2021) Do We Need to Worry That Zoom Calls Use Too Much Energy? *Forbes*, April 16, 2021. Available at: https://www.forbes.com/sites/petersuciu/2021/04/16/do-we-need-to-worry-that-zoom-calls-use-too-much-energy/?sh=233d102e64c2

Svampa, Maristella (2019) *Neo-extractivism in Latin America: Socio-environmental Conflicts, the Territorial Turn, and New Political Narratives*. Cambridge: Cambridge University Press.

Szeman, Imre and Wenzel, Jennifer (2021) What do we talk about when we talk about extractivism? Textual Practice vol. 35 no. 3, 505–523, https://doi.org/10.1080/0950236X.2021.1889829

Tsing, Anna L. (2015) *The Mushroom at the End of the World. On the Possibility of Life in Capitalist Ruins*. Princeton and Oxford: Princeton University Press.

Twine's homepage (2022), Available at (consulted August 25 2022) https://twinery.org

Unknown Fields (2018) Rare Earthenware. Available (consulted August 30 2022) at: https://liamyoung.org/projects/rare-earthenware

Videlais, D. (2021) Notes on ELO 2021 Platform as a Service a Roundtable Discussion, Blog post, May 3. Available (consulted August 30 2022) at: https://videlais.com/2021/05/31/notes-on-elo-2021-platform-as-a-service-a-roundtable-discussion-of-community-labor-and-platformization-of-twine-and-ink/

Wenger, Etienne (1998) *Communities of Practice: Learning, Meaning, and Identity.* Cambridge: Cambridge University Press.

White, Martha C. (2020) Our Digital Lives Drive a Brick-and-Mortar Boom in Data Centers, *New York Times,* December 22. Available at: https://www.nytimes.com/2020/12/22/business/data-storage-centers-coronavirus.html

Wittig, Rob (2022) *Netprov. Networked Improvised Literature for the Classroom and Beyond.* Amherst, MA: Amherst College Press.

CHAPTER 10

Media Warfare
The Coercive Coexistence of Radiation and Memory

Agnieszka Jelewska

1   Cyberwar and the New Act of Nuclear Terrorism

On February 24 2022, on the very first day of the invasion of Ukraine, the army of the Russian Federation took over the nuclear power plant in Chernobyl, as well as the so-called *exclusion zone* around it, which had been designated as such in 1986 after the reactor accident which led to the largest radioactive contamination in history. Although this nuclear power plant is no longer active, the actions of the Russian army triggered global concern. It brought back memories of the disaster that resulted in the death of many beings (those directly and indirectly exposed to radiation), caused enormous contamination of the area around the power plant and in many places in Europe due to the movement of the radioactive cloud. Consequently, politicians, scientists and journalists began to wonder why Vladimir Putin had decided to make such a move. Adriana Petryna, an anthropologist and author of the book *Life Exposed: Biological Citizens after Chernobyl* (2013), wrote an essay for *The Atlantic* shortly after the event, entitled "What Russia is Stirring up at Chernobyl". In this essay, recalling memories of traumatic experiences from years ago, she presented the following speculations and conclusion:

> Maybe Russian forces overtook the facility for the sake of convenience – after all, it's along the route from Russian ally Belarus to Kyiv, the Ukrainian capital, which is now under assault. Or maybe, as Russia's Defense Ministry claimed, the military wanted to protect the plant's infrastructure, preventing any staging of a "nuclear provocation." Or maybe, as a Russian security source told Reuters, it was a warning to NATO. ... Whatever the Russian army's reasoning, the implication for Ukrainians is clear: the potential for a repeat of the disaster, which they have spent three decades and considerable resources trying to prevent.
>
> PETRYNA 2022

However, the term "nuclear provocation" was soon replaced by "nuclear terrorism" in the political discourse when, on March 3, a Russian missile hit the industrial zone of Enerhodar, a city located just five kilometers from the largest nuclear power plant in Europe. The Zaporizhzhia Nuclear Power Plant, operational since 1972, is located on the Dnieper River in southern Ukraine and has six nuclear reactors. After the strike on Enerhodar, Russian forces moved towards the nuclear power plant at night. Members of the Ukrainian Territorial Defense Units, caught off guard, tried to stop the attack. They threw Molotov cocktails at Russian tanks in response to the shelling of civilian infrastructure, including the destruction of a school and a residential building. After resisting the Russian attack for over two hours, the Ukrainian forces finally withdrew, refusing to fight on the grounds of the nuclear power plant (Tyschenko 2022). This moment was recalled by Petro Kotinz, the CEO of Ukrainian Energoatom, in a conversation with Yulia Latynina on her YouTube channel *LatyninaTV*, which was specifically set up to track and comment on what was happening in Ukraine:

> The Russian army broke through the station's gate. Station personnel continued, in vain, to try to stop the troops. They shouted warnings via megaphone: "This is nuclear industrial infrastructure! There is a danger of a nuclear accident! Stop shooting and leave the premises! This is an act of nuclear terrorism!".
>
> LatyninaTV 2022

These words spoken by people attempting to prevent access to the nuclear power plant were picked up by the international press. The significance of this act was analyzed in a stark manner in the text *Nuclear Cyberwar. From Energy to Colonialism*, published in April 2022 by Svitlana Matviyenko:

> The occupation of both Chernobyl and Zaporizhzhia NPPs created a sense of catastrophic proximity and, in some ways, echoed and reiterated the nuclear threat articulated by Vladimir Putin on March 27, when he ordered the Russian minister of defense and the chief of the general staff to transfer deterrent forces of the Russian army to a "special regime of combat duty." These instances of "nuclear terrorism" lie at the nexus of "cyber" and "nuclear" warfare, where the two major forces of cyberwar converge for a full realization of its grimmest scenario. We should hope that we can still evade its consequence.
>
> 2022

Matviyenko is also the co-author, along with Nick Dyer-Witheford, of the book *Cyberwar and Revolution. Digital Subterfuge in Global Capitalism*, published in 2019. Here the researchers describe in detail the levels of infrastructure (and their entanglement) on which cyberwar can occur and is simultaneously planned. In this book, they propose a broad political-economic definition of cyberwar, identify the precise historical roots of this way of thinking about war strategies, and analyze the role of specific technological solutions that support them. Among other things, they highlighted the significant role that the creation of the internet played in military communication in the event of a nuclear attack (2019, 37–38). The potential for nuclear war in the 1960s gave rise to the internet and, at the same time, changed the distribution of social communication forms in the late 20th and early 21st centuries. It is well known that Paul Baran came up with the idea of packet switching techniques while working at the RAND Corporation to solve the problem of ensuring military communication during a nuclear war (Metz 2012; Dyer-Witheford and Matviyenko 2019). The newly invented electronic communication network had to be robust, be able to continue operating even in the event of multiple-leveled damage, be able to use advanced forms of adaptation to fluctuating infrastructure conditions, and be able to self-reconstruct infrastructure through replication, switching, and playback. This required the creation of conceptual foundations not only for the physical communication infrastructure but also for how communication would be realized in the network, how it would be encoded and transmitted. Therefore, Baran's project was very broad and involved both coupling existing infrastructures with the network, supplementing them with new ones, and changing the format of electronic communication. Nuclear-proof networks intertwined physical infrastructures with nuclear resilience policy, a model of digital multidirectional data transmission with unlimited expansion and the capacity to connect additional nodes to the network. These principles were first updated in the digital network developed by the Pentagon's Advanced Research Projects Agency (ARPA) and were used to connect the computer devices of scientists working on military-funded research. As Janet Abbate notes, contrary to the perceptions of computer scientists and researchers, who were under the impression that ARPA was funding research without being too concerned about its application, military imperatives were actually driving the entire research program (Abbate 1999, 76; Matviyenko 2022).

2 Cyber Warfare as a Drive of Modern Societal Transformations

According to Dyer-Witheford and Matviyenko, cyber warfare is a manifestation of the ongoing technological revolutions (industrial, electronic, and cybernetic) that reinvigorate capital, the internet being a prime example. Cyber warfare thus requires new forms and tools of technological expansion, surveillance, and defense. As Peter Sloterdjik wrote, the state of war always signifies technological acceleration (2002), and in the case of modern cyber warfare, this largely involves digital technologies, the design of computerized "autonomous weapons", and the development of new forms of AI for managing the battlefield and strategies for using new types of weapons. Therefore, it is a crucial element driving the development of capital and the economy. Cyber warfare is always oriented towards the future, as it is centered around "digital technologies, thus pointing back historically to origins in Second World War and Cold War cybernetics and forward to the new levels of networking and automation likely to characterize all social relations, including war making, in the twenty-first century" (Dyer-Witheford and Matviyenko 2019, 28). Thus, by transforming technologies, cyber warfare also transforms social relations, intensifying the construction of techno-social formations (Terranova, 2021). This term was introduced by Tiziana Terranova to investigate the technological transformations of modern societies. She writes that in the last three decades, technology and society have become completely intertwined. This new inseparability should be understood as an onto-epistemic transformation. The intertwining of the military and social levels is crucial for understanding not only the act of war itself but the entire process of predicting, designing, and simulating it. Cyber operations involve revealing weak points in communication and management systems, developing social engineering and creative simulations to generate effects in information systems that coordinate military, economic, and social behaviors (Gartzke and Lindsay, 2015; Lindsay, 2015; Gartzke and Lindsay, 2017). Therefore, the cyber warfare being developed today is also being designed for the future, along with newer and more effective strategies and infrastructures for conducting it, thereby changing socio-technological forms of existence.

A particular case of cyber warfare, analyzed and treated as a possible scenario since the Cold War, is the combination of a cyber attack with a nuclear attack. Dyer-Witheford and Matviyenko assert unambiguously: "cyber" and "nuke" are not separate (2019, 154). They never have been, since they have coexisted with each other from "the moment of conception, with the development of each dependent on the other. And the conception is not just historical; it is current." (2019, 154). As Erik Gartzke and Jon R. Lindsay wrote in their article

Thermonuclear Cyberwar in 2017, as part of the analysis of the "total potential" of this type of event:

> Nuclear weapons and cyber operations are particularly complementary ... with respect to their strategic characteristics. Nuclear weapons have some salient political properties. They are singularly and obviously destructive. They kill in more, and more ghastly, ways than conventional munitions through electromagnetic radiation, blast, firestorms, radioactive fallout, and health effects that linger for years. ... Defense against nuclear attack is very difficult, even with modern ballistic missile defenses, given the speed of incoming warheads and use of decoys; multiple warheads and missile volleys further reduce the probability of perfect interception. If one cannot preemptively destroy all of an enemy's missiles, then there is a nontrivial chance of getting hit by some of them. When one missed missile can incinerate millions of people, the notion of winning a nuclear war starts to seem meaningless for many politicians.
> GARTZKE and LINDSAY 2017, 2

However, despite the awareness – commonplace since the beginning of the Cold War – that the use of nuclear weapons will probably result in the destruction of the one who uses them, something unprecedented happened at Chernobyl and Zaporizhzhia, something that had not been anticipated or thoroughly analyzed before. The civilian infrastructure of a nuclear power plant was taken over and turned into a potential nuclear weapon.

3   The Occupation of the Zaporizhzhia NPP

The broadly spectral definition of cyberwar proposed by Matviyenko and Witheford also sheds light on what is currently happening with Russia's attack on Ukraine: cyber and nuclear war are always conducted simultaneously, as maneuvers that enable the use of an attack from outside the battlefield, while at the same time using troops on the ground. However, as Matviyenko writes, for the first time in history a nuclear plant became a weapon and was used as a potential for launching a nuclear war (2022). Information about this act of nuclear terrorism was conveyed in hundreds of images and texts, was commented on around the world, and triggered social anxiety. But it also revealed once again – and this bears emphasizing – the militarized and violent genesis of nuclear energy. Therefore, after this act of terrorism it will be extremely difficult to treat nuclear power plants as purely civilian infrastructure. The potential use of a nuclear power plant as a weapon has now been activated. "The occupation of the Zaporizhzhia NPP is not accidental. It is an imperialist zero-day exploit of cyberwar with a nuclear twist" (Matviyenko 2022).

Uncertainty and fear drove the various media narratives. Once again, media and nuclear issues were intertwined, not only as systems of informing, but even as designing, fueling, and recalling the nuclear traumas of the 20th and 21st centuries. The mediascapes (Appadurai 1990) created today by mainstream media, as well as social media, digital platforms, and other information transmission formats, have created almost immediate communication infrastructures in which the past, present, and future are visually and discursively linked. A media triggering of trauma took place, in which the past began to project the future.

This rhetorical mobilization of nuclear war was not limited to international news media. During the March attack on Zaporizhzhia, the Ukrainian President Volodymyr Zelensky delivered a message on Telegram and Instagram, calling on all Ukrainians and all Europeans, all people who know the word "Chernobyl" (Borger and Henley 2022) to raise the alarm about the occupation of the power plant by Russian forces. Later, in a message broadcast on April 26 2022, on the anniversary of the Chernobyl disaster, Zelensky suggested that the Russians do not understand what Chernobyl is, or that – unlike Ukrainians who remember – they have forgotten what Chernobyl is. Chernobyl, as a symbol of the 1980s disaster was an important starting point for addressing global public opinion, but of course, Zelensky was referring to those two places – Chernobyl as a symbol, and Zaporizhzhia as a real threat to critical infrastructure (Zelensky 2022).

In the constant hum of the mediascapes reporting on the critical infrastructure of nuclear violence, we could see the architectural plans of the Chernobyl and Zaporizhzhia power plant buildings, photos from the attacks of the Russian Federation, and CCTV recordings that showed the entry of Russian troops into the Chernobyl power plant site. Russian troops were captured by industrial cameras installed around the power plant by companies organizing tours and visits to the Chernobyl zone (Arhirova 2022; Berger 2022). Thanks to the owners of these companies, the information and images were shared online. They became a symbol not only of new postdigital communication, which allows for a direct insight into nuclear infrastructure, but also, due to the potential use of the power plant as a weapon, this type of media has been exploited to create mass fear. Industrial cameras have become yet another actor in the media infrastructure. In this broadly conceived spectral space, satellite information and images indicated that Russian soldiers had made trenches in the Red Forest, still today a radioactive area near the Chernobyl power plant, which consequently exposed them to health-threatening radiation (Ratushniak 2022; Chappell 2022). Equipment seized by the Russians from the power plants in Chernobyl and Zaporizhzhia also became elements of the infrastructure, as did the subsequent events: the imprisonment of employees of the Zaporizhzhia power plant, followed by a visit from Rosatom scientists (Russian Atomic Agency) to analyze the situation (Tirone 2022), and the simultaneous ban on access to this power plant for the International Atomic Energy Agency (IAEA). In the following months, Putin made renewed efforts to intimidate, with threats to use nuclear weapons, which was followed by the shutting down of reactors at the Zaporizhzhia power plant and the initiation of procedures to connect it to the energy network of the Russian Federation. All of these elements simultaneously contributed to the creation of the media and material critical infrastructure of nuclear terrorism. They were plugged into the transmission of media information, circulating online and connecting with images of the explosion of the Chernobyl power plant in 1986 and the atomic mushroom clouds resulting from nuclear tests conducted in the 20th century. Matviyenko describes this infrastructure, supplementing it with an account of the historically imperial and violent system of shaping relations between the "peaceful atom" and nuclear military power:

> In mid-March, the Ukrainian national nuclear company, Energoatom, reported the presence of eleven employees of the Russian state atomic energy corporation Rosatom on the premises of Zaporizhzhia NPP. Here, the Russian military and a high-level state corporation participate in a joint act of nuclear terrorism. The imperialist genealogy of this act is rooted in Soviet times, when the construction of all Ukrainian nuclear plants – the South Ukraine NPP, the Rivne NPP, the Khmelnitsky NPP, the Zaporizhzhia NPP, as well as the decommissioned Chernobyl NPP – began almost simultaneously in the XYZCs, when the USSR announced a move towards "a larger stake in the world market for nuclear energy" by "exporting enrichment services to Western European counties," envisioning "an expansion of their previously limited role" in international nuclear trade.
>
> 2022

As Paul Josephson states in his book *Red Atom. Russia's Nuclear Power Program from Stalin to Today*, the idea and concept of the "peaceful atom" was embraced by the atomic industry as a promise to develop a new economy based on "atomic-powered communism" (Josephson 2005, 5). Putin has attempted to continue this ideology in a new dimension, by using a cyber/nuclear war strategy.

Because this topic is extremely broad and can be analyzed from various perspectives, in this text I would like to focus on how the memory of nuclear regimes fades and returns, and how it is currently being fueled, rendered, and transmitted through the media, triggering fear and trauma. I am interested in the phenomenon of coerced coexistence with nuclear regimes, to which people and the environment have been subjected since 1945 in various ways and to differing intensities, both directly and through the media. Thus, a new material-media infrastructure of nuclear violence emerges as "a techno-social condition of proximity and distance, accident and security, communication and communication breakdown" (Sampson and Parikka 2020).

4   Postnuclear Media Studies Perspective

Media, as communication and data storage infrastructures, have a shared history with the development of nuclear violence. In the research conducted since 2014 with Michał Krawczak, we define the methodology for analyzing these connections as postnuclear media studies (Jelewska and Krawczak). From this perspective, it is important to analyze the provenance and genealogy of media practices that design specific types of visuality and the technologies that enable them, as well as the politics, economy, and regimes behind them. The goal of this perspective is not only to study the media and the strategies and forms of communication they generate, but also to critically redefine the nuclear ontology and infrastructure of the contemporary media sphere. The point here is not to conduct a one-dimensional analysis showing only the military and quantum-nuclear origins of contemporary and widely used media technologies – after all, this type of discourse already exists – but to reach a critical awareness of the ontogenesis and identification of the often implicit epistemic frameworks and cultural modes that have been implemented in our everyday life (Masco 2020).

Lisa Parks and Nicole Starosielski point out that it is difficult to talk straightforwardly about media nowadays, as they no longer exist in isolation but create complex communication systems and multiplying media infrastructures. As they note, "our current mediascapes would not exist without our current media infrastructures" (Parks and Starosielski 2015, 1). Parks and Starosielski describe the process of infrastructure hybridization, which is the result of intensive communication and energy development. Today, networks that were previously perceived as separate operate within a complex infrastructure.

The clearest example is the adaptation of old industrial infrastructures for the development of the media and telecommunications industry. Water, gas and transportation networks and industrial buildings are incorporated into telecommunication structures. GSM transmitters, air and water quality control stations, and transport monitoring, are now part of a single infrastructure. Importantly, these networks serve many functions – communication, control, transmission, and cultural – and contribute to shaping contemporary media culture. What is worth emphasizing is the radical change in the concept of "critical infrastructure" – if individual elements of integrated networks are subject to increasing integration, then thinking about the necessary minimum infrastructure for the functioning of society also changes. As a result of the development, entanglement and hybridization of media infrastructures, it is no longer possible to talk about separate systems – e.g. architectural, communication, energy, or cultural systems. With the entanglement of systems, their functions, policies, and social meanings have also become entangled. This is particularly evident in the case of the terrorist takeover of the Chernobyl and Zaporizhzhia nuclear power plants. Thus, there is a new need for transversal identification and disclosure of mutual co-determinants and their techno-cultural consequences. As Parks and Starosielski write:

> Critical studies of such sites draw attention to media infrastructures entanglements with environmental and geopolitical conditions, from the moment of installation through their residual uses.
> 2015, 4

5   Atomic Media Entanglements

The histories of the development of media and nuclear regimes are directly intertwined. Film cameras, still cameras and sound recorders were integral to the development of the military nuclear industry. Cameras were on board planes dropping atomic bombs and at nuclear training grounds. No other scientific project in human history has been so extensively documented by the media. Film cameras and still cameras, on the one hand, were intended to serve as scientific apparatuses, enabling people to see and record everything that humans could not experience or that would be deadly for them. The media apparatus was thus to be an inhuman witness and epistemic tool for human understanding and mastery of the nuclear phenomenon. On the other hand, constructors and politicians understood that nuclear power meant a cultural paradigm shift for humanity. For this reason, it was necessary to create propaganda content from the outset that would contribute to the realization of the idea of a new nuclear culture in various spheres of life. Both these functions (scientific-military and socio-cultural) required the preparation of appropriate tools and infrastructure.

Media devices thus became an integral part of the newly emerging nuclear laboratory infrastructure from the 1940s onwards. They became recording tools and measurement sensors for nuclear weapon tests, recording the most accurate and detailed data about the course of each atomic test that was imperceptible to imperfect human perception. In countries involved in the nuclear industry, entire laboratories and regular military-research units were established, specifically dedicated to the development of media recording technology for research purposes and the production of various media propaganda materials. The latter also provided new opportunities for shaping culture. As Jonathan Crary writes in his essay *Terminal Radiance* about the situation in the US:

> Beginning in the 1950s, film clips from U.S. nuclear tests were woven into the kitsch of Cold War consumer culture. Images of the South Pacific blasts were part of an iconography of scientific mastery that partly domesticated nuclear savagery and aligned it with fantasies of material progress and middle-class affluence.
> 2019, 59

However, in each case, these two areas – media-science and media-propaganda – intertwined with each other. Military laboratory media practices associated with conducting atomic weapons tests produced a certain type of aesthetics linked to fixed forms of propaganda narration. This type of storytelling – stretched between the tools of intimidating opponents and reasserting oneself in the momentousness of discoveries – produced narrative forms and subgenres that permeate culture and popular media aesthetics, and demand critical analysis today. The critical denuclearization of culture cannot be accomplished solely from the perspective of historical sciences but should also be pursued by various subdisciplines of media studies (including postnuclear media studies), which have the ability to critically examine the ontotechnological narrative and socio-cultural levels. As Crary points out, discussing the documentation of atomic weapons tests available on the internet today, "to watch this film and gape at the colossal radial symmetries of the detonation and its ghostly luminosities is to succumb to an aestheticization of this extreme limit of nuclear terror" (Crary 2019, 59). Thus, the persistence of various types of atomic documentation and imagery intertwined with each other in culture necessitates the adoption of a critical onto-epistemological approach. Especially today, when – thanks to the internet – the processes of hybridizing old images with new simulations have been let loose. They are blatantly subjected to the economy of repetition and the policy of ambiguous monetization, and are thus inseparable from capitalist strategies of domesticating nuclear violence.

> The video of an atomic bomb explosion replicates a pornographic image in its endlessly repeatable display of a convulsive discharge of energy on an unimaginable scale, and the Tsar Bomba film is the ultimate, unsurpassable "money shot" of a potency and expenditure beyond measure.
> CRARY 2019, 60

6 The Irreversible Coexistence of Potential Nuclear War and "Atom for Peace"

The film documenting the Tsar Bomba (AN602) explosion, mentioned by Jonathan Crary in the above quote, has become not only a sphere of monetization, but also one of the media signals announcing the launch of Vladimir Putin's nuclear regime. It was publicly released in its entirety for the first time in history on August 20 2020 by Rosatom, as part of the 75th anniversary celebrations of the Russian nuclear industry. It was a significant element of the unveiling of the vision of the Russian nuclear regime. Once a strictly classified archival film document, it is now being shared on hundreds of websites, representing an example of nuclear imperialism in all its media-material infrastructure.

In the video we can see the entire life cycle of the bomb. From its construction, assembly of individual components, transportation by a specially adapted railroad car, attachment to the Tu-95 bomber aircraft, to the dropping and explosion of the 26-ton bomb at the designated location. The propaganda-archival film has two narrative strands. The first focuses on the bomb itself and its construction, while the second is linked to the production and functionality of the research, measurement and documentation infrastructure. One of the most important elements of the overall infrastructure enabling the documentation of the test was the Tu-16A aircraft, which was transformed into a flying media laboratory. Among other things, the aircraft was equipped with radio telemetering equipment, shock wave pressure recorders, and oscilloscopes for recording the power of the explosion. Externally, film cameras and calorimeters to measure heat fluxes were mounted on the fuselage. In addition, there were several telecommunications centers on the ground for two-way communication between all measurement sites and test participants. There were also film cameras and recording equipment mounted in special metal armored enclosures at 17 and 20 kilometers from the explosion site to increase the equipment's chances of surviving the explosion. Automatic measuring equipment was installed in underground bunkers to measure the exact progress of the nuclear explosion. In the declassified video, we can also see a comparison of photos of the landscape taken before and after the explosion. The later ones show only the surface of the ground scorched by the explosion. The entrances to the underground bunkers, where the measuring apparatus was stored, were also destroyed. However, as the voiceover assures – all the measuring apparatus worked properly at all times.

The *Tsar Bomba* test in 1961 was supposed to be a turning point – a line not to be crossed, a moment when all members of the 'nuclear club' recognized that escalating the arms race would be the height of folly. However, these hopes quickly proved illusory. Andrei Sakharov, who was initially one of the leading designers of the Soviet bombs (including the *Tsar Bomba*), and later a staunch opponent of nuclear weapons development, recalls that 1962 was "one of the most difficult" years (Gorelik and Bouis 2005, 228). Sakharov had hoped that the "superpowerful blast" in 1961 would put a halt to the global race of nuclear weapons testing. This is not quite what happened, however. The US conducted another nuclear test just two weeks after the AN602 explosion. In the year after October 30 1961, about 200 more atomic tests were conducted on both sides of the Cold War conflict (Gorelik and Bouis 2005, 228).

The publication of an archival document as part of the anniversary celebrations of the Russian nuclear industry had at least several objectives. One certainly was an attempt to remind the world of Russia's nuclear military might and its arsenal of atomic weapons. However, there was another goal behind the release of the film – to present the USSR as the winner of the Cold War. Underlying this historical narrative is the myth that the USSR was the most proficient user of atomic weapons. Scientifically and technologically, it was capable of creating the most powerful weapon, but it never used it against anyone. This false argument also fuels the current policy of contemporary Russia, which acts as the inheritor of nuclear regimes and seeks to preserve its historical image of imperial legacy.

7 Nuclear Regime Infrastructures of Violence

This is just one example of the nuclear regime's infrastructure being expanded with media and archival documents in order to implement the strategy of reanimating nuclear visuality. In the online distribution of this document, the present time is looping back on itself, somehow realizing future fantasies. On the internet, this film about nuclear lineage becomes an important element of media warfare, a harbinger of what was to come two years later: nuclear terrorism. These entanglements are not insignificant for the infrastructural analysis conducted by postnuclear media studies, as they reveal what often escapes us in the overload of visuality and information. For example, the fact that while Sakharov was looking for ways to design new forms of "atoms for peace", as he was terrified of the potential for nuclear annihilation that the *Tsar Bomba* provided, Anatolii Aleksandrov, his successor at the Institute of Atomic Energy, was already developing new forms of nuclear weapons, and "gained fame for submarine nuclear propulsion and infamy for the Chernobyl reactor design" (Josephson 2005, 5). Furthermore, the secret production of plutonium suitable for weapon production was an open secret in Pripyat (Higginbotham 2020; Matviyenko 2022). The spectral overlap of facts, data, and their visualities reveals the lineage of nuclear technology as an infrastructure that continually incorporates politics, violence, and militarism. As Matviyenko aptly writes, "the nuclear power industry was ... an agent of technological modernity: it contributed to the irreversible convergence of war and peace" (2022).

The declassified footage of the *Tsar Bomba* test opens up a broad spectral view of the media-material infrastructure of nuclear power. It consists not only of recording devices, but also laboratories, military buildings, bases, aircraft carrying the bomb and equipment, the bomb itself, soldiers in the field, scientists tracking the progress of the test and those who studied its range after the explosion, and finally those who designed the weapon, as well as the politicians and the leaders who ordered it. It also includes civilians who worked at various stages of the bomb's development, such as uranium miners, those who designed the technology for processing uranium ore, and those who supplied plutonium for the test. Finally, it includes those who experienced the effects of this test, which contaminated the entire environment in the area. The infrastructure of nuclear violence does not end there, however. In this case, it also works through the media by connecting the *Tsar Bomba* to an act of nuclear terrorism. Media warfare thus has the ability to militarize social fears and direct them towards those who are unable to defend themselves. The victims of such an attack are not only those who remember the material violence, but also those from later generations who have become part of the chain of media transmission of fear of catastrophe.

8 Conclusions: Radiation and Memory in Times of Nuclear Renaissance

The occupation of Zaporizhzhia and Chernobyl generated a new form of nuclear anxiety, which unfortunately will remain with us forever – linked to the potential use of civilian infrastructure as a nuclear weapon. Therefore, this situation needs to be viewed from a cross-sectional perspective in cultural and social research, where various elements of critical infrastructure are simultaneously activated, detonated, dismembered, and disarmed. On the anniversary of the Chernobyl disaster on April 26 2023, Volodymyr Zelensky tweeted that "Radiation does not recognize borders just like the Russian Federation" (Zelensky 2023). This sentence strongly resonates in the memory of many as a looping of past and present time (Bubola and Kuznetsova 2022).

My research in the field of postnuclear media studies began many years ago with autoethnographic work, in which I collected media fragments of my own memories and stories of my loved ones about the Chernobyl disaster (Jelewska and Krawczak 2018). Then, together with the Dæd Baitz collective (Agnieszka Jelewska, Michał Krawczak, Paweł Janicki, Rafał Zapała, Michał Cichy), we created an interactive installation called *Post-Apocalypsis*. This installation was presented as part of the Polish Pavilion at the Prague Quadrennial of Performance Design and Space in 2015. It designed an experience of a contemporary vision of a simultaneously networked, global and nuclear world. Viewers entered directly into the dense space of live weather data, including from various energy hazards and disasters on Earth (Chernobyl, Los Alamos, Fukushima). The constantly updated data was processed through sonification, thus the installation was continually filled with a different audio sphere, reacting to human presence but also connecting it to weather data, speculatively related to radiation (Jelewska 2015; Krawczak 2015; Jelewska and Krawczak 2018). At that time, we tried not only to show the networked situation of datafication of subjects and energy disaster risks, but we were also interested in how the disasters and the potential for future ones should be seen spectrally, as overlapping and interfering phenomena and data. For us, they were also an expression of human and environmental traumas situated in different parts of the planet, caused by nuclear regimes and embedded in digital communication networks.

Trying to understand the lack of reliable information in 1986 and the lack of accountability by communist authorities (both the USSR and Poland) for the violence they inflicted on people and the environment, I have a sense that this situation additionally created a state of coerced coexistence with radiation in this part of Europe. It is a coexistence that is not chosen, but it nevertheless becomes part of everyday life and later memory. Back in the 1980s, radiation penetrated the water, food, and air we breathed (Phillips 2009). This made us contaminated, and not only us but entire ecosystems. The anthropologist Barbara Rose Johnston refers to this state as a "half-life", referring to the half-life of harmful radioactive elements, the consequences of which we cannot accurately predict in individual, environmental, or planetary dimensions (Johnston 2007). This is precisely the somatic memory of radiation, which transforms the organism. But there is also a media memory that renders the actual memory of such events. The situation of the Chernobyl and Zaporizhzhia nuclear power plants' occupation inseparably intertwines these levels for many people in this part of Europe. After the Chernobyl disaster, with the manipulation of information in the media, the nervous and chaotic administration of iodine solution, uncertainty and fear were culturally and medially expressed through Igor Kostin's photographs taken immediately after the explosion from a helicopter flying over the still-smoking reactor. The effect of radiation-burned film is visible in them. These media-material records of radiation, juxtaposed with our private photos taken during the celebration of May 1st, International Workers' Day, when a radioactive cloud passed over Poland, and we spent carefree time at parades and walks with our families, unaware of any potential threat, shape the media dimension of that critical infrastructure. They connect the real threat of radiation with the politics of violence, the lack of access to information, and the undefined fear and uncertainty, creating a persistent state of being-with-radiation. Today, although I observe the situation from a distance, at the same time, through media approximation, I witness images that unambiguously render the actual and potential nuclear trauma. From the perspective of postdigital reality, this trauma is also a socially shared experience, transmitted through an infinite number of cultural narratives drawing on media infrastructures. Generational nuclear trauma (Bromet 2014) also persists in media records, creating new infrastructures for the memory of nuclear regimes that, in fact, are not in the past. On the contrary, they have been reactivated, intertwining past and future with the matter of the planet.

During the Cold War period in the USSR, a popular poster depicted a worker holding a buzzing atom with electrons whizzing around it. The poster bore the slogan, "Let the atom be a worker, not a soldier" (Josephson 2005, 16; Schmid 2015, 11, 112). This slogan was also displayed on one of the residential buildings in Pripyat, and it remains there today as a memorial to the falsehoods of that era. Nuclear power plant workers were creating new collectives with the atom, working for both civilian energy needs and the military industry. Therefore, a new postcollective approach is needed to study these issues, in order to understand the mechanisms described above and counteract their work on the coercive coexistence between memory and radiation. It is necessary to create new practices that will be guided by a critical perspective, reclaiming political agency through the demilitarization and decolonization of media technologies. Only through a postcollective critique can a just social coexistence be possible. Bernard Stiegler, with the Internation Collective analyzing the state of technoculture, referred to this new need as "contributory research methods" which "are based on the constitution of research communities integrating the diverse forms of knowledge, both practical and theoretical" (Fitzpatrick et al. 2021, 119). Referring to the reality of technological and digital acceleration, he wrote that there is an urgent need to develop ways to "enter into a relationship with technology based on studying it collectively, both practically and theoretically, so that these researcher-inhabitants can understand, prescribe, transform and practise it" (Fitzpatrick et al. 2021, 121–122).

The Putinist act of nuclear terrorism has become a fact, and this should open a new chapter not only in security studies, but also in postnuclear media and cultural studies, equitable nuclear education, social radiation studies, etc. New postcollective approaches and methodologies are needed to overcome the epistemic impasse that has arisen as a result of the "cementing" of many discussions on nuclear energy in the face of political and military pressures. New and spectral sub-disciplines – such as postnuclear media studies – will also help to avoid falling into the pitfalls of mediascapes, which in many places are tangled infrastructures of media warfare. In concluding this text, I want to emphasize that we are still stuck in the same political mistake – the atom should not be seen as either a worker or a soldier – it demands new depoliticized and de-militarized socio-economic concepts and functions.

References

Abbate, Janet (1999) *Inventing the Internet.* Cambridge: MIT Press.
Appadurai, Arjun (1990) Disjuncture and Difference in the Global Economy. *Theory, Culture & Society* 7: 295–310. https://doi.org/10.1177/026327690007002017
Arhirova, Hanna (2022) Unexpected War Warning System: Chernobyl Tour's Camera. *AP News*, August 23, 2022. Available at: https://apnews.com/article/russia-ukraine-kyiv-technology-e11322452c4d41970e992257db01dbcd#
Berger, Miriam (2022) A Chernobyl Tour Group Secretly Helped Track Russia's Invasion. *The Washington Post*, August 21, 2022. Available at: https://www.washingtonpost.com/world/2022/08/21/ukraine-spy-tour-group-russians/
Borger, Julian and Henley, Jon (2022) Zelenskiy Says 'Europe Must Wake Up' After Assault Sparks Nuclear Plant Fire. *The Guardian*, March 4, 2022. Available

at: https://www.theguardian.com/world/2022/mar/04/ukraine-nuclear-power-plant-fire-zaporizhzhia-russian-shelling

Bromet, Evelyn J. (2014) Emotional Consequences of Nuclear Power Plant Disasters. *Health Physics* 106, no. 2 (February 2014): 206–210. https://doi.org/10.1097/HP.0000000000000012

Bubola, Emma and Kuznietsova, Anastasia (2022) For Chernobyl Survivors, New Ukraine Nuclear Risk Stirs Dread. *The New York Times*, August 22, 2022. Available at: https://www.nytimes.com/2022/08/22/world/europe/zaporizhzhia-chernobyl-survivors.html

Chappell, Billy (2022) 'Russian Mutants Lost This Round,' Ukraine Says After Troops Leave Chernobyl. NPR, April 1, 2022. Available (consulted May 15 2023) at: https://www.npr.org/2022/04/01/1090270567/chernobyl-russia-radiation

Crary, Jonathan (2019) Terminal Radiance. In: Baer N et al. (eds) *Unwatchable*. New Brunswick: Rutgers University Press, 59–62.

Dyer-Witheford, Nick and Matviyenko, Svitlana (2019) *Cyberwar and Revolution. Digital Subterfuge in Global Capitalism*. Minneapolis: University of Minnesota Press.

Fitzpatrick, Noel, Alombert, Anne, Tron, Colette et al. (2021) Contributory Research and Social Sculpture of the Self. In: Stiegler B. and Ross D. (eds) *Bifurcate: There Is No Alternative*. London: Open Humanities Press, 119–133.

Gartzke, Erik and Lindsay, John R. (2017) Thermonuclear Cyberwar. *Journal of Cybersecurity* 3, no. 1 (2017): 38. https://doi.org/10.1093/cybsec/tyw017

Gartzke, Erik and Lindsay, John R. (2015) Weaving tangled webs: offense, defense, and deception in cyberspace. *Security Studies* 24: 316–48. http://dx.doi.org/10.1080/09636412.2015.1038188

Gorelik, Gennady E. and Bouis, Antonina W. (2005) *The World of Andrei Sakharov: A Russian Physicist's Path to Freedom*. Oxford, New York: Oxford University Press.

Higginbotham, Adam (2020) *Midnight in Chernobyl: The Untold Story of the World's Greatest Nuclear Disaster*, Simon & Schuster.

Jelewska, Agnieszka (2015) Post-Apocalypsis. In: Kubaś A. (ed.) *Post-Apocalypsis*, Warsaw: Zbigniew Raszewski Theatre Institute, 7–13.

Jelewska, Agnieszka and Krawczak Michał (2018) The Spectrality of Nuclear Catastrophe: The Case of Chernobyl, conference paper, *Politics of the Machines – Art and After*. https://doi.org/10.14236/ewic/EVAC18.30

Johnston, Barbara Rose (ed.) (2007) *Half-Lives and Half-Truths: Confronting the Radioactive Legacies of the Cold War*. Santa Fe: School for Advanced Research Press.

Josephson, Paul (2005) *Red Atom: Russia's Nuclear Power Program from Stalin to Today*, University of Pittsburgh Press.

Krawczak, Michał (2015) Ecosystem of Post-Apocalypsis. In: Kubaś A (ed.) *Post-Apocalypsis*, Warsaw: Zbigniew Raszewski Theatre Institute, 14–17.

Latynina TV (2022) Petro Kotinz, Ukrainian Energoatom CEO with discussion with Yulia Latynina. Available (consulted May 15 2023) at: https://www.youtube.com/watch?v=LJrfjfXdPOQ

Lindsay, John R. (2015) Tipping the scales: the attribution problem and the feasibility of deterrence against cyber attack. *J Cybersecurity* 1: 53–67. https://doi.org/10.1093/cybsec/tyv003

Masco, Joseph (2020) *The Future of Fallout, and Other Episodes in Radioactive World-Making*. Durham, NC: Duke University Press.

Matviyenko, Svitlana (2022) Nuclear Cyberwar. From Energy to Colonialism. *e-flux* 126, April 2022. Available at: https://www.e-flux.com/journal/126/460842/nuclear-cyberwar-from-energy-colonialism-to-energy-terrorism/

Metz, Cade (2012) Paul Baran, the Link between Nuclear War and the Internet. *Wired*, September 4. Available at: http://www.wired.co.uk/article/h-bomb-and-the-internet

Onuch, Olga and Hale, Henry E. (2022) *The Zelensky Effect. New Perspectives on Eastern Europe and Eurasia*. London: Hurst & Company.

Parks, Lisa and Starosielski, Nicole (eds) (2015) *Signal Traffic: Critical Studies of Media Infrastructures*. The Geopolitics of Information. Urbana: University of Illinois Press.

Petryna, Adriana (2013) *Life Exposed: Biological Citizens After Chernobyl*. Princeton: Princeton University Press.

Petryna, Adriana. (2022) What Russia is Stirring up at Chernobyl? *The Atlantic*, March 2 2022. Available at: https://www.theatlantic.com/science/archive/2022/03/ukraine-russia-chernobyl-warning/623878

Phillips, Sara Drue (2009) Half-Lives and Healthy Bodies: Discourses on 'Contaminated' Food and Healing in Post-Chernobyl Ukraine. *Food & Foodways*, 10: 27–53. https://doi.org/10.1080/07409710212483

Ratushniak, Oleksandr (2022) Russian Soldiers Dug Trenches in Chernobyl Zone's Radioactive Soil. *The Moscow Times*, April 7 2022. Available at: https://www.themoscowtimes.com/2022/04/07/west-ramps-up-sanctions-as-russia-threatens-ukraines-east-a77252

Sampson, Tony D. and Parikka, Jussi (2020) The New Logics of Viral Media, *Boundary 2*. Available at: https://www.boundary2.org/2020/04/tony-d-sampson-and-jussi-parikka-the-new-logics-of-viral-media/

Schmid, Sonja D. (2015) *Producing Power: The Pre-Chernobyl History of the Soviet Nuclear Industry*, Cambridge, Mass.: MIT Press.

Sloterdjik, Peter (2002) *Terror from the Air*. Translated by A Patton and S Corcoran. Los Angeles: Semiotext(e).

Terranova, Tiziana and Sundaram, Ravi (2021) Colonial Infrastructures and Techno-social Networks. *e-flux*, issue 123, December 2021. Available at: https://www.e-flux.com/journal/123/437385/colonial-infrastructures-and-techno-social-networks/

Tirone, Jonathan (2022) Russia Forcing Ukraine Workers Into Rosatom After Nuclear Theft. *Bloomberg* 30 September 2022. Available at: https://www.bloomberg.com/news/articles/2022-09-30/russia-forcing-ukraine-workers-into-rosatom-after-nuclear-theft#xj4y7vzkg

Tyschenko, Kateryna (2022) Russian Troops Heading for Energodar Nuclear Power Plant. *Ukrainian Pravda*, March 3, 2022. Available at: https://www.pravda.com.ua/eng/news/2022/03/3/7327955

Zelensky, Volodymyr (2022) We have survived the night that could have stopped the history of Ukraine and Europe – address by President Volodymyr Zelensky. Available (consulted August 3 2022) at: https://www.president.gov.ua/en/news/mi-perezhili-nich-yaka-mogla-zupiniti-istoriyu-ukrayini-ta-y-73337

Zelensky, Volodymyr (2023) Now there is an opportunity to give new impetus to relations between Ukraine and China – address by President Volodymyr Zelensky. Available (consulted August 3 2022) at: https://www.president.gov.ua/en/news/zaraz-ye-mozhlivist-dati-novu-energiyu-vidnosinam-ukrayini-t-82501

PART 3

Transversality

∴

CHAPTER 11

The Right to Breathe Is the Right to Speak

The Transversality of Environmental Pollution and Postdigital Infrastructures

Michał Krawczak

1   Toxic Geographies

For understanding the processes of environmental pollution and, more broadly, the climate crisis, it is essential not only to gather data on planetary transformations but, above all, to study specific places where toxicity is a significant factor affecting the environment, as well as the health and well-being of people. 'Toxic geographies' is a term that was introduced into the field of human, environmental, and political geography by Thom Davies (Davies 2018; 2021; 2022; Davies and Mah 2020). This concept is used to describe interdisciplinary practices involving long-term research on places and people affected by various forms of anthropogenic pollution. Toxic geographies are defined as areas and infrastructures of pollution violence that are directly linked to the economic, social, and ecological situations of these specific places. Davies utilized various research methods, including ethnographic practices, long-term observations, and interviews with residents, in his studies on environmental pollution in the so-called Cancer Alley, an area that stretches for 137 km along the Mississippi River between Baton Rouge and New Orleans, in the River Parishes of Louisiana. As the name suggests, this place and its inhabitants have been subjected to the structural violence of pollution from the petrochemical industry concentrated in that area over the course of many years. By highlighting significant factors associated with "slow time" and "slow violence" (Nixon 2013) in the development of toxicity, Davies simultaneously demonstrated how this situation perpetuates colonial violence as a "racialised, uneven, and attritional experience of petrochemical pollution in this former plantation landscape" (Davies 2018, 1537). Within this area, there are over 200 petrochemical plants and refineries that account for 25% of petrochemical production in the United States. Cancer incidence rates caused by air pollution exceed the government-established limits of acceptable risk. Consequently, this place has become one of the indices of the climate crisis, with its effects concentrated on a specific area and its people. When viewed from this perspective, Cancer

Alley can be seen as a part of a larger infrastructure of violence, where pollution serves as a repressive force. This infrastructure, in a broader sense, is connected to the project of enduring colonialism, including corporate interests, lack of proper medical care, and the reluctance of the government and petrochemical companies to address the issues faced by the residents. Davies even emphasized that such environmental injustice can be framed as a form of "'let die' violence" (Davies 2018, 1540). The residents of Cancer Alley, left on the margins of the system and subjected to the violence of pollution, also serve as a notorious example of political-corporate practices that treat people and the environment as "pollutants", condemned to exist in a "necropolitical space of contamination" (Davies 2018, 1549; Mbembe 2003).

Back in the 1990s, Laurence Buell proposed the term "toxic discourse" to refer to critical research on pollution and progressive climate change (Buell 1998). This new methodology for environmental research was primarily based on combining analyses of aspects of environmental crisis with violence against people. It highlights:

> the interdependence of ecocentric and anthropocentric values. It underscores the point that environmentalism must make concerns for human and social health more central ... it provides a striking instance of the hermeneutics of empathy and suspicion as they are pitted against each other, and the potentially high stakes at issue in that conflict; and it reopens fundamental questions about both the cultural significance and the ethics.
> BUELL 1998, 639

Buell referred to this approach as ecocriticism, thus opening up the field for inter-and transdisciplinary research on violence against humans and the environment within an interconnected and mutually influencing ecosystem. This recognition was significant not only for humanities research but also for other disciplines because, as he wrote, the "discourse of toxicity has not been treated with the same attention as its chemical, medical, social, and legal aspects" (1998, 640). He emphasized the need to adopt toxicity as a new critical paradigm but also to engage in communal practices that are essential for understanding environmental pollution issues:

> not just individuals but communities have begun to develop what some environmental anthropologists call "disaster subcultures" (whereby community ethos and social rituals get shaped by the recollection and/or anticipation of environmental disaster). More and more it may become

second nature to everyone's environmental imagination to visualize humanity in relation to environment, not as solitary escapees or consumers, but as collectivities with no alternative but to cooperate in acknowledgement of their necessary, like-it-or-not inter-dependence.
BUELL 1998, 665

As early as the end of the twentieth century, Buell signaled the need to reformulate research methods and practices in order to shape new forms of post-collective knowledge. He understood that we are witnessing the emergence of coerced collectives formed by various manifestations of climate change, ranging from increasingly frequent natural disasters to persistent pollution and degradation of specific areas on the planet, affecting local communities and environments.

Expanding on this perspective, Davies also shows that critical discourses are insufficient today, and that engaged research practice is needed. In other words, a transversal discipline is required to shape knowledge about the climate crisis and the harm caused to both human and nonhuman entities through scientific research. The situation also calls for activist practices and *in situ* actions that allow for the analysis of the situated and detailed temporal dynamics of this violence. This seems particularly important in the case of climate change research, which should transversally incorporate a broad social context (people and the environment) within the frameworks of physical, chemical, geological and geographical disciplines. This is an extremely important requirement, because climate research in the natural sciences focuses on analyzing samples and observations from specific environments affected by pollution, as well as those that need protection (such as ice caps), or operates on large datasets, such as the Earth-Science System (ESS), to provide a global perspective on planetary changes (Jelewska 2019). On the other hand, anthropological or ethnographic approaches concentrate on studying people affected by the violence of pollution. Hence, it is crucial to advocate for the integration of these disciplines, enabling a broader and transversal approach that crosses not only the boundaries of individual studies and disciplines but also traverses places and time, connecting the human and nonhuman as witnesses and victims of the violence of toxicity.

2 Place as a Narrative Potential

In the postdigital paradigm of communication, which intertwines and hybridizes the material with the digital, most events associated with the climate crisis acquire a dual ontology. They have a real impact on places (people and the environment), but they often become media events, visual and narrative indices, and above all, mediatized phenomena. In this sense, what happens locally intertwines with moments of information flow in the network, capturing the attention of those who observe the event from a distance. In their book *Climate Change as Social Drama: Global Warming in the Public Sphere*, the sociologist Philip Smith and geographer Nicolas Howe highlight this dual structure of place in climate crisis research, which is taking shape in the postdigital reality. In this system, "place is always narrativized" (Smith and Howe 2015, 172). Events that have their situatedness "are relevant for mobilizing not just local communities but also distant spectators", leading to the formation of "shared collective representations" (Smith and Howe 2015, 172). Local situations and problems resulting from ongoing climate change become spatially expanded in the system of data and information flow. A networked approach is taken towards the problem, focusing attention on its specific dimensions, which are narrativized and visualized in media communication systems. However, although this has significance for building new postcollective perspectives on viewing the climate crisis and its consequences, the focus is often momentary. The interest of observers, journalists and researchers may diminish over time, leaving local communities with their problems and traumas. Many of these factors depend on the intensity, impact, and duration of the event – whether it is a sudden catastrophe like a hurricane, or a prolonged exposure to toxic substances penetrating the ecosystem of a specific place. The postdigital entanglements of these different events will be manifested differently, and their durations will vary. The scalability of this process, spread between the global and the local, changes when we view events from the vantage point of the network, from a distance. Their locality and globality are transversally interconnected, creating the possibility – often only temporary, unfortunately – for the emergence of postcollective practices and broader research into the causes and real consequences of these events. And even if we are aware, it as a momentary action, it can ultimately contribute to a broader understanding of local issues and efforts to provide support, solve problems, and develop strategies to improve living conditions in that place by various social and environmental organizations.

3   Black Snow in Kiselyovsk

In 2019, a video appeared on YouTube featuring women from the city of Kiselyovsk in Russia – they appealed to the Canadian Prime Minister Justin

Trudeau and the UN Secretary-General Antonio Guterres, requesting recognition as climate refugees, and seeking environmental asylum in Canada. While making this appeal, the women from Kiselyovsk accused the Russian President Vladimir Putin, with great emotion, of not responding to their previous appeals, and of failing to address environmental issues and turning their hometowns into "gas chambers". The affair was initially publicized by a local journalist, Natalya Zubkova, and subsequently gained global media coverage. Justin Trudeau publicly responded to the appeal, promising support on the condition that the women would actually relocate to Canada. Vladimir Putin did not publicly respond to the issue.

The original video, first published on Novosti Kiselyovska's YouTube channel, can no longer be accessed – it has been taken down. However, fragments of it can be found in various reports and journalistic videos on the web. A transcription of the video statements of female residents was also published in the report *Race to the bottom: Consequences of massive coal mining for the environment and public health of Kemerovo Region* produced by the Russian environmental NGO environmental group Ecodefense.

> This winter, the whole world saw our black snow. We were suffocating in our town from coal dust, from the exhaust of the open-pit trucks. Through almost the entire winter …, our children could not go outside, even for just a bit of time outdoors. Our kids felt ill from the smog, from the coal dust hanging in the air.
>
> There is a high level of oncological disease in our town. We believe it has to do precisely with the horrible ecological situation. Practically every family has someone who has either died or is sick with cancer at this moment. The realization of the high risk of falling ill with cancer while having no possibility to leave this territory makes it so that we are basically feeling backed into a corner, living in constant depression. [From a video address of Kiselyovsk residents to Canadian Prime Minister Justin Trudeau].
>
> SOLOVYOVA and SLIVYAK 2021, 9

The issue of local violence and situated toxic geography in the Kiselyovsk region of Kuzbass has thus reached a wider public audience. The site of local trauma has been shown and narrated, thereby "mobilizing not just local communities but also distant spectators" (Smith and Howe 2015, 172). The negative intertwining of industry, local economics, Russian extraction, waste management and ecology policies in this region creates extremely hazardous living conditions. This situation has been monitored for years by non-governmental organizations and activists, who have drawn attention to the violation of environmental rights and the generation of risks to residents, including notably high rates of cancer incidence and mortality (Solovyova and Slivyak 2021). Scientists have also pointed out the lack of specific and effective environmental protection policies (Kotov and Formulevich 2021).

A specific phenomenon that occurs periodically in the Siberian regions is the falling of black snow from the sky during winter (Evangeliou et al. 2018). While in previous years this situation occurred sporadically, in recent years it has been observed annually, as reported by local residents and shared on social media.[1] The black colour is a result of the accumulation of pollutants in the falling snow. Hence this black snow has become an apocalyptic symbol, around which a media narrative has emerged. On the one hand, it indicates a peculiar phenomenon that both foreshadows and visualizes global climate change; on the other, it draws the attention of the international community and environmental organizations to the issue of severe environmental pollution specifically occurring in Siberia.

4   Collectivization and Environmental Extraction

As with most places subjected to the pressures of industrialization and extractive capital, Kiselyovsk also has its colonial and collectivization history, the consequences of which persist to this day. This history, in a way, grants the authorities 'permission' to treat the residents there as objects of the local industrial infrastructure, denying them the ability to determine their own fate.

Kiselyovsk is located in Siberia, in the Kuzbass region. It is a typical industrial city, founded in 1917 as a support base for the coal industry. The economy of the entire region is subordinated to the coal industry and its associated metallurgy. It is one of the most ecologically exploited and polluted areas on the planet. Mining is carried out by means of open-pit methods, which result in massive ecological damage and land degradation. Initially, Kiselyovsk was not located in the immediate vicinity of open-pit mines. However, over the past few decades, all the deposits have been exhausted, and now the open mining pits are located right behind inhabited households. The relationship is so close that there have been cases of mining disasters being accidentally initiated by residents in their homes, such as the death in a private dwelling due to an

---

1 See the report prepared by Deutche Welle (2021a; 2021b) and videos made by local residents (Sibdepo Kuzbas 2021).

explosion of accumulated methane gas coming from open mine shafts after a match was lit.[2] The improperly and aggressively conducted exploitation of coal deposits has also become a cause of environmental and health hazards. Kiselyovsk is not unique in this regard; unfortunately, it is just a typical example of a toxic place in this region.

The industrialization and collectivization of this region in western Siberia date back to the early 1920s (Hughes 1996). After the construction of the Trans-Siberian Railway, Kuzbass became an area of high economic value due to its abundant coal reserves. The history of this region serves as an example of how industrial, social, and cultural infrastructures were intertwined in the USSR, as well as of how Soviet policies of modernization were based on colonialism, supervision, and the exploitation of human labour, combined with the degradation of natural areas. In this particular place, apart from establishing a surveillance system based on Stalinist terror, the regime also utilized the natural climate and geographic location. Cold and isolation became 'natural' elements adapted to the needs of the political regime. As Julia Landau, a historian and researcher of Soviet labor camps, writes in her article *Specialists, Spies, "Special Settlers", and Prisoners of War: Social Frictions in the Kuzbass (USSR), 1920–1950*:

> the climatic, infrastructural, and socio-geographic conditions in the Kuzbass are extremely difficult. During the long winter months, lasting from the end of September until April, the climate is harsh, with extremely low temperatures. As the region was only sparsely populated, workers and technical experts had to be attracted from other regions as well as from other countries, while an infrastructure, including housing and technical facilities, had to be built at the same time.
> 2015, 186

During the years 1922–1927, the first form of work organization appeared in the area, known as the Avtonomnaia Industrialnaia Kolonia (Autonomous Industry Colony, AIK). The first mines, sawmills and chemical factories operated within its framework. At that time, the Colony was mainly run by international communist organizations under the management of the Dutch communist Sebald Rutgers. Specialists and skilled workers were recruited primarily from the USA, Germany, and the Netherlands, while local workers also arrived in Kuzbass. The initial idea was to experiment with work organization and build internal relationships among different groups within the Colony. However, in practice,

---

2 See the report prepared by Radio Free Europe (2021a).

it turned out that local workers were under the supervision of foreign specialists. Living conditions were dire, as "workers lived in self-built zemlyanki, huts made of wood and clay, located partly in earth-holes" (Landau 2015, 188). As a result, only 20 percent of foreign workers chose to stay in the AIK, while the rest left after a few months. From the very beginning, Kuzbass became a place where several factors converged: extreme living conditions, the influx and resettlement of people brought in as a labour force, and the extraction of Siberia's natural environment. This situation took on an extreme dimension during the Stalinist era.

5 Forced Industrial Displacement

The next wave of labour organisation in Kuzbass was linked to Stalin's policy of forced industrialization.

> Huge numbers of workers were recruited, mobilized, and deported to provide the workforce needed to construct one of the biggest Soviet centres of coal production and heavy industry, deemed crucial for fuelling economic development under Stalin.
> LANDAU 2015, 186

In 1928, the AIK was transformed into the state-run monopolist Kuzbasugol Company. However, the organizational changes did not significantly improve living conditions. Most of the workers who came to Kuzbass in search of employment would give up after a few months, due to the extremely harsh working and living conditions, inadequate food rations, and housing shortages. Therefore, it was decided that this problem would be addressed systematically, through forced collectivization. Starting from the early 1930s, forced laborers were brought to Kuzbasugol, and the forced resettlements were organized by the secret police (OGPU), later renamed as the Commissariat for Internal Affairs (NKVD). To ensure that the planned economic tasks were carried out and coal production increased, it was necessary to resettle 23,000 workers to Kuzbass. Initially, they were forcibly recruited from Siberian labour camps (Gulag prisoners), but soon the majority of forced laborers came from "kulak families" (Hughes 1996). This practice served not only to ensure the influx of labour force but was also used as a form of political purge to remove so-called "class enemies". The forcibly resettled families formed a new social organization layer in Kuzbass, known as "spetspereselentsy" ("special settlers").

> Altogether, from 1930 to 1932 about 23.630 kulak families, about 61.000 people, were brought to the Kuzbass from different regions of the Soviet Union. This forced relocation was part of the larger persecution of presumed wealthier farmers, the so-called kulaks, who resisted grain requisitioning and the collectivization of agriculture. Strikingly, about 40.000 families from western Siberia were sent, not to the nearby Kuzbass, but to camps in the Narymsk region of northern Siberia. At the same time, more than 50.000 special settlers were sent from the Moscow region and Bashkiria to the Kuzbass. ... While most male heads of the so-called kulak families were executed or interned in labour camps, the rest of the families were deported to special settlements, where they were meant to live and work in custody, but often without the working-age male members.
> LANDAU 2015, 191

The "special settlers" were essentially deprived of any rights, and their families were deported in a chaotic manner, left to fend for themselves in the harsh climate. The "special settlers" also had no right of movement; they were prohibited from leaving their assigned place of residence.

Additionally, in the years 1932–1933, workers in Siberia were affected by a hunger crisis. Importantly, as emphasized by Landau, the same crisis related to resistance against forced collectivization in Ukraine (known as "the Holodomor"), which most historians agree was a deliberate genocide committed by the Russians against Ukrainians through systematic starvation. These same lethal practices were used at the same time in different parts of Russia and Kazakhstan but have not yet been the subject of in-depth studies or investigations. In fact, we know very little about the victims and the political mechanisms of controlling workers through hunger in these areas (Landau 2015). In the late 1930s, politically inspired purges also occurred, aimed at fuelling hatred between different groups of workers. Initially, foreign workers from Europe or Japan were targeted. They were blamed for the increasing number of accidents in the mines. Insinuations suggested that they were conspirators "instructed by Trotsky, together with German and Japanese spies, to induce fires and explosions in the mines" (Landau 2015, 199). By 1938, 70 percent of the leading personnel, who were of foreign origin, were "sentenced to death or to long prison sentences (though those sent to prison were also later shot)" (Landau 2015, 199). During the same period, waves of repression in Kuzbass also affected the special settlers. In the years 1937–1938, thousands of people were arrested and accused of collaborating with foreign agents. All of these actions were part of the so-called "Great Terror" policy, when thousands of people were arrested and killed by the NKVD, mainly those categorized as former kulaks and "anti-Soviet elements", as well as "national minorities". During World War II, special camps were also built in close proximity to the mines, and prisoners of war were sent there. In 1942 alone, there were 26,000 prisoners of war in these camps, mainly Germans, Poles, Japanese, Chinese, Austrians, Slovakians, and Ukrainians. This practice continued in the years immediately after the war as well (Landau 2015, 202).

From the perspective of resettlement and forced labour, a political-cultural and necropolitical foundation becomes apparent in this place that has yet to be decolonized. The history of Kuzbass is a history of the interdependence of industrial infrastructure and the voiceless and disenfranchised industrial resettlers. They were not only the lowest social class, subjected to systemic violence but, importantly for understanding the continuity of violence in this place, the practices of coercion and exclusion used against them became the *modus operandi* of the industrial and extractive environmental policies applied in this location. It is a place where the policies of forced collectivization intersected with the exploitation of workers' bodies and the natural resources of Siberia in a hybrid form. Thom Davies vividly describes such practices in relation to the entanglement of history and the present in Cancer Alley. His diagnosis is also applicable to the situation in Kiselyovsk and the Kuzbass region as a whole.

> Environmental injustice can be framed as a form of "let die" violence …, where subaltern groups in this postcolonial landscape are allowed to suffer the indignity of pollution … In other words, slow violence can be read as a form of late-modern necropolitics, where marginalized communities are exposed to the power of death-in-life.
>
> DAVIES 2018, 1549

The concept of the "subaltern", introduced by the Marxist philosopher Antonio Gramsci and referenced by Davies, refers to individuals and social groups subjected to forms of cultural and political hegemony (Gramsci 2021). This concept has been utilized by the Subaltern Studies Group and functions within postcolonial theories, where it refers to lower social classes and marginalized groups. The industrial resettlers in Kuzbass became precisely such excluded subaltern social groups. The historical forced collectivization, lack of access to political rights, and being condemned to function on the margins of the USSR, resulted in their socially disadvantaged status. In fact, although they contributed to the economic development of the USSR, they were treated as national minorities, those who were consigned to work as part of the "let to die" policy. And even though it may seem that the era of Stalinist terror has passed, infrastructural violence against the inhabitants and the environment in this place continues in new strategies and formats.

6 The Regime and Progressive Censorship

The film directed by Natalya Zubkova, the protest of women in Kiselyovsk, and the appeal to Trudeau were preceded and, in a sense, inspired by many other earlier protest actions against pollution and the dramatic socio-environmental conditions generated by the mining industry, which prevent normal functioning in the region. In 2018, a legal precedent was set in Russia when, for the first time in history, environmental organizations, together with a group of local residents, succeeded in blocking another open-pit coal mine in Kuzbass. On April 13, 2018, the court of Belovo district in Kuzbass cancelled the permission issued to a private mining company. The permit, issued in 2016 by a local governmental agency belonging to the Ministry of Natural Resources, allowed the private company to forcibly appropriate agricultural lands for coal mining. Owners were unable to refuse the seizure of their land as the permission was issued on the basis of "governmental need" (a Russian legal norm allowing the appropriation of land without the owner's consent) (Ecodefense 2018). The case was brought before the court by activists from Ecodefense with the support of the Russian group of human rights lawyers "Team 29". The court sided with Ecodefense, arguing that the private company had no legal mandate to enforce "governmental needs". The ruling was significant because in Russia the coal mining sector consists exclusively of private entities, and this provided a strong argument for activists and the representatives of local communities in attempts to enforce property rights and environmental regulations.

However, in 2021, the website of Team 29 was blocked by Roskomnadzor (The Federal Service for Supervision of Communications, Information Technology, and Mass Media), and the organization itself was included on the list of so-called "undesirable organizations" (in accordance with the law restricting freedom of speech and non-governmental activities). In 2021, Ivan Pavlov, the leader of Team 29 and a lawyer, was detained by the Russian authorities and accused of violating the secrecy of the investigation. In the same year, the authorities accused him of being a "foreign agent" and revoked his lawyer status, forcing Pavlov to flee from Russia. As mentioned previously, the original films of the women from Kiselyovsk can also no longer found in the places where they were originally published – they have been removed. Natalya Zubkova herself, after a wave of threats and intimidation, was forced to leave

Russia.[3] These actions undertaken by the Russian Federation government are a result of increasingly draconian censorship aimed at subordinating citizens and controlling their speech and actions. They are also connected to the construction of a system of total surveillance, the infrastructure of which is to be the Russian Internet (RuNet).

7   The Postdigitality of RuNet

As Françoise Daucé and Francesca Musiani note, the history of the development of the Internet in Russia is fraught with paradoxes:

> The first decade of the century, after the election of Vladimir Putin to the Russian presidency in 2000, was marked by a political-digital paradox of "half-freedom of speech", with both rapid development of a free Internet and the strengthening of vertical, unitary political governance. By 2016, nearly 75 percent of the Russian population was connected to the Internet within the country.
>   DAUCÉ and MUSIANI 2021

However, even before the end of that first decade, a special agency was established to control the internet in Russia: Roskomnadzor (RKN). This agency has the authority to control online content, block websites, and register blocked websites on blacklists. It closely cooperates with the entire apparatus of state control, intelligence agencies, and law enforcement agencies, such as the Federal Security Service (FSB). In the following decade, the control over the flow of information over the Russian internet increased even further. This situation occurred at both the legal and infrastructural levels. To understand these processes well, they must be viewed in a broader cultural, social, and political context. The processes related to the so-called "sovereignization" principle of the RuNet adopted by the Russian Federation shape not only the conditions for communication, thereby limiting freedom of speech, but are also largely responsible for creating the modal framework for digital culture in contemporary Russia in general.

---

3   Due to anonymous threats and repression by the authorities, Natalya Zubkova left Russia in 2021 (see Radio Free Europe 2021b; 2021c).

The essence of RuNet is not solely based on controlling and restricting freedom of expression. The concept of "sovereignization" of the RuNet that emerged in Russia is a techno-ideological project that aims not only to control content and communication on the network but also to exercise supervision over the infrastructure and, consequently, over society. In her article *Controlling free expression "by infrastructure" in the Russian Internet: The consequences of RuNet sovereignization,* the lawyer Liudmila Sivetc argues that when considering RuNet from a legal perspective, one must understand the real consequences brought about by administrative procedures. Legal acts such as the *Sovereign Internet law*, adopted in 2019 with the official aim of protecting the country from cyberattacks, and the *law against Apple*, passed in 2020 with the objective of having all smartphone devices in Russia to preload a host of "'Russian-made' applications", as well as the rapid isolation of the Russian-language internet after 2022 (when Russian forces attacked Ukraine), generate not only a legal framework for censorship but primarily an undisclosed infrastructural project that determines the "material" distinctiveness of the Russian network when compared to other countries. Analyzing legal acts such as *Russia's Doctrine of Information Security* (2016) and *Strategy of Information Society Development for 2017–2030* (2017), Sivetc also draws attention to the definitions of security described in these documents with regard to RuNet. The internet is perceived not only as a "critical infrastructure" but also as "one of the country's core national interests" within which "Russia possesses the right to mediate political discourse in the RuNet and aims to establish a centralized state control over the national Internet infrastructure" (Sivetc 2021). She explains that the

> critical infrastructure of the Russian Internet ... should emphasize Russian sovereignty. ... Critical infrastructure, as vaguely defined in the *Critical Internet Infrastructure Act* ..., consists of a telecommunication backbone, the Internet, and other information and telecommunication systems, as well as automatic systems controlling these networks.
> 2021

The concept of surveillance in RuNet relies on the interdependence of material infrastructures and databases, and on the ability to access metadata. This is specific in the sense that the aim is not only to facilitate data surveillance, but also to ensure access to the material infrastructure of the internet that enables communication in the first place. That is why the Russian Federation has decided to control the entire infrastructure centrally, allowing the state to maintain control not only over who uses the internet and how, but also over the physical location of all data and metadata. And ultimately, as Sivitec writes:

> over time, the Internet infrastructure merges with the infrastructure of digital speech. Online content can only be accessed through the Internet infrastructure: the chain of telecom operators and Internet access providers in the physical layer, the central protocol and standards in the logical layer, and online platforms in the application layer. Consequently, Internet infrastructure is an infrastructure for digital speech as well. This merger enables states to control digital content through Internet infrastructure. The control over infrastructure is implemented via digital locks. I offer this concept as a means of referring to various technology-based tools that governments install into Internet infrastructure to control what content is available for users.
> 2021

In addition to the "sovereignization" doctrine, which aims to create a "unified information space" under state control, there is also the "personal data localization rule" which indicates that all databases created and used must have a physical location within Russia (in some cases a physical copy of the data must be stored within Russia). By locating all data and metadata (which specify, for example, how users in RuNet participate in network communication) within the country, access to this information is possible for all authorities through physical infrastructure control. Furthermore, the so-called *Yarovaya Law* (2016) imposes an additional obligation on digital service providers to collect and store content data and to provide access to the accumulated data to intelligence agencies.

All laws regarding the internet in Russia not only result in extreme control over digital speech but also essentially define internet users as new special settlers of RuNet, where everything is physically located in a specified place without the possibility of transferring this data outside the designated area or beyond the reach of the state authorities. In this way, Russia materializes and anchors everything that is digital, enabling direct control and the establishment of communication boundaries. This internet project effectively closes down freedom of expression. What happened to Natalya Zubkova, the silenced online protest of women from Kiselyovsk, and the repression against Zubkova, Ecodefence, and Team 29, are just some of the numerous cases of curbing freedom of speech in the Russian Federation.

8   Entangled Infrastructures of Violence

As Russia develops RuNet and prohibits discussions about environmental pollution in Siberia, we are simultaneously witnessing an important international debate on expanding the catalogue of human rights. This debate concerns the emergence of new (fourth generation) human rights, beyond the historical division proposed by Karel Vasak in the 1970s (Vasak 1982). The first generation of human rights encompassed civil and political rights. The second generation included economic, social, and cultural rights, while the third generation is known as solidarity human rights. Within the reality of the climate crisis, on one hand, and the rapidly expanding network of online communication, on the other, these generations of rights are in need of redefinition. In 2022, the United Nations Human Rights Council recognized the right to a clean environment as an inalienable element of contemporary fundamental rights and called for international cooperation for its implementation. As stated on the Climate & Clean Air Coalition website, "The United Nations General Assembly has passed a historic resolution declaring that everyone on the planet has a right to a healthy environment, including clean air, water, and a stable climate" (CCAC 2022). Simultaneously, there is discussion on specifying rights related to freedom of access to information in the context of threats posed by surveillance capitalism and state regimes (such as in the case of the Russian Federation) that restrict citizens' access to publicly available information. These discussions involve incorporating digital rights into the fourth generation of human rights, focusing on the ability to freely communicate and access information. These issues are crucial for shaping fair participation in "epistemic rights in digital lifeworlds" (Risse 2021).

As the case of Kiselyovsk and Kuzbass shows, these rights are now inextricably linked. For where people and the environment are condemned to the violence of pollution, there they are most often denied the right to speak and tell their story to a wider audience. The combination of toxic environments and the lack of access to free digital speech combine in this case to create one intracultural situation of violence, which at the same time continues the violence of collectivization and the history of how this place arose as an industrial project that brought people and the environment into a state of extreme coexistence. The lack of access to clean air, the unhealthy environment, and the restrictions on speech and expression, together constitute a violation of basic human rights. Restricting freedom of speech shuts down the possibility of developing a media story for distant observers, condemning those who reside there, and their environment, to structural degradation and, ultimately, slow death.

That is why in such violent places, postcollective practices and transdisciplinary research are necessary to reclaim voices and understand the dynamics of situated violence. The Russian Federation is doing everything it can to prevent the emergence of a postcollective project of knowledge creation situated around the climate crisis in Siberia. Postcollective practices today rely on communal knowledge production, both in relation to locality and in response to global conditions. In the era of the climate crisis, postcollectives possess data on pollution, they can collect and analyse it, thereby gaining a certain agency and capacity for action.

One example of grassroots practices that have emerged in the aforementioned Cancer Alley is the Louisiana Bucket Brigade (LABB). This is a nonprofit organization based in New Orleans, Louisiana, dedicated to health and environmental justice. Founded in 2000 by Anne Rolfes, it emerged as a response to the residents' dissatisfaction with the lack of access to environmental pollution data in industrial areas. The organization collaborates with local communities and governmental entities to address air quality issues in the region. LABB's mission is to support grassroots actions that raise ecological awareness and seek to create sustainable, pollution-free areas. To achieve this, the organization has developed its own DIY methods for collecting pollution data because government methods often did not reflect the reality and were influenced by corporate interests. One of their methods involves using a portable device called a "bucket" that sucks air into a bag inside, allowing it to be analysed for harmful substances. Through various actions and socio-media practices, the organizers strive to reach communities affected by the violence of pollution and, above all, to fight against corporations by using detailed data on air pollution collected at particular times and in specific places. Thanks to these practices, some of the legal cases supported by the data and knowledge obtained by LABB have been resolved in favour of the communities in Cancer Alley.

The Louisiana Bucket Brigade is just one example of the postcollective practices that are necessary in the time of the climate crisis and industrial violence. Unfortunately, in the case of Siberia, despite important attempts to create postcollective practices for the benefit of people and the environment suffering from pollution, they have been brutally suppressed by the authorities of the Russian Federation. Blocking access to independent data and information leads to a constant state of crisis. Moreover, isolation from the global flow of information and the creation of RuNet deprive people of the opportunity to claim their rights to live in a healthy environment and to freely express themselves on issues of concern. In the climate crisis, places like Kuzbass become particularly important for understanding not only the local problem but also its global consequences. We cannot say that the environmental harm affecting both humans and non-humans in Kuzbass does not also impact the global development of the climate crisis. All these factors intertwine, creating new transversal connections between environmental pollution and the destruction of people who are forced, as in Kuzbass, into a state of extreme coexistence, where their basic rights to breathe and speak are taken away.

References

Buell, Lawrence (1998) Toxic Discourse. *Critical Inquiry* 24(3): 639–665. https://doi.org/10.1086/448889

CCAC: Climate & Clean Air Coalition (2022) *UN declares healthy environment – including clean air – a human right,* 2.08.2022. Available (consulted June 3 2023) at: https://www.ccacoalition.org/en/news/un-declares-healthy-environment---including-clean-air---human-right.

Daucé, Françoise and Musiani, Francesca (2021) Infrastructure-Embedded Control, Circumvention and Sovereignty in the Russian Internet: An Introduction. *First Monday,* April 7, 2021. https://doi.org/10.5210/fm.v26i5.11685

Davies, Thom (2021) Geography, Time, and Toxic Pollution: Slow Observation in Louisiana. In: O'Lear S. (ed.) *A Research Agenda for Geographies of Slow Violence.* Cheltenham: Edward Elgar Publishing, 21–39. https://doi.org/10.4337/9781788978033.00006

Davies, Thom (2022) Slow Violence and Toxic Geographies: 'Out of Sight' to Whom? *Environment and Planning C: Politics and Space* 40(2): 409–427. https://doi.org/10.1177/2399654419841063

Davies, Thom (2018) Toxic Space and Time: Slow Violence, Necropolitics, and Petrochemical Pollution. *Annals of the American Association of Geographers* 108(6): 1537–1553. https://doi.org/10.1080/24694452.2018.1470924

Davies, Thom and Mah, Alice (eds) (2020) *Toxic Truths: Environmental Justice and Citizen Science in a Post-Truth Age.* Manchester: Manchester University Press.

Deutsche Welle (2021a) Russia's Black Snow. *Deutsche Welle,* March 3 2021. Available (consulted June 3 2023) at: https://www.dw.com/en/coal-pollution-black-snow-falls-over-russia/video-56725957

Deutsche Welle (2021b) Black Snow in Russia. *Deutsche Welle,* March 11 2021. Available (consulted June 3 2023) at: https://www.dw.com/en/black-snow-in-russia/video-56818508

Ecodefense (2018) Coal mining is not a «governmental need», court rules in Russian Kuzbass, 13.04.2018. Available (consulted June 3 2023) at: https://ecodefense.ru/2018/04/13/coal-mining-is-not-a-governmental-need-court-rules-in-russian-kuzbass/

Evangeliou, Nikolaos, Shevchenko, Vladimir P., Yttri, Karl Espen et al. (2018) Origin of Elemental Carbon in Snow from Western Siberia and Northwestern European Russia during Winter–Spring 2014, 2015 and 2016. *Atmospheric Chemistry and Physics* 18(2): 963–977. https://doi.org/10.5194/acp-18-963-2018

Gramsci, Antonio (2021) *A Subaltern Social Groups: A Critical Edition of Prison Notebook 25*. European Perspectives. Edited and translated by JA Buttigieg, ME Green. New York: Columbia University Press.

Hughes, James (1996) *Stalinism in a Russian Province: A Study of Collectivization and Dekulakization in Siberia*. New York: St. Martin's Press in association with the Centre for Russian and East European Studies, University of Birmingham.

Jelewska, Agnieszka (2019) Spaceship Earth and the Beginnings of New Environmentalism. In: Krawczak, M. (ed.) *Post-Technological Experiences: Art, Science, Culture*. 1st Edition. Poznań: Adam Mickiewicz University Press, 26–36.

Kotov, RM and Formulevich, Ya V. (2021) The Impact of Kuzbass Industrial Enterprises on Environmental Safety. *IOP Conference Series: Earth and Environmental Science* 670(1): 012049. https://doi.org/10.1088/1755-1315/670/1/012049

Landau, Julia (2015) Specialists, Spies, 'Special Settlers', and Prisoners of War: Social Frictions in the Kuzbass (USSR), 1920–1950. *International Review of Social History* 60(S1): 185–205. https://doi.org/10.1017/S0020859015000462

Mbembe, Achille (2003) Necropolitics. *Public Culture* 15(1): 11–40. https://doi.org/10.1215/08992363-15-1-11

Nixon, Rob (2013) *Slow Violence and the Environmentalism of the Poor*. First Harvard University Press paperback edition. Cambridge, Massachusetts and London, England: Harvard University Press.

Radio Free Europe (2021a) Living On The Edge: Open-Pit Mines In Siberian City Spark Fear. *Radio Free Europe. Radio Liberty*. Available (consulted June 20 2023) at: https://www.rferl.org/a/russia-siberia-kiselyovsk-coal-mines-ecology-safety-risk/31254915.html

Radio Free Europe (2021b) Siberian Journalist Flees Her City After Attack, Threats Against Her Children. *Radio Free Europe. Radio Liberty*. Available (consulted June 20 2023) at: https://www.rferl.org/a/russia-journalist-flees-corruption-threats-assault-siberia/31127383.html

Radio Free Europe (2021c) Siberian Journalist Flees Russia After Threats, Attack. *Radio Free Europe. Radio Liberty*. Available (consulted June 20 2023) at: https://www.rferl.org/a/siberian-journalist-flees-russia-after-threats-attack/31223729.html

Risse, Mathias (2021) The Fourth Generation of Human Rights: Epistemic Rights in Digital Lifeworlds. *HKS Working Paper* RWP21-027. https://doi.org/10.2139/ssrn.3973946

Sibdepo Kuzbass [Сибдепо Кузбасс] (2021) *Black snow Kuzbass* [Чёрный снег Кузбасс], YouTube. Available (consulted June 20 2023) at: https://www.youtube.com/watch?v=a4BqU-dQQ4U

Sivetc, Ludmila (2021) Controlling Free Expression 'by Infrastructure' in the Russian Internet: The Consequences of RuNet Sovereignization. *First Monday*, April 16, 2021. https://doi.org/10.5210/fm.v26i5.11698

Smith, Philip and Howe, Nicolas (2015) *Climate Change as Social Drama: Global Warming in the Public Sphere*. 1st Edition. Cambridge: Cambridge University Press. https://doi.org/10.1017/CBO9781316217269

Solovyova, Yelena and Slivyak, Vladimir (2021) *Race to the bottom: Consequences of massive coal mining for the environment and public health of Kemerovo Region*. Environmental group Ecodefense. Available (consulted June 3 2023) at: https://ecdru.files.wordpress.com/2021/01/race_eng.pdf

Vasak, Karel (1982) Human rights: As a legal reality. In: Vasak, K. and Alston, P. (eds) *The international dimensions of human rights*. Volume 1. Westport, Conn.: Greenwood Press; Paris: Unesco, 3–10.

CHAPTER 12

Transversal Physiognomies and the Postcollective Self

Jan Stasieńko

The concept of the face as an important part of the human body in a traditional sense, seems quite distant from the category of collectivity. The face is most frequently understood as the metonymy of an independent "subject," in numerous cases perceived as a medium of a specific "truth" about a subject, as a place of conscious manifestation, and more interestingly, the expression of subconscious symptoms and signs of being distinctive and individual. The processes of technological support for the face, its reconstruction, modification and even shaping from the very beginning, evolving for a long time and in greatly distinct fields, not only seem to fit into Braidotti's category of transversality (Braidotti 2006; 2013; 2019), but also appear to be related to the concept of postcollectivity.

Although Braidotti is not concerned directly with the "posthuman" face, she points to its essential properties through the idea of transversality. While transversality presupposes the formation of subjective assemblages and systems which intersect categories, powers, and domains, as well as the free flow of vital forces and life itself, which may take various forms of states of matter and ontologies, the face in such a perspective may appear to be a place of concentration and exposure of these processes. The face could be understood here as an area of the clash of various powers, a focus of tensions and dynamics, as well as the amalgamation of biological elements, affects, technologies and communication screens. The transversal nature of the face would be revealed in its heterogeneous assemblage, in the interspecies combination of features, facial expressions and grimaces, and in the operation of the technological apparatus of its creation. Briefly, the transversality of the face would be a manifestation of the self-organising vitality of matter (see also Braidotti 2022, 136–137).

Contrastingly, these transversal physiognomies encountered in medicine, bioart, digital and postdigital art, and game and film CGI, move toward postcollectivity not only because they combine biological, material and virtual elements, but also because more and more frequently they are the effect of collective action and a specific surface for the manifestation of human and non-human affects and powers.

The face as a visible outcome of the processes of decentralisation of the human liberal subject is also an ironic symptom of its disconnection from an individual, becoming independent, and postcollectivity. Contemporary technologies of face creation in digital cinema, the use of artificial intelligence to depict it, and connecting human and non-human faces in artistic projects, are clear examples that this category is a field of intense experimentation. As a critical category, it raises questions about authenticity, integrity, communicative potential, ownership, agency, and the morphological freedom of the image.

The presented text addresses four aspects of the transversal postcollectivity of the face. Predominantly, I aimed at presenting its historical and theoretical background. Thus, I intended to prove that the face, as a result of collective action, is not always linked only to modern postdigital technologies or biological, information and machine assemblages. In a long reflection on the face, including the fundamental works of Darwin or Paul Ekman, the strands which broaden the understanding of the face as non-human can be found, also considering the collective and individual works of Deleuze and Guattari. The authors of *Capitalism and Schizophrenia* began with the imperialism of the face of a white man (Christ), which requires "dismantling," but showed the processes of facialising as the operation of abstract machines and processes independent of the subject (Deleuze and Guattari 1983). The second section analyses the medical and prosthetic processes of creating and modifying the face, which reveals the (post)collective potential of these activities and technologies, but also indicates their material context. The third section discusses the issue of facial postcollectivity using the example of digital face swapping techniques, as well as their remote control with the use of motion capture systems. These techniques currently comprise numerous dimensions and applications, ranging from digital cinema and games to political satire and propaganda. They also spark a lot of discussion and controversy, giving the question of postcollectivity an ethical as well as an ontological dimension.

The final section of the chapter includes an investigation of critical art projects in which the contexts of the transversal postcollectivity of the face are revealed. This section discusses such works and performances which focus on non-individual aspects of the face, its transversality, brevity and transience, as well as those which combine it in an unusual manner with the ideas of new materialism, ecocriticism or post-biology.

1 Transversal Postcollectivity of the Face – Theoretical Background

Certainly, the most important theoretical support for the qualities of the posthuman face defined in this manner (understood here as a transversal and postcollective face) are the reflections on this category found in the works of Deleuze and Guattari (1983; 1987). The presentation of all the contexts of the face in these authors' works is a task for a separate article or even an entire monograph, however, it has also been the subject of interest of already completed studies and articles (Bignall 2012; Zevnik 2016a; 2016b). It is worth noting that the theory of the face developed by both authors strongly resembles the aforementioned qualities of the posthuman face, although Deleuze and Guattari initially showed it as an effect of imperial abstract machines forming its structure. The research on the monstrous face of Deleuze's on-screen close-up studies (Deleuze 1986a; 1986b) and the analysis of Keiichi Tahara's photographic portraits, which Guattari describes as faciality machines (2015), are linked to this perspective.

In A *Thousand Plateaus: Capitalism and Schizophrenia*, the face is defined by numerous features and metaphors which seem like a set of categories extracted from posthuman discourse. The face is considered a policy (Deleuze and Guattari 1987, 188) and a landscape (Deleuze and Guattari 1987, 175), and in another part of the study–a map. Deleuze and Guattari also wrote about the face which needs to be dismantled (1987, 188), and even about a non-human face and a horror face (1987, 190–191). A certain part includes a definition which fits the face into the idea of a body without organs: The face crystallises all redundancies, it emits and receives, releases and recaptures signifying signs. It is a whole body unto itself … (Deleuze and Guattari 1987, 115).

In Guattari's individual works, the face recurs as a significant and useful concept–the author developed strands related to various forms of the face, for instance, diagrammatic or capitalist, and wrote about faciality as a binary signifying machine (Guattari 2010, 75–106). In turn, in the text on Tahara's photography, Guattari investigated the processes of dismantling and deterritorialisation of human faces while creating artistic portraits (Guattari, 55–66). While the extensive philosophical concepts of Deleuze and Guattari are close to a posthuman discourse, and thus to transversal and postcollective thinking about the face, the achievements of other researchers in this field seem to exhibit quite the opposite approach. The reference here is to the works of both Darwin (1872) and Ekman (Ekman et al. 1972; Ekman and Friesen 1978), whose studies on the face appear to be the essence of the anthropocentric approach, as they are the source of decoding human emotions, enabling lying and deception strategies to be revealed through the face analysis. Giorgio Agamben seems to think similarly about the face, and argues that only people have faces:

> All living beings are in the open/in openness; they show themselves and communicate to each other, but only humans have a face, only they make their appearance and their communication with others their own fundamental experience, only humans make of the face the place of their own truth.
> AGAMBEN 2020

This concept of the face as *anthropos* would therefore involve thinking of it as the emblem of an integral human subject. The face would be a distinctive and crucial element communicating a specific "truth" about the subject. It would be a face that could be decoded and read, a face which could help discover the person hidden behind it, with their intentions and desires, even against themselves. Such an approach seems to emanate from the famous works on the expression of emotions and micro-expression of the face by Paul Ekman. This researcher, developing the theory of the face since the 1970s, not only discovered the versatility of basic human emotions revealed in the face, but also examined the influence of social and cultural factors on the desire to hide natural emotions (Ekman 1973; 1980; 1985; Ekman at al. 1972). An extremely popular element of Ekman's theory is the intricately built facial expression coding system, through which the researcher, together with Wallace V. Freisen, managed to encode 10,000 different types of facial expression and assign them to basic emotions (Ekman & Friesen 1978). The system, according to the "anthropocentric paradigm," helps read emotions wherever "truth" about the human subject is required, for example, in the work of the police and intelligence services or in psychological therapy. Although we approach the desire to read human emotions, Ekman's theory includes aspects which require a broader, and also posthuman, context. Principally, from the very beginning, Ekman's work inspired studies on the expression of emotions in animals conducted by other scientists, as exemplified by the research on the facial expressions of chimpanzees by Lisa A. Parr and Bridget M. Waller (Parr and Waller 2006) or more broadly: all mammals (Descovich et al. 2017). Ekman also made an intensive reference to Darwin's fundamental work on the emotions of animals and humans – *The Expression of the Emotions in Man and Animals* (Darwin 1872).[1] Importantly, Ekman's achievements in the field of the taxonomy of

---

1   It seems that a historical issue related to the "non-human" approach to the face worthy of a broader separate study is that of the construction of animal faces in various tribal

facial movements have been widely used in 2D and 3D animation, which indicates that the study of human faces is applied not only to creating digital faces, representing human ones, but also to building the expression of various types of conventional characters, whose faces are hybrids of human, animal, and technological elements.

Agamben's reflections can be understood in a similar vein, which is critical to the anthropocentric paradigm of the face (2000). As outlined, the researcher explicitly assigned the face to people and linked it to linguistic communication skills; nonetheless, his essay on the face revealed a much more complex and non-human interpretation of it. The first suggestion of such thinking about Agamben's theory of the face can be noted at the beginning of his essay, where the author described it from a collective perspective: "The face is the only location of community, the only possible city" (Agamben 2000, 91). Further, Agamben pointed out that the face can appear wherever something reaches the level of exposition and wants to capture its own being unveiled–this means that he assigned the face to objects and even the whole Earth:

> There is a face wherever something reaches the level of exposition and tries to grasp its own being exposed, wherever a being that appears sinks in that appearance and has to find a way out of it. (Thus, art can give a face even to an inanimate object, to a still nature; and that is why the witches, when accused by the inquisitors of kissing Satan's anus during the Sabbath, argued that even there there was a face. And it may be that nowadays the entire Earth, which has been transformed into a desert by humankind's blind will, might become one single face.)
> AGAMBEN 2000, 92

The strands of transversality of the face are also indicated by those parts of the discourse in which Agamben noted the simultaneous potential of communicating the truth and simulating in the face (Agamben 2000, 94) or where he pointed out that "the face is formed by a passive background on which the active expressive traits emerge" (Agamben 2000, 98).

---

and primitive cultures, as well as in ancient Greece and Rome, most frequently as masks. Certainly, these animal physiognomies have already been the subject of numerous studies and research papers (see Edson 2005; Emigh 2011; Napier 1987; Segy 1976). Nonetheless, their interpretation in the context of the "broader than human" facial model outlined in this article could contribute to the new engaging strands, just as historical animal studies enrich the past-oriented trend of research on post-humanism. The study of the cultural representations of animal faces, see for example Fudge 2013 should also be considered.

While the works of Deleuze and Guattari seem to constitute a certain pre-criticism of facial anthropocentrism, the considerations of Ekman and Agamben could be described as its post-criticism, implying an unwitting questioning of the validity of the theses about the truth of the face and its human uniqueness. Post-criticism would show how this anthropocentricity of the face denies itself–how the theses of both researchers have evolved towards a new perception of a non-anthropocentric, postcollective and transversal face.

2   Biomedical and Prosthetic Face Collectivity

The face as a collective construct and design is very clearly revealed in complex medical procedures of its reconstruction. Primarily, prosthetic technologies in this field indicate the material context of the face, which in "typical" conditions hides behind its plastic facial expression. I have pointed to the fact that a "healthy" face, not affected by dysfunction and injuries, has a specific transparent character – it communicates feelings, mental states, supports non-verbal communication and only in the event of an injury and illness, when it is treated and prosthetically "repaired," does it become an element of a critical discourse, an area for demystification. Furthermore, it reveals its assembled structure, in which biological elements are combined with prosthetic materials of various nature. Therefore, these "non-normative" contexts and transmutations of the face are a part of the process of dismantling the face described by Deleuze and Guattari. Contrastingly, facial transplantation procedures seem to be an extremely expressive model of its hybrid construction from various biological bodies. While internal organ transplants do not have a visual context and normally do not raise questions about belonging to a specific human subject (perhaps except for the heart), face transplants seem to be an embodied process of transversal transgression – appropriation of the image of the "human" Other and blurring the existing visual identity. Therefore, both forms of facial reconstruction deserve more discussion.

Historically speaking, reconstructions with the use of prostheses began with Anna Coleman Ladd's projects, which were extremely spectacular and innovative at the time. This American sculptor joined the work for the Red Cross during World War I. Deeply moved by the tragic consequences of the war, the artist founded a facial prosthesis workshop in Paris in 1918, in which she made 185 prostheses for veterans (Alexander 2007). Her works clearly indicated the hybrid nature of the face as an object. The final effect of her treatments seemed uniform: the face appeared undamaged and entirely complete. To the contrary, it hid "unwittingly" not only the joints of biological and prosthetic elements, made of coated sheet metal, but in a more general sense, also the face as a result of an armed conflict – it was a "surface" affected by the war, like a bombed city or a blown-up trench.[2]

Nowadays, the traditions developed by Anna Colman Ladd are continued by commercial companies which create realistic face prostheses. Their products also clearly demystify the face as a uniform surface with a traditional set of familiar elements, such as lips, nose, eyebrows and eyes. Commonly, a prosthesis effectively hides the "wet" interior to which we, as observers, are not accustomed. Concurrently, prostheses from companies such as Medical Arts Prosthetics, introduced to the market since 1985, show an entirely distinct image of what is under the face. This interior shows the configuration of scarred wounds, empty spaces in the nasal and facial cavity as well as orbits. The damaged faces of the company's customers clearly deconstruct the perception of observers about the inside of the head, and simultaneously show how the head becomes a patchwork construct in which parts of the prosthetic body are held inside, owing to touch fasteners and magnets.

Contemporary prosthetic technologies appear to be an important issue from the perspective of critical studies on disability, which to a certain degree seem to coincide with the posthuman discourse. These studies indicate that "fixing" a disability is difficult to fully recognise as a legitimate and necessary process because it views disability from the ableist imperative of a handicap that needs to be eliminated (Meekosha and Shuttleworth 2009; Siebers 2017; Silvers 2003). It is looking at people with disabilities not as others to whom we show our care, but as strangers who trigger feelings of discomfort. Thus, the criticism of these ableist games with the categories of alienation and otherness, excluding approaches to the non-normative body (in this case the face) seem quite close to the critical posthumanism oriented towards non-normate others (on category of *normate* see Garland-Thomson 1997). Therefore, when considering hiding the "imperfections" of the face with prostheses, it should be noted that in the field of prosthetics of other parts of the body, especially limbs, a conscious departure from this imitative nature of prostheses can be observed. They become an emancipatory element, which is to emphasise the distinctiveness and individuality of their user, and to be an element of aestheticisation of the body with disabilities. Perhaps this is the approach for facial prostheses, so that their users do not fit in an ableist discourse and thus dismantle the face model of the normates.

---

2 Braidotti, referring to Alaimo, identifies the exposure category as useful in describing this type of phenomena, not only in terms of vulnerability to injury, but also in a more general sense of susceptibility to any type of influence from others (Braidotti 2022, 136).

The most spectacular example of the brevity and instability of the face as an element of the body, and simultaneously its collective configurability, are face transplants. The history of these treatments is rather short. It is indicated that the first such partial transplant was given to a patient Isabelle Dinoir at the Ancien hospital in 2005. This historical beginning shows various "posthuman" contexts, as if all the events related to it were a posthuman focal point of contemporary medical procedures and interspecies relations (Alberti 2017). The reconstruction of the face was carried out with the use of a fragment of the mandible and nose obtained from a deceased donor, which clearly refers to the Frankensteinian topos. Isabelle's face was bitten by her own dog, euthanised later, which seems a perverted comment on Haraway's *Companion Species Manifesto* (2009). In numerous interviews, Dinoir emphasised the great difficulty of getting used to the "alien" face. To a certain degree, the transplanted face contributed to Isabelle's death – the patient was prone to developing cancer due to the immunosuppressants taken after the procedure and, as a result of it, died in 2016, which is important after her body rejected the transplant in 2015.

In the following years, transplant technology developed to such a degree that full transplants become feasible. An anonymous patient received a new face at the Vall d'Hebron University Hospital in Spain in 2010. A spectacular testimony of transplantation as a design process is the case of Dallas Wiens, who underwent a transplant of this body part in 2011 at the Brigham and Women's Hospital in Boston (Brigham and Women's Hospital 2012). The photographs of the patient before the operation show that the face damaged by an electric shock, initially healed immediately after the accident in 2008, was a specific "blank card," a surface without any features that could only be "covered" with new details by the transplant.

3   Postdigital Collective Physiognomies

Contemporary digital technologies allow for numerous activities in the field of constructing new physiognomies and reconfiguring existing faces. Occasionally, these are sophisticated techniques and processes in which huge teams of researchers and/or designers are involved. The sizes of these teams frequently reflect well the need for effort to construct and reconstruct the face. As Darryn King wrote in "Wired": "More than 500 visual effects artists spent two years digitally building a young version of Will Smith" for *Gemini Man* (2019), directed by Ang Lee (King 2019). Nonetheless, it is worth emphasising that more and more frequently this vast contribution of "human" work is replaced by calculations performed by machine learning algorithms. This is a significant issue because the scripts of artificial intelligence contribute to the creation of a specific "non-human" aesthetics that "human" recipients have to handle.

Among the operations that affect digital faces, the advanced digital actions occurring in the contemporary CGI cinema deserve special attention. Tracking the production materials of noted Hollywood blockbusters indicates the mastery of such activities. The two technologies that currently impact the most the hyper-realistic quality of digital faces is 3D scanning, which allows for the creation of digital lookalikes of renowned actors and public figures, and the *performance capture* technology, which allows for capturing subtle microexpressions of actors' faces. Both technologies result in interesting outcomes which allow for obtaining effects that embody the key notions of post-and transhumanism.

The idea of resurrection and immortal life postulated in transhumanism can be found in digital cinema. For approximately a dozen years, there has been a trend of bringing deceased actors to life for the needs of feature films or commercials. Starting with less successful projects with the resurrected Peter Sellers, Bruce Lee and Laurence Olivier, Hollywood cinema has shown such masterpieces as Peter Cushing brought to life to "play" Grand Moff Tarkin in *Rogue One: A Star Wars Story* from 2016. All these instances, including the "alive" Paul Walker in *Fast and Furious* or the concert with the hologram of deceased Tupac Shakur at the Coachella festival in 2012, are based primarily on the careful reconstruction of the faces of late celebrities. It determines the success of the described projects.

The digital practices of character rejuvenation, such as in the remake of *Tron* (*Tron: Legacy*), are equally spectacular. In the movie, CLU–the all-powerful programme with which the characters clash, received the youthful face of Jeff Bridges. The animation of Carrie Fisher, rejuvenated for *Rogue One: A Star Wars Story,* is also stunning. This sequence brings an additional context in connection with the actress's death two weeks after the film premiere. The aforementioned 2019 film–*Gemini Man*, in which Will Smith appears in two "versions," an older and younger one, is a great example as well. In contrast, the complexly recreated figure of the android Rachel from *Blade Runner 2049* has a special power of expression. Her scene could not be played by Sean Young, who is already an aged lady, therefore the character was composed of numerous elements and reference materials including the acting by Loren Peta, trained by Young herself to act like her, an animated digital face intricately constructed by the creators of the CGI film and the voice of yet another actress, and so on. The collective process of creating a realistic character may exemplify the profound transformation of acting or the role of the actor on the set, but primarily highlights the dramatic separation of actors from their own image (Failes 2017).

Advanced techniques of face design in Hollywood are equally visible in films in which these physiognomies become the basis for building hybrid characters, not only human, but also animal or comic. Constructing characters from the bodies of two actors was characteristic of films such as *The Curious Case of Benjamin Button* and *Captain America*. The faces of Andy Serkis's characters, who played Gollum in the adaptations of Tolkien's novels or the role of Caesar–the leader of the great apes in *Planet of the Apes* series, were sophisticatedly constructed from 3D animations and recorded facial expressions using motion capture systems. The most recent spectacular face designs include the time-consuming and demanding work of numerous specialists on the image of Thanos from the *Avengers* series (primarily from *Avengers: Endgame*), whose facial expressions were given by the actor Josh Brolin.

It is worth mentioning that the arduous work on recreating the subtleties of faces known from cinematic CGI is gaining popularity due to tools which combine video game and movie production. Introduced in 2021, the MetaHuman plug-in set for the Unreal game engine was a breakthrough in terms of low-budget access to creating hyper-realistic facial animations. The creators of the tools indicated that, owing to the use of motion capture systems, it is now feasible to create vivid animated images in real time via a browser. The facial features, hairstyle and skin colour of the characters can be modified on an ongoing basis, and in this case, the metahuman category itself reflects well the possibilities of technology to bring virtual, non-real individuals to life. Hence, metapeople are the essence of transversality – their faces are driven by the facial expressions of external human actors, and their features are continuously altered.

The emergence of new digital technologies which prove the status of the face as a designed construct was initiated by involving machine learning algorithms in its visualisation. For instance, they allowed Rani Horeva to develop a project in 2018 entitled "This Person Does Not Exist" (*This Person Does Not Exist*, n.d.), which presents photographs featuring algorithmically generated faces consisting of perfectly connected parts of distinct people's physiognomies. These physiognomies came from a photo dataset frequently used by machine learning algorithms. The so-called CelebA is a collection of over 200,000 images of celebrities with 40 attributes assigned to each of them.

The development of automatic face swapping algorithms in video materials, which began with the controversy related to the deepfake algorithm, seems even more significant. This algorithm enables automatic face replacement based on photographic and film databases showing a given person.

Public figures – actors, politicians, musicians–and females in particular, as the vast majority of these materials are pornographic clips, became victims of deepfakes (Ajder, Patrini, Cavalli et al. 2019). Except for following a fairly lively discussion on copyright and image rights, as well as the risks of impersonating other people and image manipulation associated with the use of the algorithm[3] (Ajder, Patrini, Cavalli et al. 2019; Chesney and Citron 2019; Meskys, Kalpokiene, Jurcys et al. 2020; Schick 2020), the specific type of the aesthetics of "alienation," which is the outcome of algorithmic and postcollective face creation, deserves special attention. Known faces are transplanted onto bodies of dissimilar size, age and skin colour. The algorithmically animated physiognomies themselves are the result of photographs from various periods of a prominent person's life, which only intensifies the effect of alienation. There are assemblages of celebrity heads and animated characters bodies, or conversely–the bodies of porn actors have the heads of cartoon characters. In selected materials, hybrid gender intermixing can be seen.

The publicity given to the discussed algorithm and the accompanying application also led to other new technologies which develop the idea of automatic face swapping beginning to appear from 2019. An example is CannyAI studio (Video Dialogue Replacement n.d.), which introduced their own face replacement solutions allowing for lip synchronisation (a technology known as *video dialogue replacement*). Thus, the company's creators–former employees of the Israeli army have endorsed the solution as an opportunity to automatically dub movies and TV programmes or adapt training materials to different languages. The authors of the solution seek to oppose the technology that results in faces being swapped for fake news. Nonetheless, the promotional video of CannyAI was a deceitful clip for John Lennon's *Imagine*, in which phrases about the need for peace and reconciliation are sung by the digitally manipulated heads of world leaders, such as Donald Trump, Theresa May and Xi Jinping.

Another example of the successors of deepfakes is the project entitled *Photorealistic Talking Heads 2019*, created by Egor Zakharov, Aliaksandra Shysheya, Egor Burkov and Victor Lempitsky (Zakharov et al. 2019). The convincing animations developed within the project were not based on video material, but were "animations" of archival photographic portraits, for example, of Salvador Dalí or Lenin. Even more surprisingly, the same algorithm can animate the faces known from "motionless" paintings such as *Girl with a Pearl Earring* by Johannes Vermeer or *Mona Lisa* by Leonardo da Vinci. The

---

3 One of the recent, fortunately unsatisfactory examples of the political use of deep fake was the surrender speech of the President of Ukraine, Volodymyr Zelensky, faked by the Russians (see Telegraph 2022).

Myheritage.com website, where users can research their family history by creating family trees, finding relatives and browsing through countless archival documents, takes things a step further. One of the functionalities–the Deep Nostalgia™ algorithm, allows for the creation of short facial animations from archival photographs. In this way, users can "bring to life" portraits of deceased family members, which means family memories can be "tinkered" with.

Furthermore, digital technologies provide an opportunity to create performance projects in which the face becomes the surface and territory. It appears that the possibilities of projection mapping of architectural surfaces, known from urban areas, can also be applied in face mapping. One of the examples of such usage was the famous show *The Lady Gaga Experience* during the Grammy Awards in 2016. The face of Lady Gaga singing on stage became the "surface" for the VJ show. The 2014 OMOTE performance by three artists, namely Nobumichi Asai, Hiroto Kuwahara and Paul Lacroix, with the use of the *motion capture* system, was of a similar character. During the show, the artists were able to radically modify the appearance of the faces of the models on stage to make the surfaces for presenting sublime animations.

4 Postcollective Faces as Critical Art

The face in the discussed posthuman paradigm is subject to multifaceted criticism, which may be manifested in the analysis of contemporary technological and media phenomena, and also communicated in the rich creative activity of numerous artists interested in reconfiguring human and non-human physiognomies. The next part of the article seeks to discuss selected examples from the latter field, focusing on case studies in which such critical approaches emerge. Building human-animal hybrids is one of Kate Clark's key interests (Kate Clark n.d.). In her disturbing animal sculptures, the faces are replaced with human ones, which indicates a deep relationship between animals and humans, but also makes the viewer feel discomfort. To prepare her works, the artist uses the treated hides of exotic animals obtained from the secondary market, which provokes reflection on the exploitation of killed animals. Therefore, the human face is a kind of exclamation mark dot, the pinnacle of the exploited animals' grieving and an indication of the offenders. Furthermore, the multidimensional sculptures refer to the notion of diversity – the faces of the people shown are just as ethnically diverse as numerous species of animals, the bodies of which become elements of provocative assemblages. The titles given to the sculptures (*Sharp Tongue, And She Meant It, Little Girl, She Gets What*

She Wants, and so on) are critical, as they concern the human rather than the animal world.

Other artists demystify the category of faces in their projects. They apply 3D graphics and animations as well as visual effects. In his *Play-doh People* project (Azzarello 2016), José Cardoso, inspired by the works of Chris Cunningham and David Cronenberg, created a series of portraits in which, in the photographs of his relatives and himself, he builds dough overhangs, causing the effect of alienation. These overhangs radically modify the appearance of reconfigured faces, which at the same time gives the impression of damaged and painfully deformed faces.

The works of Lee Griggs (Lee Griggs n.d.) and Adam Pizurny (Pizurny n.d.) exhibit a similarly demystifying nature. With the use of 3D graphics, the first artist created a series of portraits of characters whose heads are extremely deformed by various types of rendering filters and graphic effects. We find here heads modulated into a cube and other spatial figures, heads made of streamers and ribbons, openwork and wire heads, relief heads, and so on. In contrast, Adam Pizurny treats the face as an object for animated deformation. His faces become pierced balloons, empty shells that crumble. These models change the state of matter and morph towards liquids and gases. The audiences of his animations are deeply touched by the fact that this seemingly familiar and constant element of the body can be so elusive and changeable.

The art of a specific critical portrait has a much broader character than just the works presented. For instance, Dain Yoon creates complex paintings using his own face as a surface for them (Yoon n.d.), while Christina A. West creates busts in which the eroded faces are only the surface under which the rainbow interiors of the head are revealed (West n.d.). The works of Craig Walsh, who maps the images of selected famous artists onto trees (Project Monuments: Creative Forces), are of an ecocritical nature.

Kuang-Yi Ku's projects seem to exhibit the most iconoclastic character among artistic approaches to the critical postcollectivity of the face (Ku, n.d.). This Taiwanese artist boasts three majors–one of them being a degree in dentistry; Ku even obtained a PhD in this field. The artist employs his unusual professional skills in the projects. They are embedded in the LBGTQ perspective and constitute a bioart exploration of interspecies relationships, efficiency technologies and medical procedures perceived from the perspective of sexuality and queer studies. One of his wide-reaching projects is called *Fellatio modification project*. It is a set of artistic activities in which the creator considers the possibilities of radical transformations of the oral cavity in order to increase the sensory pleasure during oral sex. The first of the projects in this series has not yet been fully related to the face, as it is a "dental" investigation of the possibility of growing specific appendages and protrusions on the palate (through cellular engineering), which increase the pleasure of the penis stimulated with such a modified mouth. The second project appears even more radical, as it is a study of the reconstruction of the entire mouthpiece into a specific "bird's beak." Inspired by gay culture, the artist proposes a series of cosmetic surgeries to extend the mandible, so that the representatives of this community subjected to treatments create a new subculture fascinated by oral sex and ready for new sensations. A "bird's beak" would also be an unequivocal manifesto of belonging to a specific sexual orientation. The project gives rise to a discussion on the limits of body modification and surgical operations, which until now have been used to eliminate disability, and also on aesthetic procedures. This time, the artist asks whether radical treatments motivated by sexual pleasure will be socially acceptable–described as radical as they do not concern only "hidden" sex organs, but also the face, which is commonly visible and associated with personality.

5   Conclusion

The examples of postcollective activities related to designing, reconfiguring, and criticising the face presented in this chapter aimed at indicating the interpretative capacity and diversity of the area of research on this part of the body in technological and cultural contexts. This diversity relates not only to the social, medical, and artistic practices that can be observed nowadays, but also to a wide spectrum of historical activities and projects. The face as a transversal system of powers and affects appears in all these activities as an area "for a moment"–a temporal construct, constituted by the force of centripetal unification processes and the centrifugal force of assemblage. As Massimo Leone, the leader of the FACETS research project, stated on the importance of the face in the digital age:

> The way in which a culture constructs the nature of a face, as well as the way in which nature underpins the cultures of the face, must be investigated with sophisticated tools, attentive to the communicative predicament of the visage.
>
> 2021, 11

In such a case, studies on the face, and in particular on its postcollective constitution, appear to be extremely significant, as they show the specificity of naturecultures influencing one of the most important body organs.[4] Furthermore, they give certain answers as to how the transversal subjectivity that emerges at the intersection of biological, technological and semiotic orders is periodically constituted and manifested (precisely in the form of a face), also as an effect and field of operation of the market, biopolitics and social discourses.

References

Agamben, Giorgio (2020) Un paese senza volto. *Quodlibet.* October 8. Available at: https://www.quodlibet.it/giorgio-agamben-un-paese-senza-volto

Agamben, Giorgio (2000) The Face. In: Agamben, G. (ed) *Means without End: Notes on Politics* (Vol. 20). Minneapolis: University of Minnesota Press, 91–100.

Ajder, Henry, Patrini, Giorgio, Cavalli, Francesco et al. (2019) *The State of Deepfakes: Landscape, Threats, and Impact.* Amsterdam: Deeptrace.

Alberti, Fay Bound (2017) From face/off to the face race: The case of Isabelle Dinoire and the future of the face transplant. *Medical Humanities* 43(3): 148–154.

Alexander, Caroline (2007) Faces of war. Amid the horrors of World War I, a corps of artists brought hope to soldiers disfigured in the trenches. *Smithsonian Magazine.* Available at: https://www.smithsonianmag.com/arts-culture/faces-of-war-145799854/

Azzarello, Nina (2016) *José cardoso's play-doh people meld molded matter with portrait photos.* Designboom. Architecture & Design Magazine. Available (consulted June 11 2023) at: https://www.designboom.com/art/jose-cardosos-play-doh-people-photography-04-29-2016/

Bignall, Simone (2012) Dismantling the face: pluralism and the politics of recognition. *Deleuze Studies* 6(3), 389–410. https://doi.org/10.3366/dls.2012.0071

Braidotti, Rosi (2006) Posthuman, all too human: towards a new process ontology. *Theory, Culture & Society* 23(7–8): 197–208. https://doi.org/10.1177/0263276406069232

Braidotti, Rosi (2013) *The Posthuman.* Polity Press.

Braidotti, Rosi (2019) Transversal posthumanities. *Philosophy Today* 63(4): 1181–1195. https://doi.org/10.5840/philtoday2020128318

Braidotti, Rosi (2022) *Posthuman Feminism.* Cambridge: Polity Press.

---

4 The U.S. Federal Health Policy defines face as an organ since 2014 in relation to first face transplantations, (see Taylor-Alexander 2014).

Brigham and Women's Hospital (2012) *Dallas Wiens, First Full Face Transplant in U.S. – Brigham and Women's Hospital.* (n.d.) Available (consulted June 11 2023) at: https://www.brighamandwomens.org/about-bwh/newsroom/face-transplant-wiens

Chesney, Robert and Citron, Danielle K. (2019) Deep fakes: a looming challenge for privacy, democracy, and national security. *California Law Review* 107: 1753–1819.

Clark, Kate (n.d.) Kate Clark. Artist's website. Available at: https://www.kateclark.com

Darwin, Charles (1872) *The Expression of the Emotions in Man and Animals.* John Murray.

Deleuze, Gilles (1986a) *Cinema 1: The Movement-Image* (Hugh Tomlinson H and Habberjam B, Trans.). Athlone.

Deleuze, Gilles (1986b) *Cinema 2: The Time-Image* (Tomlinson H and Galeta R, Trans.). University of Minnesota.

Deleuze, Gilles and Guattari, Félix (1983) *Anti-Oedipus: Capitalism and Schizophrenia.* Minneapolis: University of Minnesota Press.

Deleuze, Gilles and Guattari, Félix (1987) *A Thousand Plateaus: Capitalism and Schizophrenia.* Minneapolis: University of Minnesota Press.

Descovich, Kris A., Wathan, Jennifer, Leach, Mathew C. et al. (2017) Facial expression: An under-utilised tool for the assessment of welfare in mammals. *ALTEX*. https://doi.org/10.14573/altex.1607161

Edson, Gary (2005) *Masks and Masking: Faces of Tradition and Belief Worldwide.* McFarland & Co.

Ekman, Paul (1973) *Darwin and Facial Expression: a Century of Research in Review.* Academic Press.

Ekman, Paul (1980) *The Face of Man: Expressions of Universal Emotions in a New Guinea Village.* Garland STPM Press.

Ekman, Paul (1985) *Telling Lies: Clues to Deceit in the Marketplace, Politics, and Marriage.* w.w. Norton.

Ekman, Paul and Friesen, Wallace V. (1978) *Facial Action Coding System: Manual.* Consulting Psychologists Press.

Ekman, Paul, Friesen, Wallace V., Ellsworth, Phoebe (1972) *Emotion in the Human Face: Guidelines for Research and an Integration of Findings.* Elsevier Science. Available at: https://public.ebookcentral.proquest.com/choice/publicfullrecord.aspx?p=1838543

Emigh, John (2011) Minding bodies: demons, masks, archetypes, and the limits of culture. *Journal of Dramatic Theory and Criticism* 25(2): 125–139. https://doi.org/10.1353/dtc.2011.0025

Failes, Ian (2017) Rachael reborn: the making of the stunning scene from *Blade Runner 2049*. *VFX Voice Magazine*. Available (consulted June 11 2023) at: https://www.vfxvoice.com/rachael-reborn-the-making-of-the-stunning-scene-from-blade-runner-2049/

Fudge, Erica (2013) The animal face of early modern England. *Theory, Culture & Society* 30(7–8): 177–198. https://doi.org/10.1177/0263276413496122

Garland-Thomson, Rosemarie (1997) *Extraordinary Bodies: Figuring Physical Disability in American Culture and Literature*. New York: Columbia University Press.

Griggs, Lee (n.d.) Lee Griggs. Artist's website. Available at: https://leegriggs.com/projects

Guattari, Félix (2015) *Machinic Eros*. Minneapolis: University of Minnesota Press.

Guattari, Félix (2010) Signifying faciality, diagrammatic faciality. In: Adkins, T (Trans.), *The Machinic Unconscious: Essays in Schizoanalysis*. Semiotext(e).

Haraway, Donna (2009) *The Companion Species Manifesto: Dogs, People and Significant Otherness*. Prickly Paradigm Press.

King, Darryn (2019) Game-changing tech behind "young" Will Smith in *Gemini Man*. Wired. Available at: https://www.wired.com/story/game-changing-tech-gemini-man-will-smith/

Ku, Kuang-Yi (n.d.) *Kuang-Yi Ku–Artist page*. Available at: https://www.kukuangyi.com/

Leone, Massimo (2021) Volti artificiali/Artificial faces. Preface. *Lexia. Journal of Semiotics* 37–38: 9–25.

Meekosha, Helen and Shuttleworth, Russell (2009) What's so critical about critical disability studies? *Australian Journal of Human Rights* 15: 47–75. https://doi.org/10.1080/1323238X.2009.11910861

Meskys, Edvinas, Kalpokiene, ulijaJ, Jurcys, Paulius et al. (2020) Regulating deep fakes: Legal and ethical considerations. *Journal of Intellectual Property Law & Practice* 15(1): 24–31.

Napier, David A. (1987) *Masks, Transformation, and Paradox*. Oakland: University of California Press.

Parr, Lisa A. and Waller, Bridget M. (2006) Understanding chimpanzee facial expression: Insights into the evolution of communication. *Social Cognitive and Affective Neuroscience* 1(3): 221–228. https://doi.org/10.1093/scan/nsl031

Pizurny, Adam (n.d.) Adam Pizurny (@adam.pizurny) Instagram profile. Available at: https://www.instagram.com/adam.pizurny/

Schick, Nina (2020) *Deep Fakes and the Infocalypse: What You Urgently Need to Know*. Hachette UK.

Segy, Ladislas (1976) *Masks of Black Africa*. Courier Corporation.

Siebers, Tobin (2017) Disability and the theory of complex embodiment: for identity politics in a new register. In: Davis, LJ (ed.), *The Disability Studies Reader* (5th Edition). Routledge, Taylor & Francis Group.

Silvers, Anita (2003) On the possibility and desirability of constructing a neutral conception of disability. *Theoretical Medicine and Bioethics* 24(6): 471–487. https://doi.org/10.1023/b:meta.0000006924.82156.5b

Taylor-Alexander, Samuel (2014) How the face became an organ. (2014, August 11) *Somatosphere*. Available at: http://somatosphere.net/2014/how-the-face-became-an-organ.html/

The Telegraph (2022) Deepfake" video shows Volodymyr Zelensky telling Ukrainians to surrender. *The Telegraph*, March 17 2022. Available at: https://www.telegraph.co.uk/world-news/2022/03/17/deepfake-video-shows-volodymyr-zelensky-telling-ukrainians-surrender/

This Person Does Not Exist. (n.d.) website. Available at: https://thispersondoesnotexist.com/

Video Dialogue Replacement (n.d.) Canny. Available at: https://www.cannyai.com

West, Cristina A. (n.d.) *Busts: Unmet Series – Christina A. West*. Artist's website. Available at: https://www.cwestsculpture.com/gallery/busts-unmet-series

Yoon, Dain (n.d.) *Dain Yoon 윤다인* (@designdain. Instagram profile). Available at: https://www.instagram.com/designdain/

Zakharov, Egor, Shysheya, Aliaksandra, Burkov, Egor et al. (2019) *Few-Shot Adversarial Learning of Realistic Neural Talking Head Models* (arXiv:1905.08233; Version 1). Available (consulted June 11 2023) at: https://deepai.org/publication/few-shot-adversarial-learning-of-realistic-neural-talking-head-models

Zevnik, Andreja (2016a) Lacan, Deleuze and the politics of the face. In: Nedoh, Boštjan and Zevnik, Andreja (eds) *Lacan and Deleuze: A Disjunctive Synthesis* (pp. 74–92). Eup.

Zevnik, Andreja (2016b) The politics of the face: the scopic regime and the (un-)masking of the political subject. *Journal for Cultural Research* 20(2): 122–136. https://doi.org/10.1080/14797585.2015.1090656

CHAPTER 13

The Silicon Gender
Technological Species and the Transgression of Model Sexes

Ania Malinowska

This contribution explores the possibility of trans-organic gender opened up by the proliferation of technological species into the human context (robots, bots, digients, sims, holographic entities etc.), a proliferation that invites questions about the future of human communities and its organizing aspects. Using the slightly provocative notion of *silicon gender*, this paper aims to revisit the human element in the increasingly hybrid social environment with regard to robot culture (Semani et al. 2013) understood as a factor in mediating human cohabitation styles and their social semiotics. Central to this analysis will be the underexplored issue of *technological gender* – the immediate and most tangible effect of robot culture materialized in the robot figure (and its aforementioned derivatives), which overcomes the Western episteme of the sexes by means of its inherent genderlessness. With this, my contribution signals the potential of trans-organic gender manifested in the robot's gender otherness that surpasses the existing "model sexes". It specifically discusses how this potential of genderlessness is being lost in the process of appropriating technological entities to the existing gender templates and considers what epistemological and practical possibilities that potential could create. Drawing on cultural theories of robot cultures, this contribution discusses technological species as "subjects" that introduce gender difference beyond the organic episteme and cyborg mixed materiality, and points towards perceiving, understanding and theorizing a postmaterial gender-fluidity.

The proliferation of technological subjects (robots, digients, sims, holographs) and the inclusion of digitally engendered entities into the "human environment" have opened new possibilities for the idea of postgender societies. Anticipated through fiction, critical writing and social activism, postgenderism subscribes to a hard-won departure from binary sexes with the goal of ensuring a more transversal experience of "embodiment" for individuals and communities. In many of its forms across the ages, *postgenderism* has evolved into "an extrapolation of ways that technology is eroding the biological, psychological and social role of gender, and an argument for why the erosion of binary gender will be liberatory" (Hughes and Dvorsky 2008, 45). Postgenderists believe that being an "arbitrary and unnecessary limitation on human potential", gender – understood as "involuntary biological and psychological gendering in the human species" – can, or even should be eliminated "through the application of neurotechnology, biotechnology and reproductive technologies" (Hughes and Dvorsky 2008, 45). A big flaw in this approach to gender revolution is the approach's exclusive concentration on humans. In other words, postgenderist agendas completely ignore the cultural presence and social significance of technological objects (disembodied technologies and embodied robots). At the same time, they overlook technological gender as standard of postgenderism and a beacon in the problem of binary sexes. This is visible as much in cultural criticism as in the strategies for restructuring model genders in a social context.

When it comes to technologies, we seem to be stuck in a certain experiential paradox: on the one hand, we invite intelligent machines into our context, on the other, we undermine their "organic" and social potentials. In the era of post-automation, machine-systems are becoming more self-organized (and self-organizing); they co-create the life environment and develop their own. Parallel to human culture, specific machine (or robot) cultures emerge due to the robots' ability to act beyond their operational structuring (the transcendence of the manufacture function). Despite efforts to anthropomorphize technological species, robot cultures are idiosyncratic, impactful and demanding. They are different from the cultures of people, and challenge significant aspects of human societies, especially the perception of time (machinic time vs. human time), the mode of efficiency (calculability vs. computationality), the manner of social co-existence (collaborative vs. networked), and embodiment (cellular vs. silicone). The latter in particular poses doubts about the logic of human social policies and is perhaps the first reason for the urgency of rethinking the human way. Hybrid societies, understood as co-habitation with technological species, is not a project of a distant future. It is happening now. Technological gender (which I playfully call "silicon") is a strong premise of the transversality invariably demanded by the emergence of robot culture and the possibility of its co-existence with the human one.

The vision of human-robot society has been with us for over a century. It is only recently, however, that "hybrid culture" gained traction due to the changing role of technological objects "from that of a tool to a social entity" (Samani et al. 2013). Studies in cultural robotics discuss the distinct importance of robot culture, identifying its development in relation to human environments but also independently of human contexts. They say that apart from augmenting human functions as assistants, playmates, companions and partners, technological agents form communities of their own, creating culture of and for themselves. Samani et al. explain that "Robot Community Culture" means a multitude of cultural aspects like the "values, customs, attitudes, artefacts" created by and for the robot community or multi-agent systems. In this sense, robot culture denotes a cultural formation authored by robots and their influence.

> Robot culture refers to values that robots themselves may hold and could eventually move towards the construction of a distinct robot culture. The prerequisites for robots to evolve "culture" in the human definition would be an independent, critical and self-reflective mind that develops in a way that leads to consciousness and, ideally, self-awareness of the robot. Such a trend could lead to the creation of culture created by robots, such as robot created artefacts, ... robotic ethics and many other cultural values, and as such would be beyond the grasp of current human understanding as it would be rooted in a distinctly "robotic" condition.
> SAMANI et al. 2013

Thusly defined, "robot communities" implies that robot cultures will move beyond human cultural premises, and that instead of emulating human constructs, robots will shape standards of their own. This is a strong position against the *robotic imaginary* ("the anthropocentric vision that organizes robotics", Rhee 2018) responsible for anthropomorphic design: a manufacture idea of transferring human behaviour patterns and social stereotypes onto technical "things".

The problem with our western imaginary is that it envisages robot cultures as meant to do things *for* humans and not *with* humans (see Turkle 2006). Prevailing cultural rhetoric around robotics rely on a discourse of servitude and appropriation. From the most significant and formative concepts such as *Three Laws of Robotics* (Asimov, 2004 [1950]), *the robot slave theory* (Bryson 2010), *robot apocalypse and malicious AI* (e.g. Bostrom 2014), *companion species* (Levy 2007; 2016; Paterson 2018) – to more socially oriented, e.g. *robot personhood* (Jones 2016), *robot ethics* (Gunkel 2012; 2018), *robotic mimicry* (Breazeal 2002) – the model of social conduct deemed applicable for robot cultures is imposed through reference to the concept of humaneness. Even the more progressive (i.e., robotically inclined) critical perspectives hardly ever forget the human lens. Particularly problematic are voices preoccupied with robot ethics (e.g., Lyn et al. 2012), which tend to see robots as subjects "composed of human-complied facts" (Menzel and D'Alusio 2001, 17). Similarly, studies in artificial consciousness and emotions, (Picard 1995; Minsky 2007) reflect

THE SILICON GENDER   227

an interest in the robot's performance in terms of how it can mimic human behaviour or read human emotional states.

Until the non-human turn, the parlance around technological species was almost unanimously anthropomorphic. Once posthuman philosophy of technology emerged as a dynamic area of inquiry to offer a robot-oriented take on robot-human situations, various lines of thought and theoretical thinking (e.g., new materialism, speculative realism, object-oriented ontology) started to focus on decentering the human in favor of a concern for the non-human (Grusin 2015). Notable interventions in relation to technological subjects have proposed a disorientation (Ahmed 2006) – a radical departure from human materialism by adapting/professing *alien phenomenology* (Bogost 2012) and experiential *discognition* (Shaviro 2016). Those propositions have opted for devaluing human experiences of knowing and feeling. That includes an interest in *thalience* (Schroeder 2000) – the self-organizing properties of distributed networks – that spread from fiction into the theory of intelligent technological systems to consider the systems' qualia and affordances (including their "emotional" and operational idiosyncrasies) for defining artificial "organisms" and their related cultures.

Multiple threads of culturally sustainable social robotics (Nørskov et al. 2020) started to spread in response to philosophical social studies of technology with the aim of considering the self-organizing potential of robots and their idiosyncratic cultural criteria. They are also a reaction to the latest legal initiatives around intelligent machines: the European Parliament's bill on "electronic persons"; residency for chatbots in Tokyo; citizenship for android Sophia in Saudi Arabia; and marriages between humans and robots. Those initiatives – as they have shown a deep ignorance of robot cultures with regard to major cultural categories such as identity, agency and gender – reveal a nostalgia for variants of corporeality, subjectivity and embodiment different from that of a human.

The idea of *silicon gender* I propose in this chapter is a response to the gender paradox we have lived through for centuries: on the one hand, we cultivate human notions of the sexes, on the other we strive to transcend them. Our attempts, however, overlook possibilities that are there before our eyes. One of them is the robot thing – the embodiment of silicon gender. The uniqueness of the robot body (embodied or not) is its gender neutrality. As such, the robot body proffers an almost "infinite repository of physical experience in all possible contexts": "[m]aterially, it is inorganic and ontologically nonhuman (and, for that matter, nonanimal). It is innately genderless and possesses a form of intelligence whose singularity, once it is finally revealed, will expose to us a new dimension of sensory and cognitive experience" (Malinowska

2019, 90–91). And yet, the robot is perhaps the most undertheorized subject and certainly the most neglected concept with a potential for rehearsing the gender-free paradigm. The general problem with robots now is that, holding so much scholarly interest, they are fundamentally misapprehended, wrongly conceptualized, and critically misplaced.

Many aspects of their nature and functioning are simply missing from the conversation. Especially the issue of a robot's gender which, although widely debated in social robotics (mostly in terms of robots effective gendering), is still scarce in a wider cultural debate. When I say, "most undertheorized," I mean given proper attention from those fields of cultural critique that could analyze robots and robots' issues with regard to their actual "orientation" (sexual, material). I mean attention that could take the debate beyond the anthropocentric core: that is, beyond human categories in order to interrogate robotic beings in terms of what they ontologically are, and also what they may mean as such for human reality and cultural practice in a broad sense.

Of course, feminist studies have signaled the problem of sexing technologies through denominations of cyborgology – a posthuman school of thought that emerged in the 1980s – that have systematized the awareness of "automating gender" (as Halberstam has it in 1991). They have highlighted the impact that gender automatisms, understood figuratively and literally, have exerted on the cultural fusions of sexes and technology in social contexts. More recently, debates about the feminization of technological subjects have sparked to comment and criticize the domestication of technological species (Alesich and Rigby 2017; Sutko 2020; Fryxel 2021). Yet, those voices, although effective and most needed, do not solve the mis-conceptualization of robots as ontological beings. It is partly due to the prevalence (and perhaps theoretical monopoly) of the cyborg myth that subsumes the robotic being.

As described by Donna Haraway, a founder of cyborgology for cultural criticism, a cyborg is "a hybrid of machine and organism," i.e., an 'entity' combining a human body with non-human technological elements – an 'entity' that is inherently organic (and usually human), extended (or extending itself – literally or symbolically) by means of non-organic parts. Because it reaches beyond the structure of its own system, a cyborg alters the sense of its material self and the senses related to its materiality and organicness. A cyborg, to quote Timothy W. Luke, is "a ... lifeform ... that (con)fuses man and organism, animal and apparatus, physical matter and non-physical information, [making] thoroughly ambiguous the difference between natural and artificial, mind and body, self-developing and externally designed, and many other distinctions that used to apply to organisms and machines" (2000, 40). Being a form in-between, a cyborg is a life and a body in a transition, transforming itself from what it is (what it was born like) towards what it is inspired to be; or in other words, from what it was preconditioned, predetermined for, towards what it might become. It is a body in a constant passage, operating by the imperative of transfiguration, moving between polarities: from natural towards artificial, from human towards machinic, from organic to non-organic, from gendered to gender-neutral. Which means that as transgressive and transversal as the body is, it is never free of its original inscriptions.

So, when Haraway calls a cyborg "a creature of a post-gender world [that] has no truck with bisexuality, per-oedipal symbiosis, unalienated labour, or other seductions to organic wholeness" (2003, 150), she cannot mean a body with "no ontological grounding of Western epistemology" (2003, 153) – (even though she wants to). She can only mean a body that merely distances itself from the grounding – this distancing being propelled by the awareness that there is no transcendent authority, no legitimized interpretation, no *hors texte* but "heterogeneity ... submitted to disassembly, reassembly, investment, [and] exchange" (Haraway 2003, 164).

A robot, on the other hand, is a form that we may call epistemologically undetermined, mostly in the sense that it represents 'life' from outside the human existential system. It is inherently inorganic (or machinic as I prefer to term it) and is always already grounded in culture as a human-made artifact – a thing. Materially, a robot is a homogenous (non-hybrid) structure evolving along designed trajectories of technological progression. It is a "creature" whose development happens within ontologically uniform frames, involving only questions of complexity and function, but undisturbed by the conflicting dualities of young and old, able and disabled, homo and hetero, or finally, male and female. Robots are bodies without sex, and fundamentally (to quote Bill Vorn) "characters that are nothing more but simple articulated metal structures" (2014, 15). Of course, this gets complicated with the rapid advancements in robotics that clearly make robots "more than factory workers" (Menzel and D'Aluisio 2001,19).

Advanced or not, robots are essentially genderless creatures. The post-gender potential coming from this for the post-model-sexes reality is that, unlike any other "creatures" (except for aliens perhaps), robots have offered us a "tangible" opportunity for testing relations (social and private) unburdened by sexual polarities. Sadly, instead of taking it up, we have fought it with the systematic gendering of robots in cultural practice. What I mean by the gendering of robots is their naturalization by means of sexual "attributes" which, when appropriated, may predispose robots for certain social or cultural roles. Just as homosexuals have been naturalized to adhere to the standards of a normalcy – a process that Moe Meyer calls "bourgeois assimilationism", robots are being naturalized to the physiognomic, intellectual and emotional standards of the "domineering" species (that of humanity) to become compatible assistants, companions, and partners that we, humans tend to prefer over [companions] of our own kind.

Louise J. Kaplan defines this as the *anthropomorphic drive* – a motivation bred by human fantasies "that certain objects in the world are endowed with human characteristics" (2006, 161). It connects with a *hubris drive* inspiring those fantasies that "they are able to breathe life into inanimate objects" (ibid). It also connects with something I call *a fear/anxiety drive* – a motivation to eliminate "otherness" from the other so that it does not endanger the *status quo*. Technological development has thus been entangled with and spurred a massive conflict: on the one hand, we want innovation, on the other we are apprehensive about it. Interestingly, this apprehension has also never been gender neutral. To quote Lee MacKinnon (2016) "anxieties [that] appear around devices that outwit, or outperform their human creators" [take the form of] "anxious narratives about our reliance upon technical devices [that usually feature] female cyborgs, reflecting the particular anxiety that women too will outperform the patriarchal order that has long defined them as *other*." "It is striking", Andreas Huyssen observes, "to see how the later literature prefers the machine-woman to machine-man. ... Woman, nature, machine had become a mesh of significations which all had one thing in common: otherness; by their very existence they raised fears and threatened male authority and control" (1986, 70).

Conversely, radical feminism has masculinized technocracy, associating it with a proliferation of "master tools" that take the patriarchal subjugation of women to another level. For instance, Mary Daly speaks of "robotitude" and "roboticide" – the effects of "machinical masculinist progress [...aimed at] the elimination of female Self-centering reality" (1978: 53, 56). One way or another, the gendering of the machine has determined the placement of robots in the social context, creating a model-sexes-oriented pattern for human-machine relations. Whether through a gendered design and programming or a discursive practice, the orientation of – and towards – technological species has been squandered. I am using the term orientation after Sara Ahmed (2006) to bring up what she calls "tending towards objects", a method facilitating perspectives that open us to the idiosyncratic qualities and affordances of all subjects. In Ahmed's terms, orientation refers to the positioning of things whereby things may be objects or people or animals or technological entities "that are reachable, that are available within the bodily horizon" (2006, 2). Orientation also relates to the "natural" / "inherent" or "imposed / acquired" predisposition or preference (also sexual) with which things related spatially may impact one another, and which they may use to verify their own situations. To disorient,

Ahmed writes, "is to disturb the order of things" (2006, 3), and to disturb the order of things means to disorient oneself. Disorientation is an act of questioning the dominant (or familiar) coordinates of life – modes of perception, ways of thinking, patterns of judgment – inscribed in our orientation. Through disorientation, objects (human or non-human) rearrange themselves (and one another) and enter into relationships that exclude, or at least neutralize, the imperative of mutual appropriation. In human-robot dynamics, disorientation would mean the rejection of the anthropomorphizing model: in this instance the model of the sexes. This would call for new rhetoric around technologies and robot imageries – ones able to open acceptance of the otherness (and strangeness) of the robotic "way". Consequently, it would mean an engagement with (and adaptation to) a different way of life – a disoriented one, which, as Ahmed admits, is not an easy thing, and never a first option, as it induces fear, discomfort, and a sense of loss (as such an alternative puts us far from everything we know). Perhaps for exactly that reason the possibility of the genderless experiment offered by robots has never properly kicked in. Maybe such an experiment would be too demanding, too scary, too gruesome to embrace.

And yet, far from philosophical speculation, practical robotics is slowly taking the trouble. Echoing cultural critics, AI and robot designers more and more willingly admit that "humanoid robots are the vanguard of posthuman sexism," and that they "are being developed within the reactionary rhetorical climate" (Robertson 2010, 1). Solutions for disorientations in this regard include explanation, neutralization, or queering (Weßel at al. 2021). They mean new knowledge, new perception and new contextualization of gender for technological subjects. This is to eliminate gender-triggered judgement and inequality from human-robot interactions. Proponents of those solutions situate their strategies with regard to the general problems that gendering causes in social relations. They explain that their methods would help overcome the "totality" of model genders both for devices and for humans. The first strategy – *explanation* would employ classical pedagogics of enlightenment, assuming that

> if the function and task of the robot is adequately explained to the users, they will learn to see it for what it really is: a machine without any gender or other human features. They will no longer project anthropomorphic characteristics onto the robot to define it as a quasi-human companion but see it as a purely functional technical device. Indeed, some argue that adequate knowledge about the technical characteristics and the presumed suitability for the intended task can reduce stereotypical judgement effects.
> WESSEL et al. 2021

The second strategy – *neutralization* – would highlight the genderless nature of a robot with an aim to eschew any gender associations.

> [S]uch a robot would even help to avoid stereotypes that are pervasive in human interaction. It could be designed to look indeterminate and have features that can neither be interpreted as male nor as female. It could speak with a neutral voice and act in a gender-neutral manner. Such a neutral robot might not only solve problems regarding gender stereotypes but also intercultural conflicts of understanding gender attributes and other social categories, for example regarding race, as well as preventing possible robo-sexism in the context of sexist embodiment of a robot.
> WESSEL et al. 2021

Option three, that of *queering*, draws on the premise of feminist and queer theories "to deconstruct normalizing conceptions of identity".

> This strategy comprises a flexible and subversive (re-)combination and implementation of social categories. It suggests a non-binary and fluid gender attribution to robots that challenges common stereotypes without neglecting individual user preferences. Thus, queering might be able to acknowledge the inevitable relevance of gender aspects in human-robot interaction while at the same time challenging their conventional and normalizing application and promotion. This way, it could support an inclusive approach that also considers discriminated and marginalized groups.
> WESSEL et al. 2021

Those approaches are expected to eliminate the myopia of gender binarism and replace it with gender fluidity as a notion for conceptualizing a robot's orientation. They are also expected to help overcome the ideas of runaway technological growth making machines surpass human intelligence. It is important to foster the conviction that, being an innovation, technological entities are not a threat. Humans must start to believe that robot autonomy need not mean an extermination of the human race. Nor does it need to involve the apocalypse so often associated with it. *Silicon gender* – very different from what we have learned to regard as the sexes – will certainly defamiliarize our notions and cultures of embodiments to the point of making us believe that (to quote Burroughs) "the whole quality of human consciousness, as expressed in male in and female, is basically a virus mechanism" and that "the whole human position is no longer tenable" (Burroughs 1981, 25). Reclaiming robot cultures based on the awareness of robot values and affordances is a significant step in this process. The transformation for gender transversality will require a new robotic hermeneutics which reads gender (and gender-related categories such as subjectivity, social function, agency, cohabitation, etc.) as a bottom-up concept, and which will envisage technological species as independent and capable of developing their own emotional and social cultures and cultural values beyond human understanding. Such speculative re-readings may help bridge the gap between critical and practical robotics as well as its related design foresight. They may also help answer broader questions about the cultural role of intelligent machines.

What bearing would the acceptance of *silicon gender* (as a fourth sex) have on our post-Anthropocentric reality? How would gender irrelevance affect social organization, including the organization of labor, social relations and other inter-subject dynamics? And more importantly, how would a negotiation or elimination of major cultural categories influence the shape and functioning of hybrid societies? Changed or not, those categories have a specific resonance with technological species. To understand this resonance, engineering and design require progressive cultural thinking that accepts the reality of robot cultures as distinct from human culture.

References

Ahmed, Sara (2006) *Queer Phenomenology. Orientations, Objects, Others*. Durham and London: Duke University Press.
Alesich, Simone and Rigby, Michael (2017) Gendered robots: Implications for our humanoid future, *IEEE Technology and Society Magazine* 36(2): 50–59.
Asimov, Isaac (2004) *I, Robot*. New York: Bantam Books.
Bogost, Ian (2012) *Alien Phenomenology. Or What's it Like to Be a Thing*. Minneapolis: University of Minnesota Press.
Bostrom, Nick (2014) *Superintelligence. Paths, Dangers, Strategies*. Oxford: Oxford University Press.
Breazeal, Cynthia (2002) *Designing Social Robots*. Cambridge MA: MIT Press.
Bryson, Joanna J. (2010) Robots should be slaves. In: Wilks, Y (ed.) *Close Engagements with Artifcial Companions. Key Social, Psychological, Ethical and Design Issues*. Amsterdam, PH: John Benjamins, 63–74.
Burroughs, William S. (1981) *Cities of the Red Night*. New York: Holt, Rinehart and Winston.
Daly, Mary (1978) *Gyn/Ecology: the Metaethics of Radical Feminism*. Boston: Beacon Press.

Fryxell, Allegra (2021) Artificial eye: the modernist origins of AI's gender problem, *Discourse* 43(1): 31–64.
Grusin, Richard (2015) *The Nonhuman Turn*. Minneapolis: University of Minnesota Press.
Gunkel, David J. (2018) *Robot Rights*. Cambridge, MA: MIT Press.
Gunkel, David J. (2012) *The Machine Question Critical Perspectives on AI, Robots, and Ethics*. Cambridge, MA: MIT Press.
Halberstam, Judith (1991) Automating gender. Postmodern feminism in the age of intelligent machine, *Feminist Studies* 17(3): 439–460.
Haraway, Donna (2003) *The Companion Species Manifesto. Dogs, People, and Significant Otherness*. Chicago: University of Chicago Press.
Hughes, James J. and Dvorsky, George (2008) Postgenderism: Beyond the gender binary. *Institute for Ethnics and Emerging Technologies* 20: 44–57.
Huyssen, Andreas (1986) *After the Great Divide: Modernism, Mass Culture and Postmodernism*. Bloomington: Indiana University Press.
Jones, Raya (2016) *Personhood and Social Robotics*. New York: Routledge.
Kaplan, Louise J. (2006) *Cultures of Fetishism*. New York: Palgrave McMillan.
Levy, David (2007) *Love + Sex with Robots. The Evolution of Human-Robot Relationships*. New York: Harper Perennial.
Levy, David (2016) Why not to marry a robot. In: Cheock, AD et al. (eds) *Love and Sex with Robots*. Second International Conference, LSR 2016, London, UK, December 19–20, 2016. Revised Selected Papers, Cham: Springer, 3–16.
Luke, Timothy W. (2000) Cyborg enchantments: Commodity fetishism and human/machine interactions. *Strategies: Journal of Theory, Culture and Politics* 13(1): 39–62.
Lyn, Patrick, Abney, Keith and Bekey, George A. (2012) *Robot Ethics. The Ethical and Social Implications of Robotics*. Cambridge, MA: MIT Press.
MacKinnon, Lee (2016) Love machines and the Tinderbot bildungsroman. *e-flux*. Available at: https://www.e-flux.com/journal/74/59802/love-machines-and-the-tinder-bot-bildungsroman/
Malinowska, Ania (2019) Robot gender. A provocation, *Girls to the Front* 9: 18–22/90–93.
Menzel, Peter and D'Alusio, Faith (2001) *Robo Sapiens. The Evolution of a New Species*. Cambridge, MA: MIT Press.
Minsky, Marvin (2007) *Emotion Machine. Commonsense Thinking Artificial Intelligence, and the Future of the Human Mind*. New York: Simon and Schuster.
Nørskov, Marco, Seibt, Johanna and Quick, Oliver S. (2020) *Culturally Sustainable Social Robotics: Proceedings of Robophilosophy*. IOS Press: Amsterdam.
Paterson, Mark (2018) *Animal Automata and Living Machines in Literature and Philosophy: Robots, Replicants, and Companion Species*. New York: Routledge.
Picard, Rosalind (1995) *Affective Computing*. Cambridge, MA: MIT Press.
Rhee, Jennifer (2018) *Robotic Imaginary. The Human and the Prize of Dehumanized Labour*. Minneapolis and London: University of Minnesota Press.

Robertson, Jennifer (2010) Gendering humanoid robots: Robo-sexism in Japan *Body and Society* 16(2): 1–36.

Samani, Hooman, Saadatian, Elham and Tzu, Kwan Valino Koh Jeffrey (2013) Cultural robotics: the culture of robotics and robotics in culture, *International Journal of Advanced Robotic Systems* 10(400): 1–10.

Shaviro, Steven (2016) *Discognition*. London: Repeater Books.

Schroeder, Karl (2000) *Ventus*. New York: Tor Books.

Sutko, Daniel M. (2020) Theorizing femininity in artificial intelligence. A framework for undoing technology's gender trouble. *Cultural Studies* 34(4): 567–592.

Turkle, Sherry (2006) *A Nascent Robotics Culture. New Complicities for Companionship*. Boston: AAAI Technical Reports.

Vorn, Bill (2014) The cathartic theatre of robotic art. In: Kluszczyński, RW (ed.) *Robotic Art and Culture. Bill Vorn and His 'Hysterical Machines'*. Gdańsk: CSW Łaźnia, 15–40.

Weßel, Merle, Ellerich-Groppe, Niklas and Schweda, Mark (2021) Gender stereotyping of robotic systems in eldercare: an exploatory analysis of ethical problems and possible solutions, *International Journal of Social Robotics*. https://doi.org/10.1007/s12369-021-00854-X

CHAPTER 14

Towards a Postmonetary Collectivity

Jens Schröter

1 Introduction

We live in an age of crisis. Climate change, financial crises, pandemics ... It seems that there is nothing more important than to realize and establish new collectivities, even a new world collective, in order to survive. There are several aspects that are important for such new collectivities – here only one will be discussed (and also only addressing one detail): The question of how the capitalist organization of the economy can be overcome, given that its necessary drive to grow – and therefore its inevitable production of climate change – as well as its instability, seem to endanger all collectivity. This contribution takes the form of a speculative narrative that tries to bring to different theoretical fields into discussion. It addresses questions associated with the bottom-up self-organization of collectives and their medializations.

2 Two Ways of Conceptualizing Postmonetary Collectivities

There are two strangely disconnected currents in the discussion about alternatives to capitalism:[1] A first one, which I call the 'socialist calculation debate 2.0' (= SCD), and a second one, which I call, equally simplistically, the 'commons debate' (= CD). Although there seem to be points of contact between these fields, I have not yet been able to find a theoretical discussion that considers both.[2] What are the two positions I want to bring into discussion with each other? Let's start with SCD: The original debate took place mainly in the 1920s and 1930s (Vaughn 1980; Morozov 2019, 33–67). It was essentially about the question of whether a socialist economy, which at that time was

---

[1] Or the market economy, if one equates the two, a position which is by no means shared by all authors.
[2] Except in Simon Sutterlütti and Stefan Meretz (2018, 179–180). This reference is one of the central reasons for going into more detail on some points from this book. There are isolated references in the literature on Elinor Ostrom (see below). In the following all quotes from German are translated by the author.

understood to mean the steering of the economy top-down by central planning and/or market socialist models, could work or not. The central figures of the 'Austrian school', namely von Mises and von Hayek, vigorously contested this against their equally vigorous opponents such as Lange or Lerner. Put simply, the argument was that central planning (even if it worked with price signals) would not have and/or be able to process the *information* necessary for the economy to 'run' (especially with respect to the production of the means of production). One cannot know what should be produced – how, by whom, when, and in what way, with what raw materials, in what quantity – so that people get what they need (starting from this discussion, by the way, large parts of 20th century economic theory revolve around information, Hayek got the 'Nobel Prize' for economics in 1974; see Mirowski and Nik-Khah 2017). The discussion rippled back and forth, and the severe crisis of 1929 and in its aftermath the imposition of more regulated economies (the New Deal, postwar Keynesianism, the successes of real socialism – for in the 1950s and 1960s it was by no means so clear that this system would later collapse) seemed to disprove Mises and Hayek. Decades later: in 1989/90 the Eastern bloc collapsed, the miserable state of the planned economies became visible, and with people like Reagan and Thatcher neoliberal policies, clearly inspired by Hayek, prevailed. The end of history and the triumph of the market economy were proclaimed. Figures seem to show that absolute poverty declined. The question of an alternative to capitalism was off the table. Mises and Hayek seemed to have been proved right. But the crises came back: the crash of 2007/8, the growing extreme inequality, the climate change that was becoming unavoidable … In this atmosphere, a diverse and many-voiced discourse about 'post-capitalist' alternatives has thrived, and continues to thrive. I will go into the CD in a moment, now back to SCD.

It was increasingly asked whether the supposed certainty that the market economy was the informationally optimal economic form was really so true. Are the arguments of Mises and Hayek still valid today? Might supercomputers not be able to solve the countless equations needed to coordinate a country's economy? (Cockshott and Cottrell 1993; 1997; Cockshott et al. 2009) Can't mobile sensor technology (e.g. in smartphones) be used to collect precisely that wealth of data – and data is now being collected anyway (Google, Facebook, Amazon) – that is needed to feed the supercomputers?[3] So isn't a planned economy conceivable after all, combining the efficiency of markets

---

3 Precisely that was argued by the above-mentioned Morozov 2019. Cf. also Jasmin Kathöfer and Jens Schröter 2019.

with stability and with consideration of so-called 'externalities', such as ecosystems? Aren't large corporations functioning planned economies, in some cases larger than states? (Phillips and Rozworski 2019) Hadn't Hayek always stressed that even market economies must actually be described as decentralized planning – because every single person, every household, every company, every university plans? And if this is so, why does coordination between these units necessarily have to take place without collusion, but only via abstract price signals and then via competition? And did this picture ever correspond to reality? – after all, people can and do talk to each other. Is it really only price signals that transmit information? Numerous different approaches discuss such questions – some of them mathematically advanced. Certainly: Problems still remain. For instance, could centralized planning, no matter how well it works, supported by decentralized data collection in quasi-real time and by supercomputing (and perhaps 'artificial intelligence'), avoid authoritarian effects (which Hayek had always painted on the wall as a specter)? For the activities instructed by the plan, however democratically and cybernetically arrived at, would then have to be done and, if necessary, enforced by sanctions (Bernes 2020). It is also not clear how the transition to such an economy should proceed, since the disempowerment of capital ownership could certainly not be avoided.

In contrast to this perspective, which immediately focuses on the macro perspective of 'the economy', another discussion has developed relatively independently, which revolves around the 'commons' – we are at CD. To cut a long story short, in 1968 Hardin argued in an article that collective management of resources by a community could not work. As an example, take a meadow that is used by a number of farmers with their herds. As they all use the meadow ruthlessly, maximizing their own utility (just like the self-interest optimizers modeled by the prevailing neoclassical theory), the meadow is soon destroyed (Hardin 1968, 1244: "As a rational being, each herdsman seeks to maximize his gain."). Without market mechanisms or state intervention, common goods do not work – one can conclude. But in 2009, Elinor Ostrom gets the 'Nobel Prize' in Economics for a book published in 1990: *Governing the Commons*. In this book (meanwhile translated into German and many other languages) she shows, on the basis of theoretical considerations, historical research and numerous field studies, that – contrary to Hardin's claim – local self-governance of resources can work very well and even be superior to state and market solutions. The basic argument behind this is: If, according to Ostrom, the various users of the pasture agree and coordinate, exist as a collective, establish common rules and also control their compliance, then the meadow can be used together as common land, as a commons. There are many examples of this, some of them very long-lasting (Ostrom, 1990).[4]

From this comparison of SCD and CD, it is actually already clear why there is no discussion between these two currents: Because of scale.[5] While the discussion about the commons refers to local collectivities (some peasants communicating over a meadow), the SCD is about a whole national (or even bigger) economy. The SCD argues: Societies are too complex to be controlled by communicative agreements, that would take too long, if it is possible at all: Imagine a commons-like coordination at the level of the world society: Should 7 billion people discuss every local problem together until they have a solution? That wouldn't work, because even if everyone had only 10 seconds to speak on a given problem, it would amount to about 2220 years of discussion. This is just a caricature, of course, but it makes clear in a very simple way what complexity is and how complexity relates to time – and "Economy of time, to this all economy ultimately reduces itself." (Marx 1973, 173) It seems that the idea of separate private production – which Marx describes as typical for capitalism (Marx 1976, 132) – and later mediation of the results on local, regional, global markets is intuitively more convincing, because it is obviously logistically and medially more realistic. Complexity becomes decentralized and thus manageable. In this sense, Hayek remarked that economic problems would have to be solved by "some form of decentralization" (Hayek 1945, 524).

This would probably have been the end of the whole discussion (and especially after 1989/90 it was seen that way),[6] if the idea had not recently been formulated in the CD to propose the commons as a structural principle of a

---

4 Of course, her book has attracted much criticism, see, e.g., Walter Block and Ivan Jankovic 2016. This text is also interesting in that it emphasizes that Ostrom, with her emphasis on local organization, is herself in the Hayekian tradition, even if the authors accuse her of 'Pop-Hayekianism' (308). (See also Morozov 2019, 61).

5 And there is a difference of the historical position, see an email from Sabine Nuss from 29/08/2020: "The [SCD] also arose in a post-revolutionary spirit, when one still had system competition, i.e. really discussed how socialism and planning could be implemented beyond market signals. Whereas the [CD], if I want to start it now with Hardin and Ostrom, was rather a reaction to the question of how capitalism could be protected from undermining its own bases of exploitation, so that was a response to environmental problems that were already becoming virulent at that time." Simon Sutterlütti pointed out another difference in an email from 01/10/2020: "I think what is somewhat lost in the concrete discussion is what distinguishes us from SCD: We are against wage labor." However, this does not seem to me to be a central objection, since the coordination questions arise independently of the question of the form of work.

6 Apart from the computer socialist approaches already mentioned above.

post-capitalist society as a *whole*.[7] The question (in the light of the SCD) is *what a commons coordination could look like beyond the local meadow*. The world economy *as one collective (but not top-down)*, so to speak, would fail because of its informational complexity. So, it only makes sense to start from local commons, collectives that somehow network informationally to solve regional or even global economic and social problems. If the issue is that in Europe one might like to drink great green tea after all, networking with Chinese commons would remain unavoidable, not to mention when tackling global problems such as global warming.

I will discuss below the rather detailed proposal of Meretz and Sutterlütti in this respect. Since central planning – unlike in computer socialism – is not an option for the authors (Sutterlütti and Meretz 2018, 172–173), one must therefore assume a network (see below) of individual commons, each pursuing a specific project – for example a "local bread distribution commons" (165). One has to imagine each commons as a project-like collective operating on the basis of absolute voluntariness to produce and distribute bread, for example. They obviously need to be networked with other commons where flour, sugar, energy, baking tools are produced. Of course, questions of coordination immediately arise, to which Sutterlütti and Meretz also devote a separate section in their book (Sutterlütti and Meretz 2018, 169–189). I pick out three aspects that will be discussed in the following – without exhaustive claim: Stigmergy/Conflict Resolution, Planning, and Meta-commons.

3   Stigmergy/Conflict Resolution, Planning, and Meta-commons as Organizational Strategies of Collectivity

Sutterlütti and Meretz propose an important term: Stigmergy. This term, borrowed from research on the communication of state-forming insects, is meant to denote hint-based communication.[8] "The market is a stigmergic, cue-based system …, it signals and controls through prices." (Sutterlütti and Meretz 2018,

---

7   Helfrich 2012, 23: "Now that the limits of market fundamentalist capitalism have become apparent all over the world, the question is whether the sphere of the commons can expand to become the dominant social form." Sutterlütti and Meretz 2018, 156: "We […] ask how the whole society could be organized on the basis of commoning."

8   One must emphasize that despite the talk of 'queen' and 'workers' with respect to ant states, there is no central hierarchy in stigmergy as conceptualized by Meretz and Sutterlütti – it is a decentralized, collective control. With thanks to Hanno Pahl.

31) The clues of the market are – thus far quite Hayekian – the price signals that indicate to people, for example, what is needed:

> In commonism, too, there will be clues, and thus indirect coordination, but these clues do not communicate the logic of exploitation and ... exclusion ... but the logic of inclusion. For this, the cues cannot be one-dimensional-quantitative, but must have a multidimensional-qualitative shape. The hints will communicate, for example, where contributors are needed and what the goal of a project is. They will show a steel coordination commons who needs how much steel. They signify to a plaster commons where it is needed. They tell all innovation commons that automation of sulfur mining should be developed urgently because it is harmful to health. They allow agricultural commons to plan their production for the next year. And they point to conflicts that need to be deliberately resolved. The coordination effect here is also indirect.
> SUTTERLÜTTI and MERETZ 2018, 178

One can state: Production is to be decentralized – similar to market economies – so there is no meta-instance, such as a central planning authority, that coordinates the diverse local productions with each other and with consumption (even if the commons themselves apparently plan, see below).[9] But the coordination is not supposed to happen via quantitative prices, but via "qualitative ..., rich ... information." (Sutterlütti and Meretz 2018,180) Of course, this information must also include quantitative aspects – for example, a bread-baking commons will, after all, not only tell the flour commons *what kind of* flour it needs, but also *how much of* it is needed (by the way, this already happens in markets, it is not true that in markets only prices are communicated).[10] Since there should be no abstract unit for everything – the price – the competition mechanism also seems to be cancelled out, because a given flour-commons cannot offer the flour 'cheaper' than another, since there are no prices. Since there are no prices, there is also no exchange – the flour commons

---

9   Sutterlütti and Meretz 2018, 181: "In commonism, there will probably be no central institution that mediates needs, provides infrastructures, or enables self-organization."
10 See Cockshott et al. 2009, 326: "Posted prices are not the only telecoms system the economy has. Actual orders for commodities are another. Firms set prices and then get orders which are specified in quantities. If a business manager paid attention only to the prices she sold things at and ignored the quantities being ordered, the firm would not survive long. A priori one cannot say whether the price system or the quantity system is more significant in regulating the economy."

cannot demand money for the flour. Of course, this does not exclude that it could nevertheless demand something in exchange, but that should not be the case, otherwise it would end up being a market again (but who prevents that?). Meretz' and Sutterlütti's model amounts to decentrally coordinated planning in kind – interestingly, it was such a model of Otto Neurath against which Mises' original criticism in SCD was directed (Uebel 2005). The authors emphasize, however, that stigmergic mediation has only a limited validity:

> When people come together to produce* the means of life and the re/production needed for it, then, as a rule, the hint-based coordination between production/preservation and use is sufficient. ... However, as soon as conflicts arise between needs or over limited resources and their prioritized use, they must be mediated interpersonally. As we illustrated with the example of cumulative-hierarchical planning, conflicts of needs cannot be mediatedly decided without consequences of alienation, but must be directly negotiable.
> SUTTERLÜTTI and MERETZ 2018, 174[11]

That means that as soon as there are conflicts, communication has to become 'direct' – but especially when it comes to 'limited resources' (e.g., rare earths for computers), one is quickly at regional or even global scales, which means one would be back at the impossible 7 billion plenum. Indirect stigmergic mediation may be insufficient for conflicts, but direct interpersonal communication simply cannot be done in many cases.[12] One must communicate indirectly even in conflicts. Sutterlütti and Meretz concede that their model is about planning:

---

11 The * denotes the inclusion of reproduction in production, see p. 24, 25. The insinuation that needs are already known before the beginning of production and distribution could itself be problematic. A strength of markets 'as discovery procedures' (Hayek 1969,) can be to expand and differentiate needs, precisely because suggestions for needs come from others (suppliers), so that the ability to enjoy increases (unless one denounces these processes as 'manipulation' and as the production of 'false needs').

12 Sutterlütti and Meretz 2018, 178: "We do not have to communicate our needs to all people. We do not have to accomplish in every conflict the impossibility of thinking along the needs of all mankind." This is well and good, but in the case of complex products with distributed, global resources, this is exactly what is needed – if this is not reduced in complexity by prices (or otherwise). See also Beniger (1986, 11) on the control crisis through scaling according to Durkheim.

> A commonist society does not function via a social plan, but via self-planning, the self-setting of purposes by people. It is not a planned society, but rather a self-organizing society. Commonist mediation – commoning – does not plan society, but enables people's self-planning and self-organization.
>
> 2018, 175

Compare this with a quote from Hayek:

> This is not a dispute about whether planning is to be done or not. It is a dispute as to whether planning is to be done centrally, by one authority for the whole economic system, or is to be divided among many individuals. Planning in the specific sense in which the term is used in contemporary controversy necessarily means central planning-direction of the whole economic system according to one unified plan. Competition, on the other hand, means decentralized planning by many separate persons.
>
> 1945, 520–521

Hayek, then, sees in the 'competitive economy', the market, nothing but the enabling of decentralized planning. It is about the mechanisms necessary "conveying individuals such additional knowledge as they need in order to enable them to fit their plans in with those of others." (Hayek 1945, 521) One can casually replace 'individuals' in the quote here with 'enterprises' or indeed 'commons'.[13] The question seems very similar – and one can really ask why it should be only – and of all things – prices that provide the knowledge to coordinate local plans. Sutterlütti and Meretz criticize the poverty of price signals, Hayek would presumably praise them for this reason – as a reduction of complexity (1945, 526).[14]

One can see that this discussion raises a number of questions: For example, first, it is not entirely clear whether the mechanism of competition between different commons really does not take effect, or if it does, whether this does

---

13   Does a commons always have to consist of more than one person? Presumably yes, because if one person alone does something, nothing would be 'common'. But wouldn't that be a senseless restriction compared to markets, where I can (in principle) also act alone as one company?

14   Here, Hayek uses his famous tin example to make clear that individuals or companies do not even need to know and understand why tin has suddenly become more expensive – it is enough that they change their behavior because it has become more expensive. But as mentioned above, there are – and this is something that Hayek just does not see – also in capitalism always further information flows than just prices.

not create problems (Sutterlütti and Meretz 2018, 165).[15] Second, what is the role of the notion of 'efficiency': "And maybe copper mining ... has to be automated at great expense because it's important to us to protect the health of those involved – an expense that wouldn't pay off in the marketplace, but that we want to afford" (Sutterlütti and Meretz 2018, 185). Perhaps one doesn't want to be 'efficient' at all, and that would just no longer be a criterion under commons conditions. But here one has to be careful: an effort that 'we' want, could devour so much resources that practically everything else becomes impossible, e.g. also food supply. There must be a standard, even in commonism, above which an effort seems pointlessly costly.[16] 'Efficiency' is not the same as profitability. Third, Sutterlütti and Meretz introduce hubs (or as they are called elsewhere, Meretz 2017, 431: "meta-commons") at one point with reference to network-theoretical concepts:

> Hubs are particularly important nodes of the network. ... In capitalism, companies or state organizations are hubs. In commonism, it is the commons that perform meta-tasks. That is, tasks that allow the self-organization of other commons projects. The edges stand for the mediation between the nodes.
> 2018, 179

Obviously, apart from the conflict problem discussed above, stigmergy is not sufficient for coordination. Otherwise, there would be no need to introduce meta-commons; elsewhere it is noted that there [must] be, for example, an "infrastructure commons that plans wastewater regulation for a city, or a coordination commons that aggregates and mediates steel use in a region and can also determine conflicting requirements here." (Sutterlütti and Meretz 2018, 182, cf. Meretz 2017, 431) Clearly, commonist coordination is not reducible to the horizontal networking of collectives via stigmergic signals, but requires an additional coordinative layer.[17] At a certain level of complexity, wouldn't meta-meta-commons have to be established to coordinate the meta-commons? Is

---

15   The authors refer to problems with a bread distribution commons that leads people to establish a competing commons.
16   A completely inefficient, post-capitalist economy, for example, would also be completely unecological. (Cf. also Cockshott et al. 2009, 332–337).
17   It is very interesting that Sutterlütti and Meretz's concept of the meta-commons resembles the concept of the firm in market economies (they make the comparison themselves) – and for exactly the same reasons, see Ronald Coase 1937, 388: "But in view of the fact that it is usually argued that co-ordination [sic] will be done by the price mechanism [= stigmergic, J.S.], why is such organization [= a firm, J.S.] necessary?"

there, then, a cascade at the top of which something like a central coordinating commons would have to stand? And wouldn't that be imperative anyway, given the problems of sensibly coordinating the use of global resources and the response to global climate change, which even the market economy cannot quite solve (perhaps because it is stigmergic)?

4 Conclusion

The informational organization and coordination of collective economic processes raises considerable problems, which any proposal of post-capitalist forms of organization has to deal with. The reference to the communicative abilities of people (if they exist at all, sometimes one is not so sure ...) is not sufficient, because these abilities are limited and the interrelationships of regional to global structures are too complex to get an overview. In the SCD, the question of technology was therefore central: "The market process with its cumbersome tatonnements appears old-fashioned. Indeed, it may be considered as a computing device of the pre-electronic age" argued Oskar Lange, in order to claim that suitable computer systems could help to coordinate production (Lange 1972, 402).[18] In the CD, this topic has so far been rather left out (Tenenberg 2012, 112–121)[19] – which is not surprising, however, if one recalls the different scales mentioned at the beginning. The need for technical mediation increases with higher and more complex scales.[20] Sutterlütti and Meretz hint at this: "Commonist-stigmergic information can be conveyed in a variety of formats, images, texts, videos, augmented reality, etc. We suspect that the Internet will play an important role in providing this range." (2018, 179) It is surely no coincidence that a currently much-discussed proposal for a post-capitalist economy already has information technology in its title and, of course, discusses SCD at length (Saros 2014, 69–94). So there seem to be fundamental – media theoretical – questions at the bottom of all questions about the possibility of post-capitalist forms of organization. The question of

---

18   See ibid.: "In other words, the market may be considered as a computer sui generis which serves to solve a system of simultaneous equations. It operates like an analogue machine: a servo-mechanism based on the feedback principle. The market may be considered as one of the oldest historical devices for solving simultaneous equations."
19   On commons in innovation processes (e.g. of technology), see Potts 2018. Potts' text shows that by no means only competition is a 'discovery process'.
20   See also Luhmann (2012; 2013) – here the questions of control and planning in the face of societal complexity are repeatedly addressed.

post-capitalism is also the question of technology. Every collective is finally also a technologically mediated collective.

References

Beniger, James R. (1986) *The Control Revolution. Technological and Economic Origins of the Information Society*. Cambridge, MA: Harvard University Press.

Bernes, James R. (2020) Planning and anarchy. *The South Atlantic Quarterly* 119(1): 53–73.

Block, Walter and Jankovic, Ivan (2016) Tragedy of the partnership: a critique of Elinor Ostrom. *American Journal of Economics and Sociology* 75(2): 289–318.

Coase, Ronald (1937) The nature of the firm. *Economica. New Series* 4(16): 386–405.

Cockshott, Paul W. and Cottrell, Allin (1993) *Towards a New Socialism*. Nottingham: Spokesman Books.

Cockshott, Paul W. and Cottrell, Allin (1997) Information and economics. A critique of Hayek. *Research in Political Economy. A Research Annual* 16: 177–202.

Cockshott, Paul W. et al. (2009) *Classical Econophysics*. London and New York: Routledge.

Hardin, Garrett (1968) The tragedy of the commons. *Science. New Series* 162(3859): 1243–1248.

Hayek, Friedrich August von (1945) The use of knowledge in society. *The American Economic Review* 35(4): 519–530.

Hayek, Friedrich August von (1969) Der Wettbewerb als Entdeckungsverfahren [1968]. In: *Freiburger Studien. Gesammelte Aufsätze von F. A. von Hayek*. Tübingen: Mohr Siebeck, 249–265.

Helfrich, Silke and Heinrich-Böll-Stiftung (eds) (2012) *Commons. Für eine neue Politik jenseits von Markt und Staat*. Bielefeld: transcript.

Kathöfer, Jasmin and Schröter, Jens (2019) Money and digital media. In: Project Society after Money (ed.) *Society after Money*. London and New York: Bloomsbury, 365–386.

Lange, Oskar (1972) The computer and the market. In: Nove, A (ed.) *Socialist Economics. Selected Readings*. Harmondsworth: Penguin, 401–405.

Luhmann, Niklas (2012) *Theory of Society Volume 1*. Redwood City: Stanford University Press.

Luhmann, Niklas (2013) *Theory of Society Volume 2*. Redwood City: Stanford University Press.

Marx, Karl (1973) *Grundrisse. Foundations of the Critique of Political Economy (Rough Draft)*. London: Penguin Books.

Marx, Karl (1976) *Capital. A Critique of Political Economy Volume I*. London. Penguin Books.

Meretz, Stefan von (2017) Peer-commonist produced livelihoods. In: Ruivenkamp, G and Hilton, Andy (eds) *Perspectives on Commoning. Autonomist Principles and Practices*. London: Bloomsbury, 417–461.

Mirowski, Philip and Nik-Khah, Edward (2017) *The Knowledge We Have Lost in Information. The History of Information in Economics*. Oxford: Oxford University Press.

Morozov, Evgeny (2019) Digital socialism? The calculation debate in the age of big data. *New Left Review* 116/117: 33–67.

Ostrom, Evgeny (1990) *Governing the Commons. The Evolution of Institutions for Collective Action*. Cambridge: Cambridge University Press.

Phillips, Leigh and Rozworski, Michal (2019) *The People's Republic of Walmart. How the World's Biggest Corporations are Laying the Foundation of Socialism*. London: Verso.

Potts, Jason (2018) Governing the innovation commons. *Journal of Institutional Economics* 14(6): 1025–1047.

Saros, Daniel E. (2014) *Information Technology and Socialist Construction. The End of Capital and the Transition to Socialism*. New York: Routledge.

Sutterlütti, Simon and Meretz, Stefan von (2018) *Kapitalismus aufheben: Eine Einladung über Utopie und Transformation neu nachzudenken*. Hamburg: VSA-Verlag.

Tenenberg, Josh (2012) Technik und Commons. In: Helfrich, S and Heinrich-Böll-Stiftung (eds.) *Commons. Für eine neue Politik jenseits von Markt und Staat*. Bielefeld: transcript, 112–121.

Uebel, Thomas E. (2005) Incommensurability, ecology, and planning: Neurath in the socialist calculation debate, 1919–1928. *History of Political Economy* 37(2): 309–342.

Vaughn, Karen I. (1980) Economic calculation under socialism. The Austrian contribution. *Economic inquiry* XVIII: 535–554.

Index

agency   1–2, 4–5, 7, 9, 15–16, 35–36, 56, 61, 94–95, 97, 100–102, 114, 142, 180, 202, 207, 227, 233
agrilogistics   154
air   31, 68, 76, 81, 112, 118, 128–134, 137–141, 144, 173, 179, 191, 201–202
air pollution   112, 119, 129–130, 187, 202
anarchism (anarchy, anarchic, anarchist)   2–3, 70–71, 80, 82, 149, 153, 159
Anthropocene   21, 49, 150
Anthropocentric (post-Anthropocentric, non-Anthropocentric)   18, 21, 188, 208, 210–211, 226, 233
anthropogenic   1–2, 58, 130, 187
anti-capitalism   17–18
artwork-in-common   7, 80
assemblage (assembly, disassembly, reassembly, unassembly)   1–2, 33, 40, 71, 75–76, 91, 128, 138, 142, 148, 175, 206–207, 211, 216–217, 219, 229
authority   86–89, 92–93, 96–97, 99, 102–104, 142, 198, 229–230, 241, 243

becoming-with   129, 132
bioart   206, 218
biodiversity   3, 150, 156
bios   22
Black radicalism   16
black snow   190–192
border (border zone, borderland, border-crossing)   27–30, 33–35, 37, 40, 45, 68–70, 72–75, 77, 79–83, 155, 178

capitalism (post-capitalism, late capitalism)   4–5, 8, 10, 19, 32, 55, 58, 60, 101, 130, 142, 153, 159, 167, 201, 207–208, 236–237, 239–240, 243–244, 246
carnival (carnivalesque, carnivalization)   4, 6, 34, 37, 74
catastrophe   123, 140, 160, 177, 190
citizen science   138, 143, 145–146
climate (change, apocalypse, catastrophe, crises, havoc)   4, 7–8, 58, 112, 114, 116–117, 119–120, 122–123, 131, 138, 140, 156, 187–190, 192, 201–203, 236–237, 245

co-existence (coexistence)   2, 6–10, 111, 113, 128, 165, 172, 175, 178, 180, 201, 203, 225
co-habitation (cohabitation)   224–225, 233
Cold War   140–141, 168–169, 174, 176, 179
collective (collectivity)   1–10, 33–34, 38, 42, 48, 57–58, 60–61, 70, 75, 79–80, 83, 86, 88, 92, 100–104, 111, 113, 115, 128, 138, 141, 145–146, 148, 178–180, 189–190, 207, 210–214, 236, 238, 240, 244–246
collectivization   8, 192–196, 201
commonist   243–245
commons   9, 238–245
communism   20, 46–47, 54–55, 62, 171
communities of practice   91, 157, 160
Concrete Utopia   45, 49, 53–57
crisis   3–4, 7, 57, 86, 92–97, 103–104, 156, 159–160, 190, 195, 202, 236–237, 242
cyber warfare   168
cyberwar   165–167, 169–170
cyborg   42, 224, 228–230

data capitalism   4–5, 8
decolonial (critique, practice, struggle, subversion)   4, 6, 9, 27, 35, 40, 42–43, 87
deindustrialization   6–7, 47–48, 57–61

edgelands   69–70, 72, 80–81, 83
embodiment (embodied)   21, 35, 38, 40, 42, 48–49, 56–61, 74, 137–139, 141, 144–145, 224–225, 227, 232
environmental amnesia   7, 119–123
environmental risk   140, 142
epistemic violence   38
extractivism (extraction)   34, 101, 149–150, 152–153, 157, 159–161, 191–192, 194

face transplantation   211–213

geopolitics (geopolitical)   89, 173
geopower   145
global warming   112, 140, 190, 240

human-animal (relations)   1, 217

human-nonhuman (relations)   5, 7, 9, 34–36, 150, 189, 227
human-plant (relations)   1, 55, 115, 131
human-technological (relations)   1–2, 7–9, 27, 42, 48, 55, 57–58, 61, 69, 88–90, 92, 97, 99, 111–112, 131, 134, 138–139, 150–151, 160, 167–168, 172–174, 206–220, 224–233, 245–246
hylomorphism   16, 24

indigenous (culture, knowledge, practices)   4, 18–22, 34, 37, 45, 50, 56, 70, 77, 114–115, 154, 157
industrial(ization)   2, 6–7, 45–61, 91–92, 96–98, 101, 111, 154, 159, 166, 168, 173, 192–194, 196, 202
infrastructure   2, 8, 91, 140–143, 151–152, 158, 166–180, 187–188, 192–193, 196, 198–201, 241, 244
Interaction Pattern Design   121–122

kibbutz   2–3
knowledge (production)   1–2, 4–7, 9–10, 19–20, 35, 38, 45–61, 88–91, 98, 101, 103–104, 130, 138, 142–144, 146, 154, 157, 180, 189, 202, 231, 243

liberal democracy   90–92
local(ity)   3–5, 9–10, 35, 45, 47, 57, 96–98, 103, 138, 143, 189–192, 197, 202, 238–241, 243

material-digital   1, 4–5, 91, 101, 104–105, 150, 153, 171–172, 175, 179, 189, 199–200, 206–207, 214, 224, 228–229
media warfare (cyber warfare)   165–169, 177, 180
meta-commons   240, 244
meteorology of media   137–138, 146
monsoon   7, 128–133
mucus   128, 130, 135
multispecies postcollectives   7, 155–156

nature-relational (perspective, foundation)   120–123
neoliberalism   10, 17, 19, 21
nomadic (life, self, subject)   7, 22, 24, 114, 121

not-only-human-habitat   155–156
nuclear renaissance   178–180
nuclear terrorism   174, 177, 180

open-source intelligence (osint)   7, 87, 103–104

participatory sense-making   149, 160
penshacer   70, 75
permacultural design   8, 149, 153–156
permaculture (permacultural)   7, 8, 122, 149, 154–155, 157, 160
phantom public   94–97, 99
pollution   1, 8, 112, 119, 129–131, 187–189, 196–197, 201–203
post-communism   45, 55, 58
post-soviet   49–51
postdigital (art, communication, culture, technologies)   4–5, 8, 170, 179, 187, 189–190, 207, 213
postgenderism   224–225
posthuman(ism)   4, 18–20, 45, 51, 206–209, 212–213, 217, 227–228, 231
postmonetary collectivity   236–240
postnuclear media studies   8, 172–174, 177–178, 180
postsocialism (postsocialist)   45, 49, 54

radiation   7, 8, 165, 169, 178–180
radioactive (cloud, fallout)   165, 169–170, 179
resilience   18, 21–22, 141, 167
revolution (industrial, technological)   111, 159, 168
revolution (political)   32, 69–72, 89, 94, 113, 117, 167, 239
robot   2, 8, 224–233
RuNet (Russian Internet)   8, 198–202

silicon gender   224–233
slow violence   187, 196
sovereignization   198–200
special settlers   193–195, 200
Stigmergy/conflict resolution   240, 244
surveillance capitalism   4, 101, 201

technological gender   224–225
technological species   224–228, 230, 233

toxic (environments, places, substances)   112, 128, 130–131, 152, 190, 193, 201
toxicity (toxic geographies, toxic discourse)   130, 132–133, 187–189, 191
trans-organic gender   224
transhumanism   214
transversality (transversal)   4–6, 8, 10, 19, 173, 187, 189–190, 203, 206–208, 210–211, 215, 220, 224–225, 229, 233

violence   1–3, 6–9, 30, 35, 37–38, 41–43, 73, 95, 101, 116–117, 122, 129, 133, 170, 172, 175–179, 187–189, 191, 196–197, 201–202
vulnerability   18, 20, 130, 148, 160, 212

well-being   7, 187
worker(s)   2, 47–48, 52, 55–58, 60–61, 70, 179–180, 193–196, 229, 240

zoe   22

www.ingramcontent.com/pod-product-compliance
Lightning Source LLC
Chambersburg PA
CBHW070616030426
42337CB00020B/3821